Famous Battles and How They Shaped the Modern World c.1200 BCE – 1302 CE

To the Memory of Anthony D. Smith (1939–2016)

Famous Battles and How They Shaped the Modern World c.1200 BCE – 1302 CE

From Troy to Courtrai

Beatrice Heuser and
Athena S. Leoussi

Pen & Sword
MILITARY
AN IMPRINT OF PEN & SWORD BOOKS LTD.
YORKSHIRE – PHILADELPHIA

First published in Great Britain in 2018 by
Pen & Sword Military
An imprint of
Pen & Sword Books Ltd
Yorkshire - Philadelphia

ISBN 978 1 47389 373 3

Printed and bound in England
By TJ International Ltd.

Pen & Sword Books Ltd incorporates the Imprints of Pen & Sword Books
Archaeology, Atlas, Aviation, Battleground, Discovery, Family History,
History, Maritime, Military, Naval, Politics, Railways, Select, Transport, True
Crime, Fiction, Frontline Books, Leo Cooper, Praetorian Press, Seaforth
Publishing, Wharncliffe and White Owl.

For a complete list of Pen & Sword titles please contact

PEN & SWORD BOOKS LIMITED
47 Church Street, Barnsley, South Yorkshire, S70 2AS, England
E-mail: enquiries@pen-and-sword.co.uk
Website: www.pen-and-sword.co.uk

or

PEN AND SWORD BOOKS
1950 Lawrence Rd, Havertown, PA 19083, USA
E-mail: Uspen-and-sword@casematepublishers.com
Website: www.penandswordbooks.com

Contents

List of Contributors

Emma Aston is Associate Professor of Classics, University of Reading. She is a specialist in Greek religion and in the history and culture of northern Greece from the Archaic age to the second century BC. She is author of *Mixanthrōpoi: Animal-Human Hybrid Deities in Greek Religion* (2011), which explores the Greek depiction of deities in part-animal form. She is currently writing a book on ancient Thessaly, famous for its excellent cavalry, and her article on this subject, in the journal *Historia*, is called 'Battlefield and Racetrack: The role of horses in Thessalian Society' (2018). It is co-authored with Joshua Kerr and is the product of a UROP ('Undergraduate Research Opportunities Programme') project which commenced in 2014.

Dr Matthew Bennett, FSA (London), FRHistS, taught at The Royal Military Academy Sandhurst (1984-2014). The focus of his research is the ethos and practice of warfare in the High Middle Ages, especially chivalry, largely through the medium of Old French literature. Publications include: *Campaigns of the Norman Conquest* (2001), the *Cambridge Illustrated Atlas of Warfare: the Middle Ages 768-1497*, with N.H. Hooper (1996), *Medieval World at War* (2009) and *Medieval Hostageship c. 700-c. 1500: hostage, captive, prisoner of war, guarantee, peacemaker*, with K.A. Weikert (2016), together with over two dozen articles and chapters in peer-reviewed journals and volumes of essays.

Steven Grosby is Professor of Religion at Clemson University, USA. Among his works are, *Nationalism: A Very Short Introduction* (2005), *Biblical Ideas of Nationality: Ancient and Modern* (2002) and the edition and translation of Hans Freyer, *Theory of Objective Mind: An Introduction to the Philosophy of Culture*.

Katherine Harloe is Associate Professor of Classics and Intellectual History at the University of Reading. As well as having published numerous book chapters and articles on the influence of antiquity within the modern world, she is the author of *Winckelmann and the Invention of Antiquity* (2013) and co-editor of *Thucydides and the Modern World* (2012) and *Hellenomania* (2018). She is joint editor of *International Journal of the Classical Tradition*.

Beatrice Heuser is Professor of International Relations at the University of Glasgow. She is a specialist in Strategic and Military Studies, and has worked as Consultant at NATO. Her books include, *Reading Clausewitz* (2002), *The Strategy Makers* (2010) containing translations of early texts, and *Strategy Before Clausewitz* (2017). She is keenly interested in myths invoked in foreign policy making, treated in (edited, with Cyril Buffet) *Haunted by History* (1998).

Catherine Léglu is Professor of medieval French and Occitan literature at the University of Reading, UK. She obtained her PhD from Cambridge and has held posts at Queen's University, Belfast, and at the University of Bristol. She has published extensively on medieval lyric, satirical, didactic, and moralising texts, as well as on questions of linguistic and visual translation. Her publications include, *Multilingualism and Mother Tongue in medieval French, Occitan and Catalan narratives* (2010), *The Cathars and the Albigensian Crusade: A Sourcebook* (edited with Rebecca Rist and Claire Taylor, 2013) and *Samson and Delilah in Medieval Insular French Texts and Images: Translation and Adaptation* (Palgrave, 2018).

Athena S. Leoussi is Associate Professor in European History at the University of Reading. She is a founder of The Association for the Study of Ethnicity and Nationalism, based at LSE, and the journal, *Nations and Nationalism*. She has published extensively on the role of the visual arts in nation-building and the influence of the classical Greek cult of the body in re-defining modern European national identities. She was one of the organisers of the British Museum's exhibition, 'Defining Beauty' (2015). Her publications include, *Nationalism and Classicism* (1998), the

Encyclopaedia of Nationalism (Transaction, 2001) and *Nationalism and Ethnosymbolism* (edited with Steven Grosby, 2006).

Matthew Nicholls is Associate Professor of Classics at the University of Reading where he works on ancient books, libraries, architecture and cities in the Graeco-Roman world. He is particularly interested in the digital reconstruction of ancient spaces, including an award-winning digital model of Ancient Rome. His publications include, apart from numerous journal articles and book chapters, the two books on ancient Rome (2014) and ancient Greece (2016) that he has edited for the series *30-Second Books*.

Eric Sangar is a FNRS research fellow based at the University of Namur (Belgium) and an associate researcher at the Centre Emile Durkheim of Sciences Po Bordeaux. He is currently working on the links between collective memory and uses of history in strategic narratives, on the mobilization of emotions in the justification of violence, and on the influence of NGOs on conflict discourses. He holds a PhD from the European University Institute in Florence. The book version of his PhD thesis, entitled Historical Experience: Burden or Bonus in Today's Wars? The British Army and the German Bundeswehr in Afghanistan, was published in 2014. He has recently co-edited the volume Researching Emotions in International Relations and has published articles in various journals, including the Journal of Strategic Studies, Political Psychology, and Contemporary Security Policy.

Chapter 1

Famous Battles and their After-Life: A Framework

Athena S. Leoussi

'What force of admonition lingers in [certain] places!' *(tanta vis admonitionis inest in locis)* Cicero (45 BCE).[1]

This book is part one of a two-volume set. The set explores the collective commemoration of battles, be they victories or defeats, in the Western world. It focuses primarily on collective, civic and popular forms of remembrance and accounts of historic battles, rather than the actual events. Collective memories, as passed from generation to generation, are myths in the sense of the Greek *mythos* which means, words, or stories narrated and transmitted by word of mouth. These narratives or myths imbue events or configurations with meaning, explaining them as manifestations of particular visions of the world, be they metaphysical-religious or secular. At the same time, the collective memory of every society is perpetually transformed with the disappearance of the old and the advent of new generations. Each generation projects onto this memory its own experiences and values, thereby modifying and re-interpreting it. Thus, collective memory is not static, but in constant transition. It both transcends the life-span of its individual members and changes incessantly.

Sites of memory: the theory

The analysis of collective memory, as distinct from history, has benefited enormously from Pierre Nora's richly suggestive notion of *lieux de mémoire* or sites of memory.[2] By *lieux de mémoire* Nora refers to an almost infinite range of both physical and non-physical sites and objects which become sites of memory or reference points in the collective consciousness by virtue of their subjective, cultural significance, or, as Nora puts it, 'if the imagination invests [them] with a symbolic aura.'[3]

More specifically, Nora defines *lieux de mémoire* as 'simple and ambiguous, natural and artificial, at once immediately available in concrete sensual experience and susceptible to the most abstract elaboration.'[4] Nora's *Lieux de mémoire* range

> from such natural, concretely experienced *lieux de mémoire* as cemeteries, museums, and anniversaries; to the most intellectually elaborate ones - not only notions such as generation, lineage, local memory, but also those of the formal divisions of inherited property (*partages*), on which every perception of French space is founded, or of the 'landscape as a painting' that comes to mind when one thinks of Corot or of Cezanne's Mont Sainte-Victoire. Should we stress the *lieux de mémoire*'s material aspects, they would readily display themselves in a vast gradation. There are portable *lieux*, of which the people of memory, the Jews, have given a major example in the Tablets of the Law; there are the topographical ones, which owe everything to the specificity of their location and to being rooted in the ground - so, for example, the conjunction of sites of tourism and centres of historical scholarship, the Bibliothèque nationale on the site of the Hotel Mazarin, the *Archives nationales* in the Hôtel Soubise. Then there are the monumental memory-sites, not to be confused with architectural sites alone. Statues or monuments to the dead, for instance, owe their meaning to their intrinsic existence; even though their location is far from arbitrary, one could justify relocating them without altering their meaning.[5]

Nora's most suggestive list takes us without detours to the deep cultural significance of topography – of those physical sites on or in which great events took place. Admittedly, if these lie far in the past, there is often doubt as to the actual site thus commemorated. Until Schliemann came along at the end of the nineteenth century, the very site of Troy was in doubt, and there is still debate about the sites of famous medieval battles such as Hastings, Ourique, Aljubarrota, and Agincourt.[6] But it is mainly the transformation of battles and battlefields into metaphysical *lieux de mémoire* which interests us in these two volumes. We enquire into the meanings which battles and their sites have acquired, through the erection of monuments

2

that commemorate them and the development of cultural discourses, literary and visual about them.

Battles as *lieux de mémoire*

Nothing captures the 'us' vs 'them' feeling more strongly than conflict and among conflicts nothing can exceed the strength of feeling that is aroused in a violent physical conflict, in a battle. Moreover, people die or are maimed in battles. The natural instinct of survivors to feel at least a pinch of survivors' guilt and to feel sorry for the loss or suffering of their comrades merges with the mourning of the bereaved families to make battles a common point of reference for communities, cities, regions, nations and even for two former enemies (think of Verdun), often remembered for generations to come. Battles are thus the most obvious occasion for collective identifications to crystallize. Through their emotional charge, battles become powerful historical points of reference for entire communities whose members fought those battles and core elements in a sense of a common past. Indeed, on condition that warfare is not a monopoly of some specific estate but is socially a much broader service, one that transcends estate and class as well as ethnicity, war memories become the basis for the consolidation of 'political memory communities', including the modern nation-state. The celebrated nineteenth-century French historian Ernest Renan, in his famous lecture, *Qu'est-ce qu'une nation?*, which he delivered at the Sorbonne on 11 March 1882, emphasised the importance of the experience of common suffering for the consciousness of members of a group that they *are* a group, that they share a collective identity and common destiny. A decade after France's humiliating defeat at the hands of Prussia and its allies, he wrote, 'Common suffering unites more than joy.'[7] At the same time, Renan stressed the importance of forgetting in the process of building national unity. It is necessary for the members of the nation to forget their past conflicts and even past massacres of one another for, as John Hutchinson has observed, nations are in themselves 'zones of conflict' – communities internally divided by rival and conflicting visions and memories of both the past and the future.[8] They are thus fragile solidarities. Hence, Renan's call to forgetfulness: 'Yet the essence of a nation is that all individuals have many things in common, and also that they have forgotten many things....every French citizen has to have forgotten the Massacre of Saint Bartholomew [1572], or the massacre that took place in the Midi in the thirteenth century' (i.e., the Massacre of Béziers, of 22 July 1209, during the Albigensian Crusade, on which there is a chapter in this volume).[9]

Wars, and within wars their culminating points, battles, serve as obvious events for entire groups to remember over long periods of time, unlike individual or even local tragedies. Before the twentieth century, battles tended to be short and thus all the more remarkable events, comparable in that respect with earthquakes or floods, marking those communities affected even more than, say, long drawn-out famines or unusually bitter winters. Also, for societies that have a soft spot for narratives of courage and derring-do in the context of mortal danger, the latter so obviously found in battle, battle stories are obvious subjects for fireside storytelling, ideally with an illustrious ancestor, real or invented, thrown into the mix. As two Czech historians have remarked, 'A battle, however insignificant it might be, illustrates a catastrophe better in our imagination than a political collapse [of a regime] or an administrative act'[10] such as the adoption of a new law code or the imposition of a national language, however important the latter will be in the long term.

In commemorating their past battles, not only those experienced in their own lifetime, but also those fought by previous generations, groups cement their collective identity and sense of community. Battlefields become places for reflection, veneration and myth making for groups, as sites of memory, as discussed above, where the story of self-sacrifice in defence of family and hearth, and, by extension, the community and homeland, is being told and retold from one generation to the next, and marked by monuments to the dead in battle.[11] As sites of individual and collective sacrifice for the community, battlefields tie a group to a place – even one far away from the national territory – with almost the same intensity as the memory of the place of one's birth and childhood. Thus some battlefields – especially those within easy travelling distance on the European Continent are seen, so to speak, as corners of a foreign field that is forever one's own country, to paraphrase Rupert Brooke's famous poem. Indeed, a considerable battlefield tourism or 'thanatourism' (A.V. Seaton) which can have its sinister sides has developed around them.[12]

Following Pierre Nora, we explore in this volume and its sequel, the transformation of so many battles and battlefields into *lieux de mémoire* for a particular group – for Europe and Christendom as a whole, most frequently for a particular nation, but sometimes only for a region or a city –and their popularisation as integral parts of a specifically *group* heritage. We examine how many of the battles in our collection have become 'famous' or, indeed, 'great' not by virtue of their inherent 'greatness' but through their integration in narratives of the birth or re-birth of these groups, mostly nations. As Nora remarks, we explore how posterity confers to these events, these battles, 'the greatness of origins'.[13] The aim of these foundational narratives is to build a collective consciousness of common, *collective* origins and to forge or enhance social solidarity through appeal to common struggles in the past.

While certain battles were clearly remembered and commemorated in a variety of ways over the centuries, the great age of the political instrumentalisation of battles was above all the nineteenth century, with the spread of nationalism. This is particularly evident in the paintings of historical subjects that we find in abundance in the art of many European countries caught up in the fever of nation-building, such as G.F.Watts' *Alfred Inciting the Saxons to Prevent the Landing of the Danes*, of 1846, or Jean-Auguste-Dominique Ingres' *Joan of Arc at the Coronation of Charles VII in Reims Cathedral*, of 1854, or Ilya Repin's *Reply of the Zaporozhian Cossacks,* of 1881-91. According to the Franco-German team of historians, Étienne François and Hagen Schulze, it is noticeable that the 'deeper aim [of these paintings] was not so much the representation of truth with respect to the past, but the subjective will to bring into the present a more dream-like than real past'. This is because 'the History which they stage – the framework of which is always the nation – is a History which is systematically made subservient to the present and the future of the nation, and which draws its meaning and existence exclusively from this relationship.'[14]

Battles as (mainly national) foundation myths

The philosopher Isaiah Berlin claimed that '[O]nly barbarians are not curious about where they come from.'[15] He was mistaken, as even illiterate cultures saw the need to explain their origins through foundation myths. In fact all human societies create narratives about their origins - their past, and their destinations - their future. They construct myths in the broader sense of the term. Focusing on the past and taking the cue from the German social scientist, Max Weber, we assume that 'reality', past and present, has no concepts. History, as a sequence of events, of causes and effects, is a product of human thought - the result of reflection, remembrance and interpretation, or of abstraction and generalisation from the multitude of events which make up the flow of human life. History, therefore, belongs to the sphere of human culture. History can also be fabrication and thus mythical in this sense, creating entities where they do not exist. In this book and its sequel, we do not make a distinction between historical and fictional battles per se. Rather, we explore the ways in which certain battles have been incorporated in political narratives and especially in the grand narratives which describe the birth of nations.

The term 'foundation myth' has been coined to categorise myths that explain how a group (a tribe or *ethnie* or nation) became a group.[16] Thus, foundation myths are narratives regarding the origin or genesis of more or less continuous, intergenerational communities. Foundation myths are constitutive of nations as self-conscious cultural communities. Indeed, they are constitutive of most human communities. Most frequently, they are invoked with a national(ist) agenda. Not all nations, as enduring intergenerational communities, are founded in a red haze, as Joseph de Maistre said about the French Revolution – through the spilling of blood in the heat and danger of armed conflict.[17] A common foundation myth is a myth of common descent from a primordial ancestor – e.g. the seed of Abraham, or the seed of Shem, Ham or Japheth, or Mother Earth, as in the Greek myth of Deucalion and Pyrrha. According to this last myth, which is similar to that of Noah, Deucalion and his wife Pyrrha, after surviving a flood that had destroyed the rest of mankind, recreated the human race by casting behind them the bones of 'Mother Earth' – stones from Mount Parnassus where their ark had landed.

Foundation myths can also describe the arrival of a group in a particular place, such as the arrival of the Israelites in Palestine, the arrival of the Magyars in Hungary, or the arrival of the Pilgrim Fathers in America. We have found surprisingly few such arrival myths. Other foundation myths have been identified in political or social acts, such as the founding of Rome by Romulus in 753 BCE; or the oath of Rütli of 1291 in defiance of Habsburg overlordship for the Swiss, the symbol of collective resistance to foreign rule and the commitment to self-government; or the creation of the Kingdom of Spain from the union of the Aragonese and Castillian crowns in the marriage of Ferdinand and Isabella in the late fifteenth century.[18] But there are few examples of foundation myths which are not linked to violent conflict, from which one group – usually the group that will nurture this myth – emerges triumphant, seeing the victorious effort as the ultimate confirmation of the solidarity that binds the members of the group into a community of destiny. This brings us back to wars and battles.

The threat of extinction by a common aggressive enemy has generated communities by bringing together individuals in collective self-defence. This experience of a shared confrontation with the pathos of death has created communities of destiny in both pre-modern and modern times out of otherwise loosely tied collectivities or dispersed and even rival communities. This has been done by means of narratives of these battles which, handed down by word of mouth and later in written texts, from one generation to the next, have preserved the original solidarity and commitments of the battlefield.

Nationalism as a modern European ideology, one which emerged in the late eighteenth and early nineteenth centuries in Europe and North America, has incorporated both pre-modern and modern narratives of battles in its vision of history as a history of nations. As Anthony D. Smith has noted, most if not all nations have a myth of a heroic age as a time of resistance to foreign rule.[19] Indeed, for Smith, one of the central aims of nationalism as a movement is to secure the autonomy of a nation. Smith defined nationalism as 'an ideological movement aiming to attain or maintain autonomy, unity and identity for a social group which is deemed to constitute a nation.'[20] Smith also recognised the mythical dimension of national as indeed of all human communities. By myth he did not mean the construction *ex nihilo* of nations, but rather the subjective combination of perceptions and symbols from the past into ideal images of the identity, history and destiny of the nation.

Many uprisings in previous centuries had 'freedom from oppression' writ on their banners. For example, many towns in the medieval Holy Roman Empire rose up in revolt when laws became too restrictive or taxes too heavy, without ever wanting to form their own state. Freedom from oppression or liberty in its many guises in many contexts was perfectly reconcilable with monarchy (as long as the monarch was seen as benign) or even with the rule of a foreign elite (Robert the Bruce who fended off English pretensions to the crown of Scotland was himself of Norman origin). However, the demand for freedom of modern nationalism has been specifically oriented towards the making of new states. Its typical goal has been independent, state-based nationhood. As Ernest Gellner observed, nationalism transformed the ethnographic and political map of the modern world; it made it resemble 'not Kokoschka, but, say, Modigliani. There is very little shading; neat flat surfaces are clearly separated from each other' (Fig. 1.1).[21]

Modern nationalist ideology has inspired the formation of national independence movements across the world. Many of them pursued their independence militarily. As noted above, nationalist ideology inspired ethnic or cultural communities living under foreign rule to fight for independence. As Gellner put it, Ruritanias across the world rose against Megalomanias – against Empire.[22] The many wars of national independence that have characterised world history from the nineteenth century onwards have given rise to as many myths of *ethnogenesis* in the intense solidarity of battle.

The Wars of German Liberation from French occupation belong to this category of wars of national independence. After half a century in which the German principalities returned to their *anciens régimes*, a new series of wars – now known as the Wars of German Unification – led to the creation of the first German national state on 18 January 1871. The long road to the *Galeries des Glaces* in Versailles, where the German Reich (empire) was proclaimed, began with the Prussian defeat by Napoleon in Jena in 1806, and went through Sedan where, on 1 September 1870, the French Emperor Napoleon III was captured. *Sedantag*, as the revanche for Jena, made Sedan a new *lieu de mémoire* for the modern German nation, and was celebrated in politically unified Germany well into the Weimar Republic. Johann Gottlieb Fichte's hugely popular 'Addresses to the German Nation' which he delivered in the great hall of the Academy of Sciences in Berlin in the winter of 1807-8 and published in April 1808, helped establish the narrative of national regeneration through armed resistance to foreign rule not only in Germany but across Europe.

The Greek War of Independence (1821-1830) was mythologised in Europe most powerfully in Eugene Delacroix's *Scene of the Massacres at Chios: Greek families awaiting death or slavery*, exhibited in the Salon of 1824 (Fig. 1.2).[23] The First World War enshrined the narrative of national self-determination in international law through Woodrow Wilson's Fourteen Points which he outlined in a speech that he gave to the American Congress on 8 January 1918:

> What we demand in this war, therefore, is nothing peculiar to ourselves. It is that the world be made fit and safe to live in; and particularly that it be made safe for every peace-loving nation which, like our own, wishes to live its own life, determine its own institutions, be assured of justice and fair dealing by the other peoples of the world as against force and selfish aggression.[24]

Wilson believed, falsely, that national self-determination would bring peace to the world. Instead, it led to more conflicts as new nationalisms and sub-nationalisms would turn neighbour against neighbour, dividing communities and consuming them in the flames of mutual hatred. It also created a new problem – the problem of minorities.

The post-colonial movements that gained momentum at the end of the Second World War were wars of national independence. Taking place outside of Europe and against European imperialism, they invoked the principle of national self-determination.[25] The numerous monuments to these wars that mark the national landscapes of newly independent territories make the fight for independence an ubiquitous *lieu de mémoire*. The ruins that were left behind the more recent Yugoslav Wars are a different and more painful kind of sites of memory of the destruction of old national solidarities and the creation of new.

The key moment when nations are founded or re-affirm themselves as communities of destiny is the moment of military confrontation with the enemy. This is the moment when 'all the chips are down' and the lines of demarcation between sides, between 'us' and 'them' have to be drawn and you need to decide whom to shoot and which side to die for. After the battle, the thus bound or re-invigorated 'nation' becomes a community of memory of shared sufferings and self-sacrifices. However, as Renan has pointed out to us, there is always the option of emigrating, of exiting the national community. Nations are not permanently fixed collectivities. They depend, for their existence and persistence, on the will, the moral commitment of their members to stay together and especially to fight together. For Renan, a nation 'is an everyday plebiscite' – '*un plébiscite de tous les jours*'. The ultimate site of this plebiscite is the field of battle. For Renan, nations prove their existence through the willingness of their individual members to defend them in battle and even to die for them: 'when this moral conscience [the nation] proves its strength by sacrifices that demand abdication of the individual for the benefit of the community, it is legitimate, and it has a right to exist'.[26] It is thus blood sacrifice which expresses most decisively the desire 'to continue living together'.

Given the centrality of myths of heroic military resistance to or military liberation from foreign rule as foundational moments of modern nations, we may observe the following varieties of war-related foundation myths.

Ancient Greek, Roman and Hebrew Battles as foundation myths of modern European nations

In modern times, and particularly from the Enlightenment onwards, the ideology of nationalism has forged nations in the heat of battle, urging nations to be either free from foreign rule or die.[27] 'Liberty or Death' has been the battle-cry of many national liberation movements, from the French Revolutionaries' resistance to invasion, through the Greek War of Independence (*Eleftheria I Thanatos*) and beyond.[28] Thus, modern nationalism, as an activist ideology for national autonomy, unity and identity, has itself provided the impulse, indeed, the myth of national birth, survival and re-birth through battle. It has also revived older myths of death in battle for national freedom as, on the one hand, *exempla virtutis* – as examples of virtue, the virtue of the love of country or patriotism – and, on the other, as warnings of the cost of national freedom – death.

It is interesting that modern national foundation narratives have drawn on both pre-modern and modern battles. The classical heritage of death in defence of the community and its territory (the motherland or fatherland) has been central in modern nationalist ideology. An offspring of Enlightenment thought, modern nationalism was inspired by and revived Horace's principle of *dulce et decorum est pro patria mori* ('it is sweet and becoming to die for the fatherland'). Jacques-Louis David, in his *Oath of the Horatii* of 1784, would choose a subject from early Roman history, the seventh century BCE, to give an example of patriotism on the eve of the French Revolution that made '*la patrie*' a modern value (Fig. 1.3). Modern nationalism was also inspired by the Spartan mother's admonition to her son departing for war: *i tan i epi tas* ('bring your shield back or be brought dead on it'). Indeed, Sparta figures prominently in Renan's famous lecture of 1882, mentioned above. For Renan, 'the Spartan song-"We are what you were; we will be what you are" - is, in its simplicity, the abridged hymn of every *patrie* [fatherland]'.[29] Athens is no less invoked as an example of patriotism. Indeed, Marathon and Thermopylai became the supreme examples of modern patriotism whose roots lay in the ancient world.[30]

Under French Napoleonic occupation, historians, school teachers and poets of several European nations revived the memory of a rebellion against Roman rule to point to supposed antique origins of their national consciousness and independence. This was generally cast as an admonition to rise up against Napoleon. Heroes or rebellions included Arminius for Germany, Ambiorix for Belgium, Boudicca for Britain, Claudius Civilis for the Netherlands, and the memory of the heroic and self-destructive resistance of the town of Numantia in Spain against the Romans in 134/133 BCE (the Numantians, like the defenders of Masada, preferred to die free rather than submit to Roman rule).

Graeco-Roman antiquity was not the only source of patriotism and resistance to foreign rule in modern European thought. The wars of the ancient Israelites, through the power of the Bible and the Judaeo-Christian tradition, also contributed to the modern idea of the nation and defence of its freedom. As Anthony D. Smith stressed, 'it is to the two great ancient traditions of Graeco-Roman classicism and biblical Hebraism that we must look for much of the distinctive ideological content and character of modern nations and nationalism.'[31] Giuseppe Verdi's famous 'Jewish opera', 'Nabucco', which he composed in 1841, is a case in point. In the famous Act III chorus, "Va, pensiero," King Nebuchadnezzar's defeated and exiled Hebrew slaves yearn for freedom and their homeland. From its earliest performances in Milan and Venice, the opera was a call to arms to Italians to rise against Habsburg rule.[32]

The heritage of the national past

Ancient battles have served as models for narratives and conceptualisations of later battles. Modern national foundation myths have also drawn on the past military heroism of their own community, using their own community's past experiences of resistance to foreign rule as *exempla virtutis* for the present. For example, the battle at Masada (Fig. 1.4) has been used as a foundational myth of modern Israel. An ancient fortification in the Judaean Desert, overlooking the Dead Sea, Masada was the last stand of Jewish patriots in the face of the Roman army in 73 CE. The myth of Masada was elaborated on in the late nineteenth century by the Zionist movement. By invoking the military heroism of the Jews against the Roman occupiers of Jewish land, Masada became a part of the attempt to create a new image for the Jews, different from the image of the crushed and sickly Jew of the ghetto. It affirmed the New or revived Jew, the Fighting Jew, calling him to fight for the return and recovery of the lost land.

Later, the Middle Ages provided battles in the bloody encounters of which nations could be claimed to have been born. Medieval battles that are referred to as foundation myths for a nation include the Battle of Hastings in 1066 (after which the main ingredients of the ethnic mix of Britain were all present) and the Battle of Ourique 1137 for Portugal.[33] This date and event are fairly randomly chosen in the light of the Portuguese ruler Alfonso I Henriques' assumption of the title '*rex*' at around that time, even though it was not acknowledged by other princes for another ten years and even though at the time this was taken to imply a dependent relationship on the ruler of Leon, Alfonso VI, who called himself 'emperor' and as such claimed to be king of kings. The battle did not change much in relation to the Arabs, as after the battle, 'Alfonso Henriques went back home, leaving Moslem life in Alentejo [that is, the Muslim-occupied centre and south of Portugal] most probably undisturbed', as one later historian put it prosaically.[34]

Wolfgang Schivelbusch and Stephen Mock in their respective studies of the role of defeat in battle showed how military defeat, too, has been used to forge modern nations.[35] The sack of Constantinople by the Ottoman Turks in 1453 has given rise to myths of Greek national regeneration whose modern expression has been the *Megali Ithea* of the re-conquest of Constantinople and of the formerly Greek shores of Asia Minor. Masada, mentioned above, has been a further example of a defeat nurturing national regeneration among Zionists. The Battle of Kosovo of 1389 is yet another instance of the importance of defeat and the symbolic significance of territory as these are entwined in Serb national mythology.

Past battles as calls for the renewal of sacrifice: the uses and abuses of the past

The emerging pattern is that past sacrifice calls for new sacrifice. It is a cyclical pattern of wars without end. When we see this pattern emerging, we see battles of the past narrated in terms of political configurations of the present. Thus, the Teutonic Knights fought by Aleksander Nevskij and later by the Polish-Lithuanian Forces at Grunwald become the Germans in eighteenth-, nineteenth- and twentieth-century myths. The Ottoman armies of Kosovo Polje, Mohács, Vienna or the Shipka Pass become conflated with Turkish immigration and Syrian and Afghan refugees in the twenty-first century. Resistance by (Protestant) Englishmen and Dutchmen against (Catholic) Spain becomes conflated with a resistance to European integration perceived as a Catholic club. Napoleon and Hitler become conflated with the European Union and the rule of 'Brussels' (or even 'Belgium'). Nineteenth-century nationalism squeezed most battles into a simplified tale of two nations pitted against each other. Allies tended to be eclipsed, national complexities simplified away (e.g. the role of the Burgundians or of Flemish mercenaries or of French subjects of the English kings fighting alongside the English host in the Hundred Years' War, or the allies of Napoleon such as German Saxony in the Napoleonic Wars).

More important still were the appeals thus made to rise up and risk one's life *in war* for an imagined nation, as one's (real or imagined) forebears had done in previous wars. Curiously, in the end it seems not to have mattered much whether the battles evoked were battles one's 'own side' had won or lost, as it was the sacrifice, not the fact of victory or defeat that mattered. One almost senses that battles lost made the sacrifice all the nobler and the appeal to avenge the dead stronger. But as we shall see, there is also the twentieth-century pattern by which past wars are presented as folly and madness, and as admonitions never again to waste lives in this way.

Which Battles are famous, and what are we covering in this project?

We have conducted an informal poll among colleagues – mainly historians – from Vancouver to Moscow, Tel Aviv, and Canberra, and we encouraged them to select the ten most famous battles, admittedly with a deliberately Eurocentric focus. The result was not without its surprises, with Waterloo, Stalingrad and Verdun/Somme in the top three places (see the annex in Volume 2 for the full list): while there was significant convergence on the top six, and still some convergence on the second half dozen, after that figures plummeted.

The tenth place (with 9 votes each) was shared by six battles: the Battle of Marathon in 490 BCE, the Battle of Cannae 216 BCE, the fall of Constantinople in 1453, the defeat of the Spanish Armada off the coast of England in 1588, the Battle of Kursk 1943, and the 'Battle' (actually, operation) of Normandy 1944.

What was particularly revealing was the great number (57) of battles that only received one or at best two votes, including a list of Classical battles (Syracuse 413 BCE, Philippi in 42 BCE, Adrianople 378 CE), or the 'regional' stars such as the Spanish battles (the Fall of Granada in 1492, the Dos de Mayo 1808) or the Scottish battles (Bannockburn 1314, Flodden 1513, Culloden 1746) or confrontations with the Ottomans (the Battle of Grunwald 1410, the Battle of Mohács 1526, the Battle of the Shipka Pass of 1878, pitting the Russians and Bulgarians against the Turks, the origins of the modern Bulgarian state). Perceived as huge turning points in one country, these regional battles are often barely known in any of the others.[36]

Our two volumes come, of course, in the wake of many other works on 'most famous' or 'important' or 'decisive' battles of history.[37] These three terms are by no means synonyms. A battle (in the broadest sense) may have acquired fame through epos and literature – see for example the Trojan War, or the Battle of Roncevaux of 778 on which the *Chançon de Roland/ Rolandslied* is based – without necessarily having made much difference to a broader European or more local history at the time. A battle may be important for the epic destruction it wrought or the momentary elation of an ephemeral victory – example would be the battles of Lützen 1632 in the Thirty Years' War, Leuthen 1757 and Zorndorf 1758 in the Seven Years' War, or Austerlitz 1805 in the Napoleonic Wars – without it having truly decided the outcome of the respective war. And a battle may be decisive, or a major turning point in world history, but may only be recognised as such with the benefit of hindsight. An example is the Battle of Manzikert of 1071, the beginning of Turkish expansionism into Christian lands under the green flag of the Prophet, triggering the Crusades in reaction to it, and ultimately ringing the death knell of the Byzantine Empire. The battle is not widely known outside Greece today, and not even there.

In these two volumes, we do not aspire to engage in the academic quarrels about whether or not certain battles were actually decisive, i.e. decided the outcome of a war, or the future of history (nor are we asking speculatively what might have happened if the other side had won a particular battle). We can safely leave final judgment on the relative importance of battles to the impressive work of Cathal Nolan.[38]

Nor do we deal with 'great' battles – indeed, we would be hard pushed to define 'greatness' when linked to battle: great in scope or large numbers of fatalities?[39] Instead, we shall concentrate on 'famous' battles, battles that are widely and popularly known beyond specialists on military history.

Many works exist which deal with famous battles, but not necessarily with the most mythogenic ones. What we are interested in is battles which have become not only famous for later generations, but which have been commemorated for various political purposes, and which have one or more myths attached to them – 'myth' in the sense of 'a shorthand for a particular interpretation of a historical experience or policy, or a policy with some acknowledged historical antecedents, that is invoked in the present to justify certain policies.'[40] Or, one could say such myths are evoked to legitimize or strengthen existing rulers, regimes, states, or political movements; they can revive ancient animosities and call for a renewal of an old fight, or extend it into a new dimension, in new circumstances. By referring to particular well-known battles, and casting them in terms of mythical sacrifice, mythical triumph of the good cause over the bad, mythical heroism, myth-makers turn battles into models for emulation, in support of one given approach, one proposed course of action, one policy, over another. Our aim in this project is to highlight the diversity of political interpretations of battles and the existence of fluctuations in the fame of battles, over time.

The French scholar Anne-Marie Thiesse has remarked that 'Nothing is more international than the way national identities have been created.' Her work has identified a whole series of patterns of the re-interpretation of past events to construct a supposedly specific national history that can be found in several countries.[41] Many myths of battles owe their existence to nineteenth and twentieth-century nationalist movements and wars, as they were produced for nation-building and national solidarity strengthening purposes. Modern national 'myth-makers' tended to be poets, painters, composers, novelists, folklorists, teachers and other professionals, such as the physician Elias Lönnrot, (1802-1884) who created the Finnish national epic the Kalevala (1835). They also include political agitators and leaders, and, once an independent nation existed, school-book authors. Indeed, many of the propagators of these myths tended to be school teachers, a pattern captured well in Erich Maria Remarque's opening chapter of *All Quiet on the Western Front*. These myth-makers incorporated battles, real or legendary, in their accounts of the birth, history and destiny of their 'nations', usually the cultural communities into which they themselves were born, whose character they also tried to define and crystallise through text, image and sound.

So which battles have we chosen? Size does not determine the fame of a battle, and numbers of casualties do not necessarily determine its mythogenic potential. As Sir Edward Creasy, a Victorian historian who wrote a popular volume on 'decisive battles of the world' rightly observed, '...it is not the number of killed and wounded in a battle that determines its general historical importance.'[42] If massacres can count as battles, then the Massacre of Glencoe, for example, where members of the Clan Macdonald were cut down by Hanoverian troops, was an outstanding 'success' in terms of myth-making, as the *Punch History of Scotland* noted: 'with a death roll at about forty, it may be the most famous massacre per fatality in history.'[43]

Nor does fame always generate myth. There are famous battles without myths that incite emulation or renewed confrontation. Cannae, a battle won by the Carthaginians under Hannibal against the Romans in 216 BCE, has been referred to often for Hannibal's ingenious tactics, often consciously copied in subsequent centuries, but it is not referred to as incitation to renew the war – both political entities, the Punic and the Roman empires, have long since disappeared and with them their enmity.

The naval Battle of Lepanto in 1571 was a powerful myth of Christian victory over Muslim expansionism, commemorated by a series of murals in the Vatican in Rome and many other works of art in different parts of Christendom. Certainly, there have been interpretations of Lepanto as arguments for Habsburg or papal leadership. However, these have not been used politically for much beyond the seventeenth century; neither have they ever had much popular resonance. Today the commemoration of Lepanto has little traction as a myth.

By contrast, Trafalgar has been enduringly myth-creating (or 'mythopoetic'). Trafalgar's most lasting international legacy is that it suggests the desirability of a large-scale, fleet-on-fleet naval battle, which taken out of context became the coveted gold standard for many subsequent countries over several generations. Much of the history of naval procurement and naval strategy of the following two centuries, from the USA to Japan, can be explained by this myth. In Britain, the commemoration of Trafalgar long encapsulated the Royal Navy's self-confidence (and arrogance, some might say), even when it was shrinking in the sequential cut-backs of the second half of the twentieth century and the early twenty-first century. Nevertheless, a conciliatory posture was adopted at its 200th anniversary, which was celebrated by graciously inviting the French, now long-standing friends and allies, to participate in the revels. But so much has been written about Trafalgar and its importance in English folklore and identity that we need not do so here.[44]

We have chosen battles for this project on the basis of two criteria: first, battles which are not only famous, but which have engendered one or several myths, usually successively (i.e. not all at the same time), making their memory persist over a long period of time; secondly, battles that have strong political, and, most frequently, national implications. We start with the Trojan War, Homer's account of which in the Iliad, along with the Bible, is a key text for Western civilisation as a whole. We continue with Marathon and Thermopylae that have similarly given rise to myths shared throughout Europe. These are followed by the Jewish Wars which have inspired and continue to inspire political action among Christians and Jews, alike. We include an unusual take on the Battle of the Teutoburg Forest, myths about which were, even in its own time, harnessed to political purposes and, in the nineteenth century, to the consolidation of the first German nation-state. It is worth noting that the the Battle of Hastings did not make it into our top ten. However it is the only battle, according to the great authority of W.C. Sellers and R.J. Yeatman, whose date any English schoolchild always remembers.[45] Still interpreted in some quarters as catastrophic defeat of the (good) Anglo-Saxons by some (bad) Continental force, variously cast as French (and thus at the beginning of a tradition of anti-French sentiment) or Upper Class (in a Marxist interpretation according to which the Anglo-Saxons would henceforth be Lower Classes dominated by a foreign, Norman-French aristocracy), it is one of the main stepping stones to many a Briton's rejection of all things European (and their vote in 2016 to leave the EU). Other stepping stones of British suspicion of continental Europe include, the defeat of the (Catholic, Continental, Spanish) Armada in the Anglo-Spanish War, the defeat of (Catholic, Continental, French) Napoleon, and the defeat of (Continental, Authoritarian) Germany in the world wars (with the Somme as central British point of reference), symbolising the fight against Britain's three favourite enemies. A chapter is devoted to key battles in each of these wars, but also to the last direct naval attack on Britain, the Battle of Chatham 1667, rich in symbolism also for the Dutch. Finally for Britain, we have include Culloden 1746, the last battle on British soil, with its many different myths.

The battles of Crécy of 1346 and Agincourt, of 1415, might well have featured in our two volumes. The invocation of English victory against the French at 'Cressy' by supporters of UK's exit from the European Union on the occasion of the 2016 United Kingdom European Union Membership referendum, is a good contemporary example of the variety of ends which battles may be called upon to legitimise. It also shows the creation of new myths about old battles as well as the endurance and transfiguration of particular battles in collective memory as metaphors or myths of new experiences. (Interestingly, the referendum was described by Tim Shipman, political editor of *The Sunday Times*, as an 'all-out war').[46] Agincourt has recently been claimed as a nationalist symbol by Brexit proponents and is termed 'the battle that made our nation'.[47] But the English on the whole see their victory much as a sporting event, won by themselves, against their favourite sporting adversary, the French. Battle as sport is a myth that already features in the historic prelude of Henry V's campaign of 1415 as his request that the succession to the French crown be discussed was met by the French Dauphin (crown prince) with the dispatch of a cask of tennis balls, a reflection of the newly invented fashionable game at the French court. Famously, this was taken up by Shakespeare, and thus forms the beginning of his *Henry V.*[48] Otherwise, Agincourt has been exhaustively covered from the point of view of our own project in the recent work by Anne Curry.[49]

Moving further into the Continent, everybody is familiar with the exhortation, 'Kill them all, God will know His own' which unleashed the

Massacre of Béziers in 1209. We explore the wide range of political myths and forms of popular culture which have been developed in relation to this massacre, down to the present day. We have also included the Battle of Coutrai of 1302, no doubt the most important in Belgian collective memory and instrumentalised for different political movements. On a much larger scale, the battle for the relief of Vienna in 1683 has left important mythical bequests not only in Austria and Poland, but throughout Central and Southern Europe. We bring in also America with the Battle of Gettysburg of 1863 to show how the memory of civil war has been used to unite a divided community. We end with the great battles of the two World Wars which devastated Europe in the twentieth century, and which also became *lieux de mémoire* for the dream of a pacified and united Europe, the Battle of the Somme in 1916 and the Battle and Siege of Stalingrad over the long winter of 1942-43. Their importance is also reflected in the high ranking they received in our little poll of important battles in European history.

Battles and Popular Audiences

But how much do memories of such battles resonate among the audiences that are addressed? To get a very rough estimate of this, we conducted small sample polls among 17- to 19-year old pupils in their last year of school, with History as a special subject, in England and in Germany. These confirmed that the Trojan War is, to this day, a key point of reference of our civilisation. Admittedly, this poll conducted among A-level students was only conducted with few participants ("small-n", "n" being the number of participants) and in only two schools, and is therefore not necessarily representative. However, the fact that the results of the small surveys of the English and German school pupils match those of the survey of academics may well be indicative of general, popular European agreement that the three most famous battles in European history are the battles of Waterloo, Stalingrad and either Verdun/Somme. Knowledge about battles of Antiquity – Thermopylai, Cannae – was surprisingly good as well in the English school, and around a third had heard of the fall of Constantinople 1453 and the Siege and Battle of Vienna 1683. Admittedly, even when a good number of pupils had heard of a battle, this did not guarantee that they knew who won – there was significant uncertainty, for example, on who had carried the day at Austerlitz 1805 or at Leipzig 1813. And of the few who knew of Lepanto – celebrated for so long and so prominently around the Mediterranean as the great triumph of Christendom over the Muslim

Turks – were rather of the opinion that the Ottoman navy had prevailed. Likewise, those few English pupils who had heard of Castillon wanted to claim this as an English victory.

Overall, we feel that our selection of 'famous' battles in our two volumes can be justified, and that they will ring bells in the minds of a general readership. We hope, however, that the myths constructed around them will provoke some surprises, perhaps confirm some hunches, but will inspire further reflection on the subject of collective identities and clichés of inherited, perpetual antagonisms.

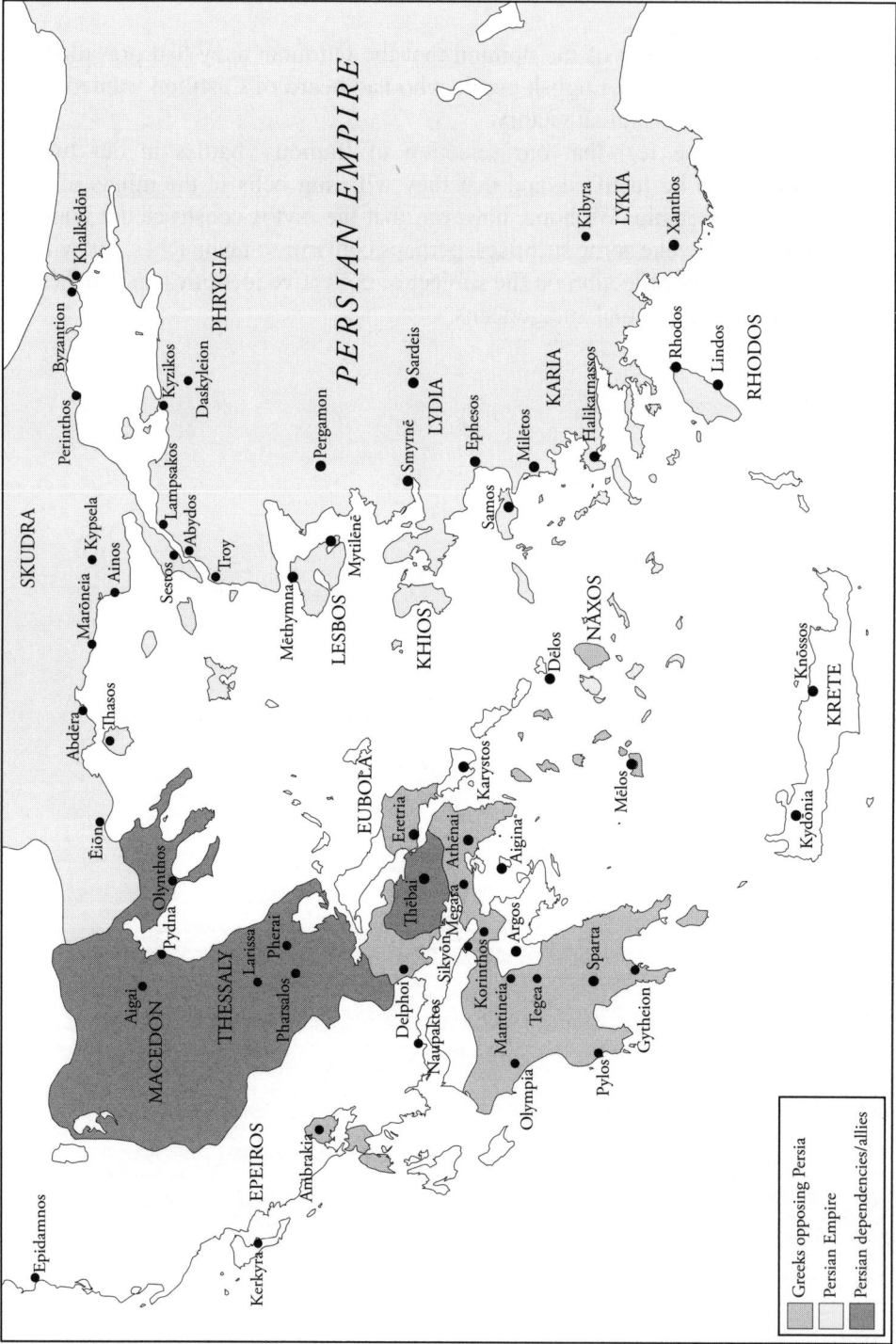

Chapter 2

The Siege of Troy[1]

Katherine Harloe

No matter how often I try, I can never manage to understand how
cities, fortresses, landscapes, sanctuaries, can lie forgotten for
centuries, preserved, if at all, only in writings which no one any
longer credits with truth content; until a few fanatics with their
Homer in hand begin to scratch in the earth at places designated
2,500 years before… But recently I have come to understand the
source of the passion that drove Heinrich Schliemann and Arthur
Evans… The steps of the ancient forum where the apostle Paul
may well have preached to the Corinthians, with the pillars of the
far more ancient temple of Apollo in the background: this picture
affords more insight than books can into the way various strata
of belief are linked to various strata of rocks. What kind of faith
will the people of the future (assuming there *are* people in the
future) read out of our stone, steel, and concrete ruins? How will
they account for the hubris of the gigantic metropolises, in which
people cannot live without paying the penalty? Of the maze of
themes which we, its contemporaries, perceive in our civilisation,
will only a few remain? Power. Wealth. Delusions of grandeur.

Christa Wolf, *Cassandra: Conditions of a Narrative*

In the beginning: Homer

The Trojan War may – or may not – have happened, but whatever events took
place around the city of Ilion in about 1200 BCE have long been eclipsed
by the legends subsequent ages have made of them. Principal among our
sources for the ten-year siege and its culmination in the city's destruction
are the *Iliad* and *Odyssey*, two epic poems the ancients attributed to a

single, divinely gifted poet called Homer. In fact, only one ancient source attests to the use of this name before the sixth century BCE – and even there it denotes the author of a *Thebaid* ('song of Thebes'), rather than one of Troy.[2] By the classical period, however, Greeks were (with a few exceptions) convinced of both Homer's existence and the truth of his songs, their authenticity guaranteed by divine inspiration from the Muses. The traditional comparison of the role of the Trojan epics in Greek culture to that of the Bible in Christendom, although hackneyed and in some ways misleading, remains useful in giving a sense of the respect Homer was accorded. Only Hesiod, an almost equally shadowy figure traditionally considered the author of two didactic poems, *Theogony* and *Works and Days*, was spoken of with comparable reverence.[3]

Despite their monumental scale – the *Iliad* is some 16,000 lines long, the *Odyssey* 12,000 – neither poem recites the entire story of the war. Rather, the Siege as a whole provides the 'essential background' (Sherratt)[4] to the particular events narrated in each: in the *Iliad* the momentous consequences of the quarrel that arose between Agamemnon, commander-in-chief of the besieging Greek forces, and Achilles, his champion fighter, over the division of war booty; in the *Odyssey* the challenges faced by the resourceful Greek warrior Odysseus on his way home to his palace in Ithaka, his son Telemachus and his loyal wife Penelope. While the ancient biographical legends that grew up around Homer make him an eyewitness to the fighting, who handed down its story to his children, the consensus today is that the poems derive from traditional stories of gods and heroes that were transmitted around the Mediterranean for centuries in song before being written down around the seventh or sixth century BCE. Analyses of their language and of the material culture described in them agree in dating Homer (who, if he ever existed, was the master-poet who gave these stories their canonical form) to the late eighth century, while also indicating they derive from storytelling traditions that stretch back as far as the middle of the second millennium. Certain elements, such as the motif of the siege, the death of a boon companion, or immortality denied, find parallels in the even older textual and visual traditions of Egypt and Mesopotamia.[5] At some point in the historical period Homer's poems were incorporated into a sequence with other Troy poems: the 'Cycle' thus created narrated the entire story of the War, from the initial sewing of discord between Athena, Hera and Aphrodite at the marriage of Peleus and Thetis to the returns of the other major Greek heroes to their native lands. These 'Cyclic Epics' were considered inferior to the *Iliad* and *Odyssey* in antiquity and now survive only in summaries and fragments. They nonetheless inspired later authors whose works treat of the Trojan War, among them the great trio of Athenian tragedians: Aeschylus, Sophocles, and Euripides.[6]

The Homeric narrative of the Siege was thus already the product of long processes of telling and retelling which stretched across the centuries and over different regions of the Mediterranean world. Although tradition and memory are often understood as the unreflective and unselfconscious repetition of past elements in an unchanging context, oral traditions possess a certain (though by no means unbounded) fluidity, such that a singer can produce notably different performances of what purports to be 'the same song' on discrete occasions.[7] As a product of oral tradition, the Homeric narrative of the Trojan War – which is our oldest, and the source from which all others derive – raises in particularly sharp form a number of questions pertinent to many of the famous battles and their myths discussed in this volume. How far does Homer's narrative preserve a kernel of historical truth, an echo of a real siege and sack of a city in the late Bronze Age? In what ways, over the centuries of its transmission, was the material reshaped (whether deliberately or otherwise) to suit particular audiences and agendas? Did this story, which projects back into prehistory an image of independent Greek cities united in a righteous war against a common enemy, serve primarily as a source of cohesion and collective identity for Greeks of the historical period, or was it sometimes a site of discord and contestation? What, finally, is the role of physical location, of *place* in all of this? The geography of the Homeric poems is twofold: on the one hand, the *Iliad* and *Odyssey* take in the whole of the early Greek world, from the Asia Minor seaboard to the mysterious (possibly mythical) Ithaka in the west.[8] On the other, the *Iliad* in particular points to a particular site in north-western Anatolia: an ancient, ruined city guarding the entrance to the Dardanelles straits, whose once-proud citadel remained visible until it was levelled and built over in the Hellenistic and Roman periods, to be rediscovered in the 1870s by Heinrich Schliemann.

These questions do not only apply to the Homeric version of the myth. They echo through the centuries, for the tale of the Trojan War has inspired political, social, literary and artistic imaginations in all subsequent ages, even for those with no access to Homer's Greek. In medieval and Renaissance Europe, dynastic rulers bolstered their authority by tracing their lineage back to Greek and Trojan heroes, much as the Roman emperors had before them. By the sixteenth century, Odysseus and (surprisingly, to modern readers) Agamemnon were studied as models of good kingship. More recently, the story has attracted those who have sought to develop critical perspectives on military might and glory: not the triumph of victors, but the tragedy of the vanquished, the dehumanization of fighters and the vulnerability of defenceless civilians, or those pressed by an enemy within.

Antiquity: political competition and cohesion

As we have already seen, the origins of the *story* of the Trojan War are almost as obscure as the events of the war themselves.[9] The evidence points to the Siege being one of a number of heroic battle sagas that circulated around Dark Age Greece, alongside the stories of the sack of Thebes, the labours of Hercules, and the voyage of Jason and the Argonauts, amongst others. Our best explanation of how and why the Trojan myth came to achieve the prominence it so evidently had by the sixth or fifth century BCE starts from a number of significant political and socio-economic changes of the eighth century BCE, at the end of what is traditionally (but increasingly misleadingly, given what archaeology can now tell us) known as Greece's 'Dark Age'. Principal among these were population growth and concentration around regional centres on the Greek mainland; the establishment of new Greek settlements overseas to both west and east; the growth in importance of interregional religious sanctuaries, such as those of the god Apollo at Delos and Delphi; and the establishment of both interregional and 'Panhellenic' festivals, the most famous of which is, of course, the Olympic Games (traditional date of establishment: 776 BCE). Alongside these developments, which brought Greeks from different regions into increasing contact with each other and with non-Greeks, we find cultural changes: the spread of writing using a modified Phoenician alphabet rather than the forgotten Linear B script of Mycenaean Greek; the appearance of heroic, narrative scenes on Greek pots; and evidence of a new interest in the distant past, as manifest in cult practices centred around Bronze Age burial sites.[10]

Hesiod, whom ancient and modern scholarship alike treat as the oldest Greek author besides Homer, also provides evidence that the tale of Troy belongs to this context. In the myth of the Five Ages of Man given in his *Works and Days*, composed perhaps a little after 700 BCE, he names the sieges of Troy and Thebes as the outstanding exploits of that 'godly race of men-heroes, who are called demigods' which followed upon the Gold, Silver and Bronze eras and preceded his Iron age:

> Evil war and dread battle destroyed these, some under seven-gated Thebes in the land of Cadmus while they fought for the

sake of Oedipus' sheep, others brought in boats over the great gulf of the sea to Troy for the sake of fair-haired Helen. There the end of death shrouded some of them, but upon others Zeus the father, Cronus' son, bestowed life and habitations far from human beings and settled them at the limits of the earth; and these dwell with a spirit free of care on the Islands of the Blessed beside deep-eddying Ocean—happy heroes, for whom the grain-giving field bears honey-sweet fruit flourishing three times a year.[11]

If, as has been argued, this 'age of heroes' constitutes an innovative insertion into an older myth of metallic ages with oriental roots, it attests to a contemporary interest in investing the Trojan War with the significance of cosmic history.[12] Hesiod's second mention of the myth, in an aside as he counsels his brother Perses on the risks of seafaring, is equally revealing:

For never yet did I sail the broad sea in a boat, except to Euboea from Aulis, where once the Achaeans, waiting through the winter, gathered together a great host to sail from holy Greece to Troy with its beautiful women. There I myself crossed over into Chalcis for the games of valorous Amphidamas—that great-hearted man's sons had announced and established many prizes—and there, I declare, I gained victory with a hymn, and carried off a tripod with handles.[13]

This is a joke, for the strait that divides Aulis from Chalcis is so narrow that today it is bridged at the shortest point. But Hesiod's description of a competitive gathering of poets from different regions points to the kind of occasion on which songs about the Trojan War might have been performed and become known among diverse audiences. Ancient commentators preserve an alternative version of the last line of this passage, according to which Hesiod declares that he gained victory 'in Chalcis over godlike Homer'. This is also the conceit of the intriguing ancient sophistical work known as 'The Contest of Homer and Hesiod.'

The evidence noted above combines to suggest that the myth of the Trojan War began to grow in cultural importance during a period when Greeks were coming into increasing contact with Greeks from cities and regions other than their own, as well as non-Greek peoples, and were also increasingly concerned with their own heroic past. Some scholars seek to explain this by suggesting that the story played a role in grounding a developing notion of pan-Greek identity: 'the idea of a past in which all Greeks combined together in a single, heroic and successful enterprise, under the leadership not of an overlord or emperor but of a *primus inter pares*'.[14] Yet Homer's tale could also be given other, more divisive meanings: the sixth-century tyrant Kleisthenes (eponymous grandfather of the founder of the classical Athenian democracy) was said to have banned public recitations of the *Iliad* and *Odyssey* in the city of Sikyon while it was at war with Argos, 'since [in the poems] Argives and Argos are principally celebrated'.[15] It may also have played a role in Persian efforts to dissuade Greek cities on the Ionian coast of Asia Minor from revolting against their rule. Homer's inclusion of Miletos and Mykale in the catalogue of Trojan allies, rather than that of Greek ships, in Book 2 of the *Iliad* provided one way of grounding such appeals in notions of ancient allegiance.[16] The idea that Xerxes presented himself as an avenger of Priam also provides a way of making sense of the elaborate rituals he carried out at Troy and on the shores of the Hellespont in 480 BCE, on his way to invade Greece.[17]

Herodotus, who reports both Kleisthenes' act of political censorship and Xerxes' activities at Troy, implicitly seeks to define his own achievement against that of Homer. His *History of the Persian Wars* also narrates a glorious military victory achieved by individual Greek cities united against an eastern enemy, and its opening chapters are devoted to explicating a distinction between those past events he *knows* to have taken place, because he has ascertained their truth by his own inquiry (*'historiē'*) and stories told by others, about whose truth he reserves judgement. The story of Troy belongs in the latter category, and Herodotus is keen to highlight discrepancies between Greek and Persian accounts of events.[18] Herodotus is also one of our earliest extant authors to make the claim – which goes back at least as far as the sixth-century BCE lyric poet Stesichorus, and which has echoed down the centuries to Christa Wolf – that Argive Helen never arrived at Troy with Paris, remaining instead in Egypt for the war's duration.[19] This is a rationalisation, since Herodotus cannot believe that the Trojans would sacrifice their city rather than give up the woman they had stolen. He does not refrain from accusing Homer of having known the true story of events but electing to tell an alternative version because he found it better suited to poetry.[20] He concludes that the true lesson of the Trojan War is a moral one: the inability of the Trojans to give back the woman they did not possess, and the Greeks' refusal to believe their protestations that they did not have her, demonstrate 'that vengeance sent by the gods in retribution for terrible wrongs is also terrible'.[21] For Herodotus, then, as for Hesiod before him, we see the Trojan War invested with more than historical significance, its destruction cited as proof of a coherent and just cosmic order.

Throughout the ages the Trojan War has also been given new interpretations linked to the more immediate political and cultural circumstances of each generation of readers. The slants given to the story – and even the heroes favoured – have differed in different periods. Despite the popularity of the *Iliad* in military circles, as an exposition of the ethic of the warrior-hero, an equally prominent strand of contemporary interpretation sees the *Iliad* as an anti-war poem: Caroline Alexander has likened Achilles' refusal to continue to fight for Agamemnon and Menelaus to Muhammad Ali's refusal of the Vietnam draft on the basis that 'No Viet Cong ever called me nigger'.[22] The same comparison is invited by the reproduction of the famous image of Ali towering over the unconscious Sonny Liston on the cover of a recent translation.[23] This moral of justified civil disobedience was certainly overlooked by those ancient military and political leaders who paid their respects at the site of the Siege on their journeys of conquest between Europe and Asia. Xerxes' activities at Troy have already been noted; he was followed – so ancient writers report – by Alexander the Great, Julius Caesar, and the Roman emperors Hadrian, Caracalla, Constantine, and Julian.[24] As Philippe Borgeaud (2010) notes, the highly embellished (in some cases, entirely fictional) narratives of these pilgrimages testify to the continuing resonance of the legend for Hellenistic and Roman leaders. Lucan's fictitious account of Julius Caesar's visit – a detour from chasing the defeated Pompey east over the Hellespont after the Battle of Pharsalus in 48 BCE – provides a particularly interesting example.[25] To some extent it replicates a motif of filial piety found already in narratives of Alexander the Great's visit, for Alexander claimed descent from Achilles through his mother and modelled himself on the War's greatest hero in various ways.[26] But the crucial reference point for Lucan's Caesar is no longer a Greek but a Trojan: it is to the household gods of his ancestor Aeneas that Caesar sacrifices.[27] Through this, apparently entirely invented, episode, Lucan projects back into the Civil Wars period that connection between the fall of Troy and the foundation of Rome that had become a central plank in the dynastic portrayal of the Julio-Claudian emperors. The important literary precedent was, of course, Virgil's *Aeneid*.[28]

27

Medieval and modern responses: genealogies and eternal truths

The Roman practice of deriving one's ancestry from Trojan War heroes caught on in a big way in medieval and Renaissance Europe. While Homer's poems were hardly read in the Latin West until the end of the fifteenth century (the first printed edition was published in Florence in 1488/9), the myth lived on through Virgil, the Latin verse summary known as the *Ilias Latina*, and plentiful allusions in other ancient poets and commentators. Widely disseminated and influential too were Latin translations of what purported to be two eye-witness accounts by warriors present at the Siege: Dictys of Crete and Dares of Phrygia.[29] These in turn informed works such as Benoît de Sainte-Maure's mid-twelfth century *Roman de Troie*, the origin of the romantic story of Troilus and Cressida retold by Boccaccio, Chaucer and Shakespeare, amongst others; and Geoffrey of Monmouth's *Historia Regum Britanniae*, a major source of Arthurian legend which also traced the lineage of the British Kings back to a supposed descendant of Aeneas named Brutus. The passion for finding Trojan ancestors was perhaps greatest in France, where both the Valois monarchy and various lesser dukes claimed descent from Francus, son of Hector, and other warriors on both the Greek and Trojan sides.[30] The greatest fruit of this tradition is Pierre de Ronsard's *Franciade*, commissioned in the mid-1500s by Henri II: it tells the story of Francus in order to furnish the French kings with a national epic to rival Virgil. Yet by 1572, the year Ronsard's poem began to appear, such myths of origin were falling into disrepute. Appealing to an Aristotelian distinction with a distinctly Herodotean pedigree, Ronsard himself admitted the challenge of reconciling the requirements of poetry and history, and ultimately classed his version of the story, alongside the *Iliad* and *Odyssey*, as 'romance'.[31] (Fig 2.1)

Those sceptical of the traditional stories of Francus, Brutus and the like pointed to the complete absence of reference to them in the ancient sources. As Ronsard's case shows, appreciation of the character of Homer and Virgil as poetry rather than historical chronicle was growing, and for some 200 years the Siege was generally assumed to be a product of poetic invention rather than a story with any basis in historical reality. This scepticism did not dent the authority of Homer's narrative in a different sense: as a repository of moral and political wisdom. It was for their educational value to princes (the *Iliad* as a paradigm of martial valour, the *Odyssey* of prudence) that the humanist Guillaume Budé recommended the study of Homer to Henri's father, François I, and the Bolognese painter

Francesco Primaticcio created a cycle of Ulysses frescos to decorate the royal apartments at Fontainebleau.[32] Aspects of this approach, which treats the myth as expressing eternal verities of the human condition, survive in today's very different cultural context, proving particularly popular in the United States. In two books, *Achilles in Vietnam* and *Odysseus in America*, the psychiatrist and PTSD specialist Jonathan Shay has appealed to the tale of Troy to illuminate the psychological and social challenges faced by traumatized veterans of military conflicts.[33] The New York theatre director Bryan Doerries takes this approach to its logical conclusion, staging readings of Sophocles' Trojan War tragedies (principally *Ajax* and *Philoctetes*) to audiences of veterans as almost a form of group therapy.[34]

Since the 1990s there has been renewed interest among both poets and creative nonfiction writers in the Trojan War as a paradigm of military conflict and devastation. This interest is no doubt prompted by the increasing number of 'hot' wars in which Western powers have again been involved since the fall of the Soviet Union, as well as by the centenary of the First World War. Greek tragedies' unremitting focus on the catastrophe of the War's aftermath has proved particularly popular, but there have also been reworkings of Homer.[35] Caroline Alexander's aforementioned reading of the *Iliad* as the first anti-war poem (2009), finds a poetic counterpart in Alice Oswald's *Memorial* (2011), a tour-de-force which extracts and reworks the *Iliad*'s similes and battle descriptions while obliterating its main story. The result is a mesmerising, repetitive incantation which if anything heightens the original's emphasis on death and loss.[36] Oswald herself interprets the *Iliad* as 'a kind of oral cemetery – in the aftermath of the Trojan War, an attempt to remember people's names and lives without the use of writing'.[37] *Memorial*'s poppy-red cover art and publication just before 11 November 2011 invite parallels with the organised, institutional remembrance of twentieth-century war dead. Oswald thus joins a tradition of poets, from Michael Longley, through Seamus Heaney and W.H. Auden, to the First-World War poets Rupert Brooke and Patrick Shaw-Stewart, who have used the Trojan War as a reference-point for commenting on the conflicts of their own day.[38]

History rediscovered: Robert Wood, through Heinrich Schliemann to the present

One of the most famous poetic responses in the English language to Homer's account of the Trojan War is John Keats' sonnet *On first looking into Chapman's Homer* (1816):

Much have I travell'd in the realms of gold,
And many goodly states and kingdoms seen;
Round many western islands have I been
Which bards in fealty to Apollo hold.
Oft of one wide expanse had I been told
That deep-brow'd Homer ruled as his demesne;
Yet did I never breathe its pure serene
Till I heard Chapman speak out loud and bold:
Then felt I like some watcher of the skies
When a new planet swims into his ken;
Or like stout Cortez when with eagle eyes
He star'd at the Pacific—and all his men
Look'd at each other with a wild surmise—
Silent, upon a peak in Darien.

Although Keats was to die in Rome he never visited Asia Minor, and the voyage of discovery prompted by his exposure to George Chapman's Homer translation occurred in the imagination. The physical rediscovery of Ilion would begin in earnest with Heinrich Schliemann's excavations in the 1870s. Yet in 1816 Keats was already behind the times. By then, Western visitors had been making their way to Constantinople and down what is now the west coast of Turkey for some 150 years. Most were diplomats or clergy on postings to the Ottoman Empire; many were also enthusiastic tourists and amateur archaeologists. The travel accounts they published sparked a new interest in the historical reality of the Trojan War, and provide the intellectual background to Schliemann's endeavours.[39]

Robert Wood in particular is worth noting as precursor of Schliemann. An Irish-born minister's son who travelled to Greece and the Levant in the 1740s and 50s, Wood is also significant for having visited, and published, accounts of the impressive ancient ruins of Baalbek and Palmyra.[40] More immediately relevant to our story is his enthusiastic meditation on Homer's descriptions of landscape and manners, first published in 1769 and then in a much expanded edition in 1775.[41] Wood struck a new note in an age where Homer's writings were considered mere 'fable'. Wandering around the plain of Troy, and seeking to match the descriptions found in the *Iliad* with the evidence of his eyes, he insisted that Homer was true to both the geography and the social customs of the lands in which his story was set: 'We shall admit his antient title of *Philosopher* only as he is a *Painter*'.[42] Schliemann claimed that similar convictions had motivated his Trojan explorations. In the autobiographical introduction to his *Ilios: The City and Country of the Trojans* (1880), he alleges that his interest in rediscovering the historical site of the Siege was sparked by a childhood spent listening to the story of the Siege at his father's knee:

> He... related to me with admiration the great deeds of the Homeric heroes and the events of the Trojan war, always finding in me a warm defender of the Trojan cause. With great grief I heard from him that Troy had been so completely destroyed, that it had disappeared without leaving any traces of its existence. My joy may be imagined, therefore, when, being nearly eight years old, I received from him, in 1829, as a Christmas gift, Dr. Georg Ludwig Jerrer's *Universal History*, with an engraving representing Troy in flames, with its huge walls and the Scaean gate, from which Aeneas is escaped, carrying his father Anchises on his back and holding his son Ascanius by the hand; and I cried out, 'Father, you were mistaken: Jerrer must have seen Troy, otherwise he could not have represented it here.' 'My son,' he replied, 'that is merely a fanciful picture.' But to my question, whether ancient Troy had such huge walls as those depicted in the book, he answered in the affirmative. 'Father,' retorted I, "if such walls existed, they cannot possibly have been completely destroyed: vast ruins of them must still remain, but they are hidden away beneath the dust of ages." He maintained the contrary, whilst I remained firm in my opinion, and at last we both agreed that I should one day excavate Troy.[43]

A personal fortune built in overseas trade enabled Schliemann to realise his alleged childhood dreams. Following a tip from Frank Calvert, who owned part of the site and had conducted trial excavations there the previous decade, Schliemann began digging at Hisarlik in 1870.[44] During eight excavation seasons between then and 1890, he and his collaborators discovered nine superimposed settlement layers dating back to the third millennium BCE. Schliemann in fact dug through the Troy VI/VIIa – the layers now thought to contain the 'Homeric' city – to Troy II (now dated to the third millennium), and in May 1873 uncovered a rich hoard which he smuggled back to Germany and put on display under the sensational banner, the 'Treasure of Priam'. He went on to excavate other sites mentioned in Homer: Mycenae (where he also discovered gold treasure), Ithaca, Tiryns, and Orchomenos. (Fig 2.2)

Schliemann's reputation as an archaeologist is controversial. His methods were unscientific and sometimes legally dubious (neither his first excavation at Hisarlik nor his removal of 'Priam's Treasure' to Germany occurred with the Ottoman authorities' permission). His accounts of his finds were sensationalised, and he destroyed much historically valuable material in his eagerness to uncover the earliest strata of Trojan civilisation. Yet it was his commitment, drive, and (not least) financing that produced the great discoveries at Hisarlik and Mycenae, and the stratigraphy established by his collaborator, the respected German archaeologist Wilhelm Dörpfeld, is still considered valid today.[45] Schliemann's knack at popularising his finds also brought Troy and Mycenae to life for a broader audience. Despite its questionable relationship to Homer's texts (it dates around 300 years too early), the golden 'mask of Agamemnon' Schliemann discovered at Mycenae is today among the most iconic objects in Athens' National Archaeological Museum.[46] The fate of 'Priam's Treasure' is more interesting still: after vanishing from the Berlin Royal Museums in 1945 it resurfaced in the early 1990s in Moscow's Pushkin Museum. Arguments between Germany and Russia over its 'restitution' are ongoing.

After Schliemann's death in 1890 the excavations were continued by Dörpfeld, whose work was followed by that of Carl Blegen in the 1930s and, most recently and impressively, Manfred Korfmann, whose excavations from 1988 to 2002 uncovered an extensive lower citadel, defensive ditch, and gate consistent with a Bronze-Age Anatolian city of the size and importance suggested in Homer.[47] Evidence from other ancient Anatolian civilisations has also strengthened the case for identifying Hisarlik with the Troy of legend. For example, some thirty documents excavated at Hattusa (modern name: Boğazkale) in north-central Turkey, ancient capital of the mighty Hittite Empire, mention a kingdom 'across the sea' named Ahhiyawa which enjoyed trading and diplomatic relations with the Hittites from the early fourteenth to the end of the twelfth century BCE. While often cordial, interactions between the two powers were punctuated by episodes of conflict and contestation for influence over regions of the western Anatolian seaboard. Since the 1920s, when documents were first deciphered and published, scholars have debated whether 'Ahhiyawa'- a name that bears a striking resemblance to Homer's 'Akhaioi' ('Achaeans') – refers to one or a group of Mycenaean Greek kingdoms.[48] One of these texts, the so-called 'Tawagalawa Letter', is a diplomatic missive addressed by the Hittite Emperor to the Great King of Ahhiyawa, appears to refer to a former dispute between the two powers over 'the matter of the land of Wilusa', a name that scholars since the 1920s have identified with Ilion/Troy.[49] If the dating of this letter to the late thirteenth century is correct it tallies with destruction of Troy VIIA, the settlement Blegen identified as the Homeric city. Together with the other Hittite sources, the Tawagalawa Letter thus provides a tantalising glimpse of a possible kernel of historical truth at the heart of the Trojan War legend.

Conclusion

In 1998, in the wake of Korfmann's spectacular discoveries, UNESCO declared Hisarlik a World Heritage Site. The award citation on the UNESCO website reads as follows:

> Troy, with its four thousand years of history, is one of the most famous archaeological sites in the world. In scientific terms, its extensive remains are the most significant and substantial demonstration of the first contact between the civilizations of the Near-East and the burgeoning Mediterranean world. Moreover, the siege of Troy by Mycenaean warriors from Greece in the 13th century BC, immortalized by Homer in The Iliad, has inspired great creative artists throughout the world ever since.[50]

Visitors to the site today have the opportunity to climb inside, and pose for pictures in front of, a replica Wooden Horse, while a similar effigy (the scene property from Wolfgang Petersen's blockbuster 2004 movie, *Troy*) graces the seafront in nearby Çanakkale. (Fig 2.3)

Over the millennia during which the myth of the Trojan War has entranced listeners and readers, the pendulum of historical interpretation has swung and returned: from the ancient conviction that the Siege really happened, through modern understandings of the myth as either as 'fable' or as true in some higher, moral or philosophical sense, to the nineteenth and twentieth centuries' renewed interest in its possible historicity. The image of Troy recovered by contemporary archaeologists and historians is complex, pointing east to the Hittites and south to Egypt as well as west to mainland Greece. UNESCO's citation nonetheless betrays that it is the myth of the Siege as told by a Greek poet that has placed Ilion on the map of modernity. As the Bronze-Age specialist Susan Sherratt comments:

> It is because Homer's Trojan War, as a powerful and infinitely adaptable ideological motif and just about the most famous

"event" of history (after the Flood) on which one can hang a long and glorious ancestry, is so deeply embedded in the collective psyches and cultural traditions and national inheritance and sense of self-identity of so many Europeans, that anyone even thinks of caring whether it represents real history or not.[51]

For Oliver Taplin

Chapter 3

The Battle of Marathon and European Identity[1]

Athena S. Leoussi

These days, when we hear the word 'Marathon', we reach for our trainers, but this was not always the case: in the summer of 490 BCE, in Athens, 'Marathon' was a call to arms. It made Athenians reach for their full hoplite armour and march to the plain of Marathon to repel the invading Persian army. They were successful. The Persians were pushed back and returned home. (Fig 3.1)

The jury is still out on many great events in human history. For example, when the President of the USA Richard Nixon asked, in 1972, during his historic visit to China, the Chinese Prime Minister, Zhou Enlai, what he thought had been the impact of the French revolution of 1789 (almost 200 years before) on Western civilisation Zhou, who was himself an avid student of French history, replied: 'too soon to tell.'[2]

Unlike the French Revolution, the verdict of history regarding the impact of Marathon on Western civilisation is clear and unequivocal especially within history's slow and long unfolding of consequences. Marathon had a profound and immediate significance for the Greek world that fought it and as the modern world embraced the ancient Greek world, and came to see itself as Greek, Marathon acquired a wider and more enduring significance – it became a battle in *European* history.

The profound and enduring significance that the Battle of Marathon has had both for the Greek world of antiquity and the modern Western world, was emphatically reaffirmed in 2010. In that year, scholars across Europe and America marked 2,500 years since the Battle of Marathon with conferences, colloquia and workshops (even though the celebrations should probably have been held in 2011, since there was no year 0).[3]

As the organisers of one of these conferences put it, their aim was to 'celebrate what was on any reckoning a key moment not just in

Greek but in European history'.[4] The aim of this essay is to explore what Marathon meant, not only to its contemporaries, but also to later generations. Why is Marathon such a 'key moment' in Greek and European history?

Marathon acquired many layers of significance. These layers of significance can be divided into military, political and cultural. I shall look at each one in turn.

First, I shall look at the battle itself, and its military significance. The key ancient source for the Battle of Marathon is Herodotus' book, the *Histories*. This was written in 445 BCE some fifty years after the event. As Herodotus wrote in his introduction to the *Histories*:

> These are the researches of Herodotus [sic] of Halicarnassus, which he publishes, in the hope of thereby preserving from decay the remembrance of what men have done, and of preventing the great and wonderful actions of the Greeks *and* the Barbarians from losing their due meed of glory; and withal to put on record what were their grounds of feuds (my emphasis).[5]

So, with Herodotus, the 'Father of History', History emerges as a new field of study - the study of 'feuds' – the study of battles. History was Military History. And History begins with the Battle of Marathon. Marathon is the first fully recorded historical battle, not counting the Trojan Wars or the battles against the Amazons and those between Centaurs and Lapiths which stood between reality and imagination.

Let us now look at the grounds of the feud between Athenians and Persians. Why did the Persians set out to invade Athens? It must be made clear from the outset that there was no woman involved – there was no *cherchez la femme*. The Battle of Marathon was not a battle for the return of a Helen, an Io, a Medea or a Europa. In any case, as Herodotus remarked, the Asiatics were 'men of sense': they would not 'make a stir' about the carrying off of their women. But the Asiatics were different from the Greeks. To quote Herodotus, concerning the Trojan War,

> Now as for the carrying off of women, it is the deed, they say, of a rogue: but to make a stir about such as are carried off, argues a man a fool. Men of sense care nothing for such women, since it is plain that without their own consent they would never be forced away. The Asiatics, when the Greeks ran off with their women,

never troubled themselves about the matter...[6]

By contrast, '...the Greeks, for the sake of a single Lacedaemonian girl, collected a vast armament, invaded Asia, and destroyed the kingdom of Priam.'[7]

So, why did the Persians invade mainland Greece in 490 BCE? What drove them was revenge for Athenian assault on the Persian Empire. In the summer of 490 BCE, the Persian king Darius sent an Expeditionary Force across the Aegean to punish the Athenians and Eretrians for helping the Greek cities of Ionia, on the Western edge of his mighty empire, in present-day Turkey, revolt against him and his satraps, his local rulers. The Ionian Revolt was a failure, but it had to be punished.

Darius did not lead this expedition. Its commanders were Datis the Mede and Artaphernes, son of the Artaphernes who was satrap at Sardis.[8] The Persian fleet first raised Eretria to the ground, then sailed to the plain of Marathon and started disembarking. The choice of Marathon for the landing of the Persian fleet was strategic. Marathon was a part of Athenian territory, in Attica, and opposite Eretria. The Persians were led to Marathon by Hippias, whom the Athenians had exiled for his tyrannical rule. Exiled Hippias had taken refuge in Darius' court. As Herodotus informs us, Marathon was a good place for horses, and thus a good place for the Persian cavalry. Horses could be easily manoeuvred on the large plain.[9] Also, Hippias had family connections at Marathon so that the locals were expected not to make a fuss over a Persian landing.

Why did the Athenians make a fuss and resist the Persians? Neither Athenian resistance nor the location of Athenian military engagement with the Persians were inevitable. Marathon was a choice. In fact, the Athenians were faced with a number of choices upon learning the news of the Persian destruction of Eretria and disembarkation at Marathon:

First, not to resist the Persians and save their lives and homes – they could thus 'medize' (i.e., collaborate with the Persians). The Athenians would not be the first Greek city-state to accept Persian rule – the Thebans, the Parians had done it (see also Chapter 4 on Thermopylai in this volume). Indeed, as Paul Cartledge has noted, not only were the Greeks perpetually divided, but also, more Greeks aided the Persians than resisted them.[10] Second, to fight. Here, two options were open to them: a) to stand siege behind their city walls, in Athens; and b) to go to Marathon and confront the Persians there. At Marathon they would also able to block the narrow exits of the plain that would enable the Persians to advance to Athens.

Herodotus tells us of the decisive part that Miltiades, one of the ten generals who led the Athenian army, played in the events that followed Persian disembarkation at Marathon. First, Miltiades persuaded the Athenian Assembly to fight at Marathon. Second, Miltiades convinced Callimachus, who was the 'Polemarchos', the overall military Commander, that the Greek army should fight, and that they should do so sooner, rather than later. Indeed, once at Marathon, and after five days of stalemate, the ten generals of the Greek army became divided about what to do. It was decided that a vote should resolve the matter. Five generals voted '…not to risk a battle, because they were too few to engage such a host as that of the Medes'. Miltiades, however, was with the other four. Callimachus' vote thus became crucial. And Callimachus sided with Miltiades. And third, Miltiades devised a military strategy which, although risky, secured Athenian victory.

Herodotus gives us the arguments with which Miltiades persuaded Callimachus to fight: 'For if you agree with me that we should fight, you make your country free and your city the best in all Greece. But if you choose not to fight, we will lose it all.'[11]

It is worth quoting the entire text of Miltiades' arguments to Callimachus, as presented to us by Herodotus:

> With thee it rests, Callimachus, either to bring Athens to slavery, or, by securing her freedom, to leave behind thee to all future generations a memory beyond even Harmodius and Aristogeiton. For never since the time that the Athenians became a people were they in so great a danger as now. If they bow their necks beneath the yoke of the Medes, the woes which they will have to suffer when given into the power of Hippias are already determined on; if, on the other hand, they fight and overcome, Athens may rise to be the very first city in Greece. How it comes to pass that these things are likely to happen, and how the determining of them in some sort rests with thee, I will now proceed to make clear. We generals are ten in number, and our votes are divided; half of us wish to engage, half to avoid a combat. Now, if we do not fight, I look to see a great disturbance at Athens which will shake men's resolutions, and then I fear they will submit themselves; but if we fight the battle before any unsoundness show itself among our citizens, let the gods but give us fair play, and we are well

able to overcome the enemy. On thee therefore we depend in this matter, which lies wholly in thine own power. Thou hast only to add thy vote to my side and thy country will be free, and not free only, but the first state in Greece. Or, if thou preferrest to give thy vote to them who would decline the combat, then the reverse will follow.[12]

So, Miltiades gave two main reasons why the Athenians should fight: first, for freedom and second for the glory of Athens. And the Athenians set out to fight. As noted above, Miltiades was the architect of Athenian victory. This was not a simple matter. Miltiades' forces were limited and much inferior in size to those of the Persians. The Persian force has been estimated at 300,000 men as against approximately 10,000 men in Miltiades' camp. The Athenian number of soldiers was just 9,000 men; nearby Plataea had sent 1,000 hoplites. There were no Spartans: Athens had sent Pheidippides (or Pheilipides), a good runner, to Sparta to ask for help. But the Spartans told Pheidippides that they could not send reinforcements immediately because of a religious law which forbade military operations until the full moon. And the full moon was six days ahead.

Miltiades decided not to wait for the Spartans. He devised a military strategy which was new and which led to Athenian victory.[13] Miltiades organised his hoplites into phalanxes. The hoplite phalanxes were close-order formations of hoplites advancing in step. The hoplites were an infantry force of well-trained, heavily armed men, wearing a bronze helmet, armour, breastplate, and greaves and carrying a large round shield, a sword and a roughly two-meter long spear. No stone throwers or any other kinds of light infantry were used.

Miltiades's strategy was to reinforce the wings of his battle line and make the middle thinner. Having fought with the Persians in the past, he knew that 'Persian practice' was to place 'the commander with his best troops in the centre of the battle line'. Miltiades hoped to strike the centre hard on both its flanks avoiding a 'frontal assault'.[14]

The Persian force consisted mainly of lightly-armoured archers. But the Persian archers were famous for their lethal skill. It is not certain how many horses, if any, the Persians had on the day of the battle. Herodotus informs us that the Persian army was *khoris hippeis* (without cavalry) on that day. It is likely that most of the Persian horses were back on the ships.

It is not certain who attacked first, on the day of the Battle of Marathon. But when the Athenians and Plataeans did engage, they did so, at first with a marching step. And only when they came within bow-shot of the Persian archers, they broke into a run, shouting, *Eleleu! Eleleu*! the Greek battle cry.[15]

According to Herodotus:

> The Persians saw them [the hoplites] charging at a run and prepared to receive the charge, thinking that the Athenians were completely crazy, seeing how few they were and how they were charging at a run without their cavalry or archers.[16]

But the strong wings of the Greek army broke the Persian centre from its flanks and chased the Persians 'all the way to the shore'.[17] The Persians suffered heavy losses, re-embarked on their ships and sailed off around Sounion, to Phaleron, at the southern coast of Attica, to sack Athens from there. They thought that it would be easy to sack Athens since only women, children and the elderly had been left. However, the Greek army ran back the 26 miles from Marathon to Athens to defend their city and when the Persians saw them, Herodotus writes, 'they departed and sailed away to Asia'.[18] Herodotus also gives us the number of casualties on each side: 'There fell in this battle of Marathon, on the side of the barbarians, about six thousand and four hundred men; on that of the Athenians, one hundred and ninety-two'.[19]

Let us now look at the significance of Marathon as a military event for each of the two warring factions - the Persians and the Athenians. What did the Persians and Athenians think and say about Marathon? In the Persian version of the event, Marathon was of no significance, as far as the Persian Empire was concerned. It was an 'insignificant skirmish on the beach'.[20] For the Iranian historian, Abdollah Razi, writing in 1982, the importance of Marathon had been exaggerated by the Greeks.[21] For another modern Iranian historian, A.H.Zarinkoub, the Persians were not even defeated at Marathon; they were just forced to withdraw. And although many of them died, none of them was taken prisoner.[22] Robert Graves, the great classicist and poetic critic of the First World War, and especially of what he saw as the lies that were told by governments to both British and German publics about the purpose of that 'Great War', shared the Persian/Iranian view of Marathon. In his famous poem, 'The Persian Version', which he wrote around the time of the Second World War, from the point of view of the Persians, Graves criticised the Athenian version of Marathon, as follows:

Truth-loving Persians do not dwell upon
The trivial skirmish fought near Marathon.
As for the Greek theatrical tradition
Which represents that summer's expedition
Not as a mere reconnaisance in force
By three brigades of foot and one of horse
(Their left flank covered by some obsolete
Light craft detached from the main Persian fleet)
But as a grandiose, ill-starred attempt
To conquer Greece - they treat it with contempt;
And only incidentally refute
Major Greek claims, by stressing what repute
The Persian monarch and the Persian nation
Won by this salutary demonstration:
Despite a strong defence and adverse weather
All arms combined magnificently together.[23]

As 'the Persian version' suggests, for the Athenians, Marathon meant more – much more. As Miltiades had predicted, it became the foundation stone, first, of the freedom and second, the glory of Athens: it made Athens 'the best in all Greece'.

This was so for a number of reasons. First, Athenian victory was clear: it turned the Persians away. At the same time, Marathon was not an end, but a beginning. The Persians returned, ten years later, led by Xerxes, to avenge Marathon (if we accept Aeschylus' account in the *Persians*). So, Marathon was the first of a series of struggles of free Greek city-states, led by Athens and Sparta, against a number of Persian invasions, known as the Greco-Persian Wars. These ended with the final victory of Greece at Plataea in 479 BCE.[24]

Second, the Athenians at Marathon not only defeated the Persians, but - and as importantly - conquered the *fear* of the Persians. Nobody had defeated the Persians before. At Marathon the Athenians proved that 'the Persian power was not invincible'.[25] Marathon was a strategic triumph devised by one man and this man was an *Athenian* general - Miltiades. With Miltiades, Marathon was the first battle that a Greek army fought exclusively with hoplites: heavily armoured foot soldiers – there were neither horsemen nor archers. Furthermore, and as Evans has noted, 'The charge of the hoplite phalanx was another innovation'.[26] Athenian recognition of Miltiades' crucial role at Marathon was expressed in words and deeds. As I shall discuss below, Miltiades was honoured with great works of public art: for example, in both Delphi and Athens statues and paintings that recount and memorialise his victory, becoming *lieux de mémoire* of his as well as his city's achievement.

And third, Marathon was a superhuman achievement in the famous and brave advance at a run.[27] There was a dramatic disproportion in the powers in play and also a matching disparity in the casualties of the two sides. As noted above, Herodotos had reported that there were 192 dead on the Greek side, as opposed to around 6,400 on the Persian side, even though modern historians are rather sceptical about the actual numbers.[28] The Athenian decision to bury the Athenians who died in that battle at the site of the battle, instead of the usual place, the *Kerameikos*, the public cemetery of Athens, expressed the special status that the victory at Marathon and its site held in Athenian consciousness.

Marathon was of great political significance for Athens: Firstly, it contributed to the invention of the myth of Athens. Athenian interpretations of and propaganda about their victory had far-reaching political consequences both for Athens and Greece. Athens claimed Marathon as an exclusively Athenian victory, despite the admittedly small, Plataean reinforcements. As Herodotus noted, the Athenians claimed to have defeated, 'all alone', 'forty-six nations' at Marathon - the multi-ethnic Persian army.[29] Furthermore, with Marathon, the Athenians claimed to be not only the saviours of their own city, but also the saviours of 'the whole of Greece'.[30] They had risked their lives for the whole of Greece.

Secondly, Marathon became embedded in Athenian consciousness of itself as a great military power, able and entitled to be the leader of Greece. Combined with Athenian-led victory at Salamis, in 480 BCE, Marathon justified Athenian claims to hegemony over other Greek city-states. In 478 BCE, the hegemonic position of Athens was unequivocally established through the formation of the Delian League, a confederacy of Greek city-states, under Athenian leadership.

Thirdly, The Athenians made Marathon a lesson in 'patriotism'. As Plato noted in his Socratic dialogue, *Menexenus*, the Athenians became *thithaskaloi* (teachers) of the whole of Greece.[31] The Athenians made patriotism – the fight for the freedom of one's country - an Athenian virtue, and a lesson for later generations of Athenians and Greeks to imitate.[32] We find this exemplary status of Marathon in the writings of Lysias (his *epitaphios*, or funeral oration), Demosthenes, and, as noted above, Plato.[33] Athens did not medize and, unlike the Eretrians, won the battle.

Furthermore, and as Herodotus noted, Marathon showed the superiority of Greece over the Barbarians. Fourthly, and as importantly, Marathon was a hoplite triumph in a political sense: the Athenian army was an army of free men. It was a citizen-army - every citizen a soldier.[34] This was seen as, and it was, a very different kind of army to that of the Persians, whose soldiers were subjugated peoples forced to fight for their despot.

Marathon entered Greek cultural memory not only through the written word, but also through great works of public art. These were designed to ensure that Marathon would be known and remembered by future generations not only of Athenians, but also of other Greeks – that it would become a pan-Hellenic *lieu de mémoire*. Marathon was memorialised in Athens, Marathon, and in Panhellenic and international Greek sites, such as Delphi and Olympia, immediately after the battle and in the years that followed it. At Marathon, on the site of the battle the Athenians constructed a memorial column and a burial mound for the 192 Athenians who had died, there (Fig. 3.2). Pausanias, the Greek traveller and geographer of the second century CE, whose *Periegesis Hellados* (*Description of Greece*) is an invaluable guide to ancient ruins, gives us an account of the ways in which the site of the Battle of Marathon was transformed into a memorial site – a site marking Athenian victorious resistance to the Persians. He writes, in Book I, Chapter 32:

> The tomb of the Athenians is in the plain and on it stand stelai bearing the names, listed by tribes, of those who fell. There is another tomb for the Plataeans of Boeotia and for the slaves; for slaves fought then for the first time. There is also a separate monument for an individual, Miltiades, son of Kimon.... There is also a trophy of white marble. The Athenians say that they buried the Medes, and indeed it is a sacred duty to cover a human corpse with soil, but I was unable to find a tomb, nor was there any mound or other visible sign, but they brought them and threw them haphazard into a trench.[35]

At Delphi, Athens, and most probably Miltiades' son, Kimon, with the approval of either the Assembly or the *Boule* of Athens, commissioned a Marathon monument, now lost, but also mentioned and described by Pausanias. Kimon dominated Athenian politics in the 470s and 460s BCE. Kimon's Marathon monument must therefore date either from the 460s BCE or the 450s. It was an expensive monument in bronze, consisting of an inscribed base carrying, originally, thirteen statues. These included Athena, Apollo and Miltiades. It was probably made by Pheidias.[36]

At Delphi was also found a thanks-giving inscription to Apollo referring to Marathon, carved on a rectangular limestone base, dating, according to Davison, either from the 480s or 460s BCE.[37] It reads, in translation, 'The Athenians to Apollo, after their victory over the Medes as first fruits of the booty of the Battle of Marathon'. Whether this inscription belongs to the Kimonian Marathon monument or not, is a hotly contested matter among classical archaeologists. According to Neer, this inscription has been confirmed, following recent archaeological evidence, as being part of the great Athenian Treasury in Delphi, a building that was made of gleaming white Parian marble, and thus not the base of Kimon's monument.[38] According to Neer, this discovery proves Pausanias' claim that the building of the Athenian Treasury was a thank-offering for the Battle of Marathon.[39] Neer thinks the Kimonian base is lost.[40]

In any case, these and other extraterritorial memorialisations of Marathon at Panhellenic shrines, such as Delphi, as well as Olympia, were significant not only as manifestations of Greek religious practices (dedications of individuals or poleis to the gods who had assisted them in victories in battle), but also for creating and propagating narratives or 'myths' of both personal and civic power – of the power and achievements of both Miltiades and the city-state of Athens.[41]

In Athens, the *Stoa Poikili*, also commissioned by Kimon, included a depiction, now lost, of the Battle of Marathon. However, above all, the greatest memorial to the battle, the *lieu de mémoire par excellence*, stood on the Athenian Acropolis (Fig. 3.3).[42] The temple of Athena Parthenos and other buildings that adorned the Acropolis of Athens, the lower town and the Athenian countryside, were built after the end of the Persian wars, during the 440s and 430s, by Pericles.[43] Pericles' building programme which brought about a renaissance in the arts, affirmed the power, glory and prosperity of Athens that began with Marathon. It also included a monument to the Polemarch Callimachus, who was killed in the Battle of Marathon - the Nike of Callimachus.

The legend of Marathon did not stay within the confines of Greek culture; neither was it lost with the end of the ancient world. What is fascinating about Marathon as a 'famous battle', is its long and illustrious after-life, and especially its diffusion across and survival into the modern Western world. Indeed, Marathon would acquire a crucial significance for the modern Western world, especially from the eighteenth century onwards. Marathon assumed huge proportions as it came to be seen by modern Western thinkers as a European foundation myth.

This identification of Europe with Greece owes much to Herodotus himself: 'For Asia, with all the various tribes of barbarians that inhabit it, is regarded by the Persians as their own; but Europe and the Greek race they look on as distinct and separate.'[44] European opinion has not changed much in this respect. For Marathon is believed to have helped preserve the cultural division between Asia and Europe.

In modern Western thought, Marathon has been regarded as significant not only for protecting what Athens had achieved until then, but also, and more importantly, for what it enabled to come: and what was to come was the rise of Periclean Athens. Marathon has been integrated in a narrative that begins with that battle on the beach and culminates in the 'golden age' of Pericles, Pheidias, Plato, Aristotle and the great dramatists. In this age of political, artistic, literary and philosophical creativity, Western thinkers have seen the roots of their own, European civilisation. For example, Eduard Meyer, the great late-nineteenth-century German ancient historian and author of the monumental *Geschichte des Altertums (History of Antiquity)* of 1884-1902 (with a third edition in 1913) emphasised the world- historical significance of the Persian Wars if not as cause, at least as 'pre-condition' for the development of western culture. Max Weber, a contemporary of Meyer, who also engaged with the problem of the sources of modern Western culture and published a critical essay on Meyer, summarised Meyer's argument as follows: for Meyer, the outcome of that 'meagre' contest at Marathon, was 'the indispensable "precondition" of the development of the war of liberation, the salvation of the independence of Hellenic culture, the positive stimulus of the beginnings of the specifically western historiography, the full development of the drama and all that unique life of the mind which took place in this – by purely quantitative standards – miniature theatre of world history'.[45] Weber did not doubt 'the "significance" which the culture of classical antiquity has had for our own spiritual and intellectual discipline'.[46] However, he objected to Meyer's narrow approach to the history of antiquity which sought to eradicate from this history 'that which is no longer historically "effective" in the contemporary world' – anything that does not explain the contemporary world.[47]

Had the outcome of the Battle of Marathon been different, which was also possible, a different cultural development would have taken place. For Meyer, Persian victory would have led to 'the development of a theocratic-religious culture, the beginnings of which lay in the mysteries and oracles, under the aegis of the Persian protectorate, which wherever possible utilized, as for example among the Jews, the national religion as an instrument of domination'.[48] But this did not happen. As Weber remarked, agreeing with Meyer, with Greek victory, first at Marathon and finally at Plataea, there was 'the triumph of the free Hellenic circle of ideas, oriented towards this world, which gave us those cultural values from which we still draw our sustenance'.[49] Finally, Weber admitted that the continuing vitality and appreciation of these Hellenic 'irreplaceable values' by modern Europeans, who are not Athenians, makes the Battle of Marathon an object of more serious historical analysis than does 'a scuffle between two tribes of Kaffirs or Indians'.[50] However, for Weber, this was not the *only* reason for studying ancient history.

Marathon as a model of modern nationalism

Apart from classical studies and early sociology, Marathon inspired modern European nationalism: the armed resistance to foreign rule for the preservation or acquisition of national freedom. Marathon became the blueprint on which some of the leading European nations modelled their own foundation myths. 'Freedom or Death' became the battle-cry of all those Wars of Independence which began in the nineteenth century and continue to the present day. The Greek War of Independence was one of them, and, as William St Clair and others have shown, it was inspired by Marathon.[51]

But even before the Greek War of Independence, in 1791, the French Revolutionaries, caught up in the heat of Enlightenment classicism and Austrian invasion to restore the absolute rule of the French King, Louis XVI, identified with the Greeks of the Persian Wars. As they declared, 'The invading Austrian hosts resemble the liberticide hordes of despotic Xerxes', while 'The French armies are lionhearted Romans and Athenians, ready to die at Thermopylai or to conquer at Marathon'.[52] During the same revolutionary period, the French town of Ris changed its name to Marathon: 'Marathon is the name we have taken; this sacred name recalls to us the Athenian plain which became the tomb of a 100,000 satellites, but it recalls to us with still greater sweetness the memory of the Friend of the People, Marat…'[53] In addition, Marathon inspired the French *levée en masse*: the citizen-army that fought both the defensive wars against Austria, but also the imperial wars of Napoleon.

Marathon also became as foundational for the modern English nation. In nineteenth-century England, we find national identification with the young Greek men who fought at Marathon – the *Marathonomachoi*. The acquisition from Lord Elgin by the British Parliament, in 1816, of major sculptures from the Parthenon for the 'nation' played a major part in this process. British educated opinion saw in these sculptures from that great temple of Athena Parthenos which, as we saw, was the apogee of Pericles' building programme of commemoration of Greek victory in the Persian Wars, and especially of that first, Athenian victory at Marathon, the supreme expression and confirmation of their own values - those of personal and national freedom. As symbols of freedom as well as artistic beauty, the British Museum's Parthenon sculptures became British national symbols. Writing in 1890, Jane Ellen Harrison, the great nineteenth-century classicist and feminist, hailed the Parthenon sculptures in the British Museum as 'our national pride' – for they spoke the language of freedom.[54]

English or British identification with the horsemen of the Parthenon frieze is most striking (Fig. 3.4). It is possible that they represent the *Marathonomachoi*.[55] Of course, at Marathon, the Athenians had no cavalry. These are the horses of the Panathenaic festival which included horse and chariot races. But their riders were emblematic of those freedom fighters, those Athenian citizens who fought and won at Marathon. And these Athenian heroes, that 'handful of free men [who] had withstood a horde of barbarian slaves', as Harrison described them, became the national symbol of the English. The Parthenon horsemen inspired the image of St George, patron saint of England, that appeared, as a new motif, on the reverse of the new gold sovereign of the late summer of 1817 - two years after Waterloo, which was seen as a specifically British victory against Napoleon, and one year after the acquisition of the Parthenon sculptures (see the chapter on Waterloo in the second volume). The new design for the gold sovereign shows St George not, as might have been expected, in the form of an armoured mediaeval knight, but as an Athenian hero from the Battle of Marathon (Fig. 3.5). He is muscular and naked, except for a billowing cape, and mounted on his horse, killing the dragon, below him. St George *Marathonomachos*, as we might describe this new image of St George, remains, with only slight modifications, the flagship coin of the Royal Mint. It was designed by the Italian gem engraver, Benedetto Pistrucci, a devout classicist. Pistrucci had come to London in 1815 and, by all accounts, it was he who suggested St George and the Dragon as a suitable subject for the proposed new sovereign. The Royal Mint gives the following account of the visual sources of Pistrucci's design:

Pistrucci's approach to the design represented a refreshing departure from previous gold coins whose style had been traditionally heraldic. It seems he may have found inspiration in the magnificent Elgin Marbles, the beautiful marble carvings that Thomas Bruce, the 7th Earl of Elgin, brought to England in the early 1800s... Pistrucci's St George is strongly reminiscent of these marble relief sculptures, his horse adopting an aggressive attitude towards the wounded dragon yet effortlessly kept in check by his master. His design of a naked Greek horseman mounted on a Parthenon-style horse is, indeed, one of great classic beauty... To the delight of collectors, artists and historians, it continues on the gold sovereign to this very day.[56]

Marathon and modern democracy

Marathon saved Athens not only from the tyranny of foreign rule, but also from Athenian tyrants. As resistance to the tyranny of Hippias, Marathon enabled the further growth of the spirit and institutions of democracy that had been set in motion by Cleisthenes's reforms of 508-7 BCE. This growth culminated in Pericles' own democratic reforms of 462 BCE. These secured the government of Athens, through the Assembly and the Courts, by the average Athenian and not by the aristocracy.[57]

In his famous Funeral Oration, which Thucydides has reported in his *History of the Peloponnesian War*, Pericles, alluding to Marathon, made a direct connection between the democratic freedoms, prosperity and beauty of Athens and Athenian independence. He also upheld Athens and its way of life as a model for the rest of Hellas - 'the School of Hellas'. On these grounds, he urged Athenians to continue to fight the Spartans, '...believing that to be happy is to be free and to be free is to be brave, do not think lightly of the perils of war'.[58] Pericles' funeral oration became the touchstone of Western liberalism from Abraham Lincoln to Winston Churchill, and beyond. As Sir Edward Creasy put it, writing in 1851: '[Marathon] secured for mankind the intellectual treasures of Athens, the growth of free institutions, the liberal enlightenment of the Western world, and the gradual ascendancy for many ages of the great principles of European civilisation'.[59] Unveiling the 4.68 m high, restored Nike of the Callimachus Monument in the new Acropolis Museum, in 2010, as part of the celebrations of the 2,500 years since the Battle of Marathon, the Greek minister of Culture and Tourism, Pavlos Geroulanos, noted that democracy was also integral to the decision to fight the Persians: as the ten generals were equally divided, it was the Polemarch's eleventh vote that tilted the balance and decided the course of action. As the minister stressed, 'Today we are not unveiling the monument of just another general but a monument to a democratic process that changed the course of history.'[60]

It is often overlooked that Marathon enabled a *double* political legacy of Athens: on the one hand the Periclean idea of the rule of the demos, and, on the other, the Platonic idea of the rule of oligarchy and the philosopher-king. In this latter idea, the philosopher attaches his *own* vision of the world to the state, making this vision compulsory and killing millions in the process, in the belief that the end justifies the means. Both of these Athenian political legacies found adherents in modern Europe dividing the continent between totalitarian Platonists (Hitler, Lenin, Stalin) and Periclean democrats, who would found and defend 'open societies'.

However, while democracy prevailed in Athens, it enabled the growth of free thought. This meant 'fearless questioning' - the scepticism and critical approach which began most consistently with Socrates and gave birth to modern science. This questioning even of the most sacred, religious belief, this openness to metaphysical criticism, which, admittedly, came gradually and at the cost of Socrates' own life, is humorously exemplified in Aristophanes' comedy, *The Clouds*, in an exchange between Socrates and Strepsiades:

> Socrates: '…there is no Zeus: don't you be so obtuse.
> Strepsiades: No Zeus up above in the sky? Then you first must explain, who it is sends the rain; or I really must think you are wrong.
> Socr. Well then, be it known, these send it alone: I can prove it by argument strong. Was there ever a shower seen to fall in an hour when the sky was all cloudless and blue? Yet on a fine day, when the clouds are away, he might send one, according to you.[61]

This new and more liberal view of religion that came after Marathon, was also embodied in Pheidias' conception of the Parthenon. As Harrison noted, 'Pheidias and Perikles were the friends rather of philosophers than priests.' Therefore, 'the Pheidian conception of the gods' was an 'even, temperate balance between faith and freedom, a certain fearless questioning as far removed from irreverence on the one hand, as on the other from ignorant dogmatism'.[62]

Marathon entered modern European popular culture in 1896.[63] When the French Baron Pierre de Coubertin revived the Olympic Games of Greece, in Athens, he included in them the Marathon run. Recent scholarship adds weight to the view that the Marathon run was a run from Marathon to Athens, not of the runner Pheidippides, as legend had it, but of the entire Athenian army, running to Athens after the Persian re-embarkation at Marathon, to stop the Persians from disembarking at Phaleron and marching on Athens (Fig. 3.1). The first Marathon run at the 1896 Olympic Games retraced that historic route.[64]

Marathon remains a part of popular culture having expanded into a global Marathonomania in the twenty-first century, with over 500 Marathons being run every year as independent events by ordinary people across the globe.[65] It is worth ending this survey of the myths surrounding the Battle of Marathon, with John Stuart Mill's famous words of 1846:

> The interest of Grecian history is unexhausted and inexhaustible. As a mere story, hardly any other portion of authentic history can compete with it. Its characters, its situations, the very march of its incidents, are epic. It is an heroic poem, of which the personages are peoples. It is also, of all histories of which we know so much, the most abounding in consequences to us who now live. The true ancestors of the European nations (it has been well said) are not those from whose blood they are sprung, but those from whom they derive the richest portion of their inheritance. The battle of Marathon, even as an event in English history, is more important than the battle of Hastings. If the issue of that day had been different, the Britons and the Saxons might still have been wandering in the woods.[66]

Mill's judgment about that battle which took place some two and a half millennia ago, is still valid today. We find it quoted repeatedly and with approval by different contributors to the book, *Marathon – 2,500 Years*, published in 2013, and based on a conference held in 2010 to mark the 2,500th anniversary of Marathon. As the editors of that book, Chris Carey and Mike Edwards observed, Mill's view of Marathon is quoted with approval by four of their contributors. In this way they recognised the embeddedness of that battle on the beach in the modern 'collective European consciousness'.[67]

Chapter 4

Thermopylai 480 BCE:
Geography and Landscape

Emma Aston

'The merits of these men, who would not regard them with wonder?'[1]

Introduction

In the popular imagination, the Battle of Thermopylai (or Thermopylae) has a Manichean quality: the key to its enduring appeal is that it seems to represent the clash of extremes, of opposites. Zack Snyder's 2007 film *300*, adapted from the graphical novel by Frank Miller, abounds in the imagery of antithesis. The Spartan king Leonidas is visually austere, verbally curt, wholly masculine, driven by a fierce and simple warrior code. His opponent Xerxes, Great King of Persia, is the reverse in almost every way: heavily adorned, sexually ambiguous, surrounded by bizarre hordes of grotesquely armoured troops, the deformed and the monstrous, war-rhinoceroses and grovelling slaves. Their values are antithetical also: the Spartans stand for freedom, integrity and valour, the Persians for insane ambition, servitude and perversion. When the two forces meet at the pass of Thermopylai their struggle has an elemental quality, black versus white.

Such imagery, though taken to its extreme by Snyder, is not wholly new. The 1962 film *The 300 Spartans* certainly reveals some of the same themes, in particular the battle between freedom and slavery. Such symbolic resonance has in fact been part of Thermopylai's depiction over centuries of Classical tradition. One thinks of Jacques-Louis David's 1814 painting *Leonidas at Thermopylae*, in which a calm, self-possessed Leonidas gazes out at the viewer from the dark ravine of the pass (a geographically inaccurate but evocative setting).[2] Or *The Battle of Thermopylae* (1823) by Massimo D'Azeglio, in which the Persian hordes swarm up over the cliffs towards the small, determined band of Spartans who wait to confront them. (Fig 4.1)

There is a core meaning of Thermopylai universal and enduring enough to be recycled in wildly different times and situations.[3] Thermopylai was evoked by supporters of Greek independence in the early nineteenth century;[4] by Confederate leaders during the American Civil War;[5] by the present pro-gun lobby in the United States;[6] even by members of the Nazi party in the mid-twentieth century.[7] Its popular resurrection is never-ending. The key to its endurance is the simplicity of its essence: the fight for liberty at all costs, even at the expense of great personal sacrifice. It is this which guarantees the lasting usefulness of the battle as a symbol by which communities can articulate and celebrate their own collective history.

This paper will argue two things: first, that the symbolism of Thermopylai is rooted in an ancient celebration of the battle which began almost as soon as the dust had settled over the bodies of the fallen; and second, that in fact Thermopylai is of all battles the least suited to being cast as a simple struggle of good and evil. As I hope to show, the simplification of the conflict, both ancient and modern, belies the extraordinary complexity of its geopolitical implications in the early fifth century BCE.

First, however, a brief reminder of the salient historical facts. The invasion of Greece by Xerxes in 480 BCE came a decade after the attempt by his predecessor Dareios; the Athenians had defeated Dareios at Marathon in Attica, in a battle which would form a cornerstone of Athenian self-esteem for generations to come, not least because Sparta, her rival for influence in Greek affairs, took no part in the battle, being detained by a religious festival at home. Thermopylai, a decade later, was another matter. Though the famous 300 Spartans were not the only warriors involved, theirs was the chief fame.

Thermopylai lies south of the rich plains of Thessaly, and forms a gateway into central Greece. The Thessalians abandoned their initial intention to resist the Persian onslaught, in circumstances described more fully below, and the Greek line of defence was established at the pass of Thermopylai, where a narrow strip of passable land lay between steep mountains and the sea. There, it was judged, Xerxes' army would have to come on its southward march, and there a small Greek force, led by Leonidas and his Spartans, positioned themselves. Our chief narrator of the ensuing battle, Herodotos,* depicts the Greeks as proving an immoveable obstacle to the

---

* Throughout this chapter, the author has chosen to use the Greek spelling of Greek words, e.g. 'Herodotos' and 'Thermopylai', rather than the more familiar Roman spellings ('Herodotus' and 'Thermopylae' etc.).

Persian advance, until the treachery of a certain Ephialtes, from the local community of the Malians, hands Xerxes the means to defeat and annihilate the defenders: a narrow goat-track by which picked Persian troops can get behind Leonidas' position and so trap him and his men and destroy them. The result is, historically speaking, curious: a Greek defeat which has none the less been remembered as a triumph, even a victory of sorts, moral if not military. And this process, that of endowing the battle with a special symbolic force, began on the battlefield itself.

Thermopylai and the monumentalisation of Greek heroism

Today the site of Thermopylai is dominated by the modern 'Leonidas monument': a bronze effigy of the Spartan king rests on a marble base bearing his most famous utterance: ΜΟΛΩΝ ΛΑΒΕ – 'Come and take them', his supposed riposte to the Persian demand that he and his men give up their arms. In 1997, he was joined by a monument commemorating the contribution of the Thespians (of Boiotia) during the battle, who are represented by a figure of the god Eros, winged and headless like the Victory of Samothrace (no coincidence, surely). So no modern traveller could pass Thermopylai without immediately grasping its historical and cultural importance. (Fig 4.2)

Indeed, the physical monumentalisation of the site began immediately after the battle, with the formal interment, under a mound, of the Greek war-dead. This *polyandrion* (shared tomb) was accompanied by inscribed verses. One of these celebrated the courage of the whole defending force, but another, dedicated to the fallen Spartans specifically, has achieved a special fame, not least because it is the work of the poet Simonides, who specialised in commemorative commissions and was especially active in the wake of Xerxes' invasion:[8]

Ὦ ξεῖν᾽, ἀγγέλλειν Λακεδαιμονίοις ὅτι τῇδε κείμεθα, τοῖς κείνων ῥήμασι πειθόμενοι.

'Stranger, announce to the Spartans that we lie here obedient to their laws.'[9]

Though this verse is brief, as befits its setting and function (and perhaps the famous terseness of the Spartans who speak in it), Simonides composed other poems celebrating major Persian War battles, and it is clear from these that he saw himself in the role of a new Homer, guaranteeing *kleos aphthiton*

53

(undying fame) for the fallen, who were thereby raised to the status of heroes.[10] It should be remembered that his poems were often designed to be performed regularly on public occasions of commemoration.[11] Through such commemorative practices, legendary warriors and historical warriors became as one, and the burial-mound of the Spartans had a similar effect: such tumuli were a feature of the heroic dead.[12] And indeed, Herodotos' account of the battle contains many Homeric touches: the struggle over Leonidas' body strongly recalls the scene in the *Iliad* in which the Greeks struggle to recover Patroklos' corpse.[13]

Ancient visitors to Thermopylai and the surrounding area do not fail to mention the visible monuments of the battle. Strabo, for example, writing his geography of Greece in the age of Augustus, comments:

'περὶ δὲ τὰ στενὰ ταῦτα οἱ περὶ Λεωνίδαν μετὰ ὀλίγων τῶν ὁμόρων τοῖς τόποις ἀντέσχον πρὸς τὰς τοσαύτας τῶν Περσῶν δυνάμεις, μέχρι περιελθόντες δι᾽ ἀτραπῶν τὰ ὄρη κατέκοψαν αὐτοὺς οἱ βάρβαροι. καὶ νῦν τὸ πολυάνδριον ἐκείνων ἐστὶ καὶ στῆλαι καὶ ἡ θρυλουμένη ἐπιγραφὴ τῇ Λακεδαιμονίων στήλῃ οὕτως ἔχουσα ᾽ὦ ξέν᾽ ἀπάγγειλον Λακεδαιμονίοις ὅτι τῇδε κείμεθα τοῖς κείνων πειθόμενοι νομίμοις.᾽

It was at these narrows that Leonidas and his men, with a few who came from the neighbouring areas, held out against all those forces of the Persians, until the barbarians, coming around the mountains through by-paths, cut them down. And today their *polyandrion* is to be seen, and stone slabs, and the oft-quoted inscription on the slab of the Lakedaimonians, which is as follows:

'Stranger, announce to the Spartans that we lie here obedient to their laws.'[14]

Rather more complex is the account of Pausanias, the second-century CE travel-writer, a Greek writing in the context of Roman imperial control. Pausanias has an intense interest in the glory days of his people, which he sees written onto the landscape he tours,[15] so it is unsurprising to find that he lavishes on the battle a really elaborate excursus. However, his framing of the event is particularly interesting. It occurs in the context of his description of Delphi (not far from Thermopylai, of course). Delphi inspires Pausanias to describe in great detail the invasion of Greece by the Gauls under their leader Brennos, and it is as a fore-runner to this episode that the Persian War battle is brought in. Time and again the Gauls are compared to Xerxes' Persians, and the Greeks who opposed the Gauls to those who stood in the pass with Leonidas. Echo after echo is created between the two battles, centuries apart. Brennos, for example, makes use of the very mountain track which allowed Xerxes to turn the pass, and is similarly assisted by locals; as before, the Phokians fail to prevent this manoeuvre. Once again, a stand in the pass fails to stop the aggressor: Brennos and his surviving fighters get through to menace Delphi itself, that crux of Hellenic identity. (As in 480 BCE, though, the very rocks of Parnassos rain down on the barbarians.) For Pausanias, plainly, Brennos is a new Xerxes, and an opportunity for dusting off and adapting Herodotos' commemoration of the Persian invasion while bringing it closer to his own age.

Perhaps the most striking detail in Pausanias' account, however, occurs when the attacking Gauls are raked by missiles from Athenian triremes steering close to the shore. Their losses are great, and yet they omit one crucial aspect of Greek battlefield etiquette: the taking up of the slain for burial.

τότε δὲ ἐν ταῖς Θερμοπύλαις οἱ μὲν Ἕλληνες μετὰ τὴν μάχην τούς τε αὑτῶν ἔθαπτον καὶ ἐσκύλευον τοὺς βαρβάρους, οἱ Γαλάται δὲ οὔτε ὑπὲρ ἀναιρέσεως τῶν νεκρῶν ἐπεκηρυκεύοντο ἐποιοῦντό τε ἐπ' ἴσης γῆς σφᾶς τυχεῖν ἢ θηρία τε αὐτῶν ἐμφορηθῆναι καὶ ὅσον τεθνεῶσι πολέμιόν ἐστιν ὀρνίθων.

ὀλιγώρως δὲ αὐτοὺς ἐς τῶν ἀπογινομένων ἔχειν τὰς ταφὰς δύο ἐμοὶ δοκεῖν τὰ ἀναπείθοντα ἦν, πολεμίους τε ἄνδρας ἐκπλῆξαι καὶ ὅτι ἔστι τεθνεώτων οὐ δι' ἔθους οἶκτος αὐτοῖς. ἀπέθανον δὲ παρὰ τὴν μάχην τεσσαράκοντα μὲν τοῦ Ἑλληνικοῦ, τοὺς δὲ τῶν βαρβάρων οὐχ οἷόν τε ἦν ἀκριβῶς ἐξευρεῖν· πολὺ γὰρ καὶ τὸ ἀφανισθὲν κατὰ τῆς ἱλύος ἐγένετο ἐξ αὐτῶν.

After the Battle of Thermopylai the Greeks buried their own dead and despoiled the barbarians, but the Gauls sent no herald to ask leave to take up the bodies, and were indifferent whether the earth received them or whether they were devoured by wild beasts or carrion birds.

There were in my opinion two reasons that made them careless about the burial of their dead: they wished to strike terror into their enemies, and through habit they have no tender feeling for those who have gone. In the battle there fell forty of the Greeks; the losses of the barbarians it was impossible to discover exactly. For the number of them that disappeared beneath the mud was great.[16]

The fact that the barbarian Gauls are indifferent to the memorialisation of their battle-dead, content to see them vanish into enveloping mire, highlights how essential memory and commemoration were to the Greeks, and their special importance at the site of Thermopylai. Though this was a long-standing cultural priority in Greek culture, the Persian Wars really placed collective monumentalisation of battlefields at the centre of Greek military habits. Poets and historians, were of course, part of this process. Simonides' epitaph asked every passer-by to remind the Spartans of the sacrifice of the defenders with Leonidas; there was no time-limit on that instruction. Herodotos presents his *Histories* as ensuring that the great deeds of men – whether Greek or barbarian – should not be forgotten; and Pausanias, centuries after him, was 'piggybacking' on the Herodotean narrative to boost his own literary credentials as the commemorator of the Greek resistance against the Gauls. For the Greeks, memory was an essential part of battle and its legacy, and Thermopylai is a powerful and formative example of that.

A quite recent discovery gives us yet another 'version' of the Battle of Thermopylai. This time the invaders are not Persians, or Gauls, but Goths. In 2007, in the Austrian National Library in Vienna, were found some substantial new fragments of the third-century CE writer and statesman Publius Herennius Dexippus.[17] These include an account of the invasion of Greece by the Goths under their leader Cniva, in CE 250/1. In this narrative, certain aspects chime strikingly with what may be recognised as the 'canonical' themes of the Battle of Thermopylai in its several guises. First there is the desperation of the defenders, described as using whatever rough weapons come to hand;[18] second, the leaders of the defence, in their battle-oration, evoke the glory of Leonidas' last stand to put heart into their men.[19] It is a geographical inevitability that a pass like Thermopylai should see a lot of fighting; but the constant recycling of Persian War motifs is very striking. This is partly a literary device used by the authors of the accounts, but one can also imagine that to fight at Thermopylai without recalling Leonidas would have been well-nigh impossible, not least because of the visible monuments to his achievement and that of his fellows described above.

That said, long after those monuments were displaced or effaced, battles taking place on the site almost always acquired the 'Thermopylai treatment'. In 1941, for example, New Zealand and Australian troops held off a German advance at the Brallos Pass, a short distance from the place where Leonidas and his fellows were slain. Eventually the ANZAC forces had to withdraw, but only after a whole day of resistance and significant German casualties. The reported words of Brigadier George Vasey of the Australian 19th Brigade – 'Here we bloody well are, and here we bloody well stay' – are pure Leonidas, though whether consciously or not it is impossible to say.[20]

Thermopylai and oppositional Greek identity

What is it about Thermopylai as a battlefield which encourages so many powerful reiterations and re-adaptations of history on the site?

At first glance, it may seem to serve as a symbolic frontier of Hellenism. In Herodotos' account,[21] the coalition of Greek states against Persia first respond to the approach of Xerxes by sending a force up to the pass of Tempe, with a view of establishing their line of defence there. They do so at the urging of the Thessalians, who plead with them to help protect their land. However, a set of murky circumstances persuades the coalition to withdraw from Tempe and to make their stand at Thermopylai instead. At this, the Thessalians, despairing of being able to hold out without aid, collaborate with the Persians entirely. Herodotos exonerates them from moral blame, but not so the Aleuadai, the ruling family of Larisa, who are depicted as actively encouraging Xerxes to invade.[22] In any case, once the line of defence moves to Thermopylai Thessaly is left out in the cold, sacrificed to Persian occupation. Is this an implicit reflection on where the boundary of 'true Greece' really lay?

The questionable loyalty and indeed identity of Thessaly is a theme which surfaces periodically in subsequent Greek literature. Pausanias did not include the region in his *Description of Greece*; in the third century BCE the geographer Herakleides had included it, but had made a curious little defensive justification for doing so as if his contemporaries might find fault with him.[23] There is a specific reason for this: ever since the time of Philip II of Macedon and his son Alexander the Great, Thessaly had been widely seen as part of Macedonian territory, and this of course did render its Greekness questionable in the eyes of its detractors. I have argued elsewhere that the later fifth and the fourth century BCE saw an increasing identification of Thessalians with their 'barbarian' northern neighbours, and in this process the Persian invasion of 480 is often evoked.[24] Kritias, writing at the end of the fifth century BCE, apparently remarked that the Thessalians sympathised with the Persians because they were inherently rather *like* them: corrupt, indulgent, undemocratic.[25] So in this view, drawing the line at Thermopylai was appropriate: the Thessalians deserved to be left outside because they were not true Greeks.

It is certainly the case that the Persian Wars helped to forge a new perception of Greek identity and its limits. As Edith Hall has shown, the threatening presence of a foreign invader allowed the Greeks to redefine their own ethnicity through a process of symbolic opposition: to be Greek was to be *not* Persian, and Persians were increasingly conceived as the polar antithesis of the Greeks: effeminate, greedy, cunning, autocratic, untrustworthy, cruel.[26] The Thessalians suffered in this new definition, since they were thought to fail the antithesis-test: they had too much in common with the Persians to count as proper Greeks. This is a very different situation from the one which prevailed in the Archaic period. In the seventh and sixth centuries, the very concept of Hellenicity arguably arose in central and norther Greece,[27] and the so-called Hellenic stemma places a Thessalian ancestor-figure at the heart of Greek origins. Fragments of the seventh-century genealogical poem the *Catalogue of Women* (attributed, with questionable veracity, to Hesiod)[28] let us reconstruct the story as Greeks of the time saw it: after the great flood, the hero Deukalion ruled Thessaly and fathered three sons, Aiolos, Doros and Xouthos. These sons were the ancestors of the three great tribes of the Greeks: Aiolos of the Aiolians who peopled Thessaly, Boiotia and parts of Asia Minor, Doros of the Dorians and Xouthos of the Ionians.[29] So a Thessalian ruler stands as the *Stammvater* of all Hellenes.

Thessalian heroes also dominated the Homeric epics and other Archaic verse, central to the shared cultural experience of the Greeks: most famously, Achilles was from Phthia in southern Thessaly.[30] This heritage of ethnic centrality was however, lost to Thessaly in the aftermath of its medism,[31] when siding with Persia was enough to compromise all Hellenic credentials, however deep-rooted. The decision to hold Thermopylai may be seen as symbolic of this shift: the door of Greece slams shut, and Thessaly is left shivering on the outside.

In fact, however, we have to be cautious in viewing the actual site of the battle in this binary way, as the junction between Inside and Outside, Greek and not-quite-Greek. Both Herodotos' nuanced account and the geopolitical realities of the early fifth century were far more complicated than this. Indeed, Thermopylai was anything but a simple frontier: rather, it was at the heart of a cluster of central Greek communities whose loyalties and allegiances challenge our preconceptions about the Greek response to Persia. While the Battle of Thermopylai has come to stand for heroic resistance, in fact the location of the battlefield was charged with murky agendas and motivations.

Thermopylai and the complexity of Greek responses to Persia

So far from being on the boundary between loyalist and traitor, Thermopylai was in fact surrounded by medising communities. Herodotos lists the pro-Persian Greeks thus:

> τῶν δὲ δόντων ταῦτα ἐγένοντο οἵδε, Θεσσαλοὶ Δόλοπες Ἐνιῆνες Περραιβοὶ Λοκροὶ Μάγνητες Μηλιέες Ἀχαιοὶ οἱ Φθιῶται καὶ Θηβαῖοι καὶ οἱ ἄλλοι Βοιωτοὶ πλὴν Θεσπιέων τε καὶ Πλαταιέων.

> Among those who gave these things [i.e. earth and water] were the following: Thessalians, Dolopians, Ainianes, Perrhaibians, Magnesians, Malians, Phthiotic Achaians, Thebans and the rest of the Boiotians except for the Thespians and the Plataians.[32]

The reader will certainly be forgiven for failing to recognise many of these communities: in terms of large-scale historical events, they are extremely obscure! They may be viewed on the map. The Perrhaibians, Magnesians and Phthiotic Achaians are on the edges of Thessaly, to the north, east and south respectively, and were subordinate to the Thessalians from the time of Thucydides at least.[33] As for the Dolopians, Ainianes and Malians, these were small *ethnē* (tribes, peoples) in the Spercheios valley itself, very close to Thermopylai. And Boiotia of course lay to the south, between Attica and Phokis. So Thermopylai actually nested in the midst of medising communities. One of them supplied the man – the Malian Ephialtes – who showed Xerxes the path which let his soldiers attack Leonidas and his forces from behind, and so brought about the doom of the defenders.

The ambiguity of Thermopylai's position increases when we factor in the role of Delphi. What bound together the medising states listed above is that they were all members of the Delphic Amphiktyony, the collective of twelve *ethnē* which oversaw the management of the sanctuary of Apollo.[34]

Sparta and Athens were represented in the Amphiktyony too, but they – and their votes on the Amphiktyonic council – were outnumbered by the medising members. Moreover, not only was Thermopylai in the midst of pro-Persian states, the Amphiktyony actually held regular meetings a spear-throw away, at Anthela (see map). So the Spartans and the other participating Greek loyalists staged their heroic last stand near the sacred headquarters of a collective whose members had overwhelmingly backed the other side.[35]

The pro-Persian sympathies of the Amphiktyony may or may not have contributed to the fact that the Oracle's pronouncements concerning the Persian invasion were very discouraging, on more than one occasion advising the Greeks to give up the struggle and capitulate to Xerxes.[36] The Oracle itself did not of course suffer any depletion of its standing as a result of the medism of so many of its Amphiktyony; on the contrary, it was the site of some of the most energetic character-rehabilitation campaigns and triumphal posturing performed by the Greeks once their victory over the Persians was assured. This is the other salient fact about Thermopylai. Its own commemorative monuments and inscriptions surely drew power from their relative proximity to Delphi, in which the built landscape of the sanctuary reflected the Greeks' triumph back to them with a new spate of buildings and dedications. Those by individual states competed to proclaim most loudly their wartime achievements, and there was also a collective dedication by all the states of the coalition, derived from a tithe of the Persian spoils. They also made showy offerings at the other pan-Hellenic sanctuaries, as Herodotos records:

συμφορήσαντες δὲ τὰ χρήματα καὶ δεκάτην ἐξελόντες τῷ ἐν Δελφοῖσι θεῷ, ἀπ' ἧς ὁ τρίπους ὁ χρύσεος ἀνετέθη ὁ ἐπὶ τοῦ τρικαρήνου ὄφιος τοῦ χαλκέου ἐπεστεὼς ἄγχιστα τοῦ βωμοῦ, καὶ τῷ ἐν Ὀλυμπίῃ θεῷ ἐξελόντες, ἀπ' ἧς δεκάπηχυν χάλκεον Δία ἀνέθηκαν, καὶ τῷ ἐν Ἰσθμῷ θεῷ, ἀπ' ἧς ἑπτάπηχυς χάλκεος Ποσειδέων ἐξεγένετο.

Having brought all the loot together, they set apart a tithe for the god of Delphi. From this was made and dedicated that tripod which rests upon the bronze three-headed serpent, nearest to the altar; another they set apart for the god of Olympia, from which was made and dedicated a bronze figure of Zeus, ten cubits high;

and another for the god of the Isthmus, from which was fashioned a bronze Poseidon seven cubits high.[37]

The golden tripod was melted down by the Phokians in the 4th cecentury BCE, but the bronze serpent column was taken to Constantinople by Constantine the Great, and survives. The names of the coalition-members are inscribed on the coils of the snakes! The inscription runs thus:

> These fought the war: Spartans, Athenians, Korinthians, Tegeans, Sikyonians, Aiginetans, Megarians, Epidaurians, Orchomenians, Phleiasians, Troizenians, Hermionians, Tirynthians, Plataians, Thespians, Mykenaians, Keans, Melians, Naxians, Eretrians, Chalkidians, Styrians, Eleans, Potidaians, Leukadians, Anaktorians, Kythnians, Siphnians, Ambrakiots, Lepreans.[38]

An impressive tally, until one recalls that these are thirty states among some 1,500 in Greece proper. Loyalists and medisers were massively outnumbered by those who simply contrived to keep their heads down.

However, the first victory commemoration at Delphi was not by the coalition of anti-Persian states but by the Amphiktyony, a gesture which (as Scott plausibly argues) was an attempt at character-rehabilitation and the assertion of Greek loyalty; with this may be compared the dedication by Alexander I of Macedon, another mediser, also distinctly apologetic in intent.[39] But individual medising Amphiktyonic states, Thessaly included, are absent from the flurry of triumphant or justificatory post-war dedications at Delphi. We should not make too much of this: the communities living closest to the sanctuary were never its most enthusiastic dedicators. However, we can perhaps imagine that the tone of the Amphiktyonic meetings, and of sanctuary organisation generally, had changed since the last of Xerxes' forces left Greek shores. Athens and Sparta, twin leaders of the resistance, had come to the fore, and with their rivalry would go on to dominate the course of historical events through the fifth century. They must have gained massive symbolic ascendance over the other delegates on the Amphiktyonic council.

That said, in practical terms the medisers got off quite lightly. A promise made in 480 BCE to punish them once victory was complete and to give their confiscated wealth to Apollo at Delphi was not actually carried out in full.[40] A Spartan expedition to Thessaly after the war to punish the Thessalians for their disloyalty ended in farce when the Spartan commander, Leotychidas, succumbed to the lure of Thessalian gold and was persuaded to withdraw.[41] Thessalian coinage starts to flourish for the first time in the decades after the Persian defeat; this is not indicative of a region demoralised or suffering economic repercussions. Moreover, more fundamentally, it is worth bearing in mind how used the Greeks were to being at war with each other, in one way or another. They were not, of course, a nation; they were a collection of independent and semi-independent city-states and other types of political unit, and had never felt obliged to refrain from Greek-on-Greek conflict. Joint military enterprises were, by contrast, extremely rare.

Conclusion: the simplification of Thermopylai

The aim of this paper has been to show that the simple power of Thermopylai as an idea is not in fact matched by its geopolitical role and situation in early fifth-century Greece. So far from standing on a clear-cut frontier between loyalty and treachery or between Greek and barbarian, the site of the battle was at the very heart of pro-Persian territory, and for the historian acts as a reminder not to adopt a black and white view.

Herodotos is not unwilling to disclose the murkiness of the Persian Wars: he revels in it. The following remark about the loyalist stance of the state of Phokis, Thessaly's southern neighbour, illustrates this beautifully. The context is a Thessalian attempt to strong-arm the Phokians into medising.

οἱ γὰρ Φωκέες μοῦνοι τῶν ταύτῃ ἀνθρώπων οὐκ ἐμήδιζον, κατ᾽ ἄλλο μὲν οὐδέν, ὡς ἐγὼ συμβαλλόμενος εὑρίσκω, κατὰ δὲ τὸ ἔχθος τὸ Θεσσαλῶν· εἰ δὲ Θεσσαλοὶ τὰ Ἑλλήνων ηὖξον, ὡς ἐμοὶ δοκέειν, ἐμήδιζον ἂν οἱ Φωκέες. ταῦτα ἐπαγγελλομένων Θεσσαλῶν, οὔτε δώσειν ἔφασαν χρήματα, παρέχειν τε σφίσι Θεσσαλοῖσι ὁμοίως μηδίζειν, εἰ ἄλλως βουλοίατο· ἀλλ᾽ οὐκ ἔσεσθαι ἑκόντες εἶναι προδόται τῆς Ἑλλάδος.

The Phokians were the only ones in the whole region who would not take the Persians' side, and their only reason for this (as I find, from my reckoning) was their hatred of the Thessalians. [2] If the Thessalians had aided the Greeks, then the Phokians would certainly have medised. They replied to the offer of the Thessalians that they would give no money. It was open for them to medise like the Thessalians, if for any reason they wanted to, but they would not willingly betray Hellas.[42]

The Phokians evoke the rhetoric of loyalty, but Herodotos reveals it as a sham. The Phokians don't love Greece. They just hate the Thessalians. Flashes of deadly realism like this punctuate the *Histories*, even though Herodotos is also plainly captivated by the glory of resistance and by the magnitude of the Greek achievement. Osborne beautifully sums up the reality of interstate relationships in Greece:

> What then had the Greeks saved themselves from by defeating the Persian invasion? They had saved themselves from an imposed end to inter-city conflict. The liberty which they had gained was the liberty to continue to interfere with each other's liberty.[43]

Herodotos would not, at heart, have been astonished by such a verdict.

No other ancient author, however, matches Herodotos' complexity. The simplification of the Persian Wars and of Thermopylai specifically was accomplished in Classical Greece – it is not a modern phenomenon. This process was fuelled by nostalgia. By the early fourth century BCE, Greeks – Athenians especially – could look back on their victory against the odds, and sigh with longing.[44] For them, the invasion of 480 was the moment at which the Greeks achieved perfect unity in the face of seeming disaster: they forgot entirely, in the glow of hindsight, all the bickering, back-stabbing and jockeying for primacy which really beset the Greek response to Persia. Bickering and back-stabbing were features of their *own* time, not the time of Leonidas and his fellow-heroes.

A common theme of evocations of Thermopylai through the ages is the use of history as a means of escape from the complexity and compromise of one's age, through reference to what is seen as a simple ideal couched in a simple event. Leonidas is prized in this regard because, like nearly all famous Spartans, he is given to short, punchy statements; he has the rugged austerity of speech and manner which other Greeks, especially Athenians, admired and envied.[45] He is eminently quotable,[46] as a conversation with a fan of the film *300* will quickly reveal, and no knowledge or understanding of the man's full historical context is needed to appreciate his symbolic power. Likewise, the elaborate verses of Simonides are known only to Classicists, but his two-line epitaph echoes through the centuries: 'Go tell the Spartans that here we lie, obedient to their laws'. He has tailored his art to the laconism of its recipients, and in doing so has achieved just the kind of immortality the poet's words were meant to ensure but didn't always capture.[47] In the same way, Thermopylai's real oddness – its uncomfortable muddying of Greek allegiance; states scrambling to capitulate as the Persian armies approach; old attitudes discredited and old certainties overturned – is left for historians to pick over. The wider world understandably prefers the shining emblem of honour and glory.

Chapter 5

The Wars of the Ancient Israelites and European Culture

Steven Grosby

It is curious that there were so many appeals to past battles of Jewish wars throughout the history of predominately Christian Europe. One wonders why this was so. In an examination of those wars and the memory of them, two questions arise. What was the purpose of the frequent and varied retrievals of those past events from one culture into a later and different culture; and what was the significance of those appeals for the development of European culture? It appears that often this cultivated recollection of those past Jewish battles and wars was in the service of a pursuit of freedom, usually the freedom of a European nation. There are, however, a number of complications having to do with both this retrieval of the past and the pursuit of freedom that merit consideration, including the very nature of freedom.

What freedom means is not so straightforward. It could mean to be relieved from current burdens by restoring a previous condition before those burdens were imposed, as conveyed by our use of the word 'to liberate (from)'. In this instance, the individual would be relieved of crushing debt or liberated from slavery, thereby restoring the condition before the individual was in debt or enslaved. This appears to be the meaning conveyed by those approximately 4,000 year-old terms, the Sumerian *amargi* and the Akkadian *anduraru*, which scholars often translate as 'freedom'.[1] Because those terms from ancient Mesopotamian culture convey a restoration of a previous way of life, we may characterize their meaning of freedom as being traditional. A different understanding of freedom is conveyed when the term indicates a course of action where the individual, confronted with a problem, takes initiative to do something different, that is, when the individual has latitude of action to do something new.

When we today use the term 'freedom', we use it with both meanings, even though we may for the most part understand the term to convey the ability of the individual to embark on a new course of action that is determined solely by the individual. Whatever ambiguity of meaning might be lurking within our use of the term 'freedom', it means little apart from the ability to determine or control one's fate. To be free from coercion, to have control of one's life, is one of the most fundamental dispositions of the human heart.

When an individual acts, the individual does so based upon what he or she wants to do or thinks he or she should do. Human beings are not like bees in a hive or ants in a colony, where instincts determine entirely how the activity of the single bee or ant meshes with the hive or colony. The individual human being has the capacity to act independently, to make choices, to be open to the world in weighing alternatives. This anthropological ability to choose how to act is also referred to as freedom, as in 'free will'. The choice of the individual may be guided by the desire to restore what has been lost, to embark on a new and different pursuit, or some kind of combination of restoration and innovation. This latter combination is usually what takes place, because no individual, even when embarking on a new initiative, can be entirely free from his or her past.

Innovations are based upon previous accomplishments and the memory of past accomplishments. To be sure, the understanding of that past may be changing and selective, as it is subject to continual re-evaluation in response to the current interests of the individual. Be that as it may, every individual lives with a cultural inheritance, however changing and ambiguous, from their family, nation, and civilisation. Thus, while individuals act independently, they are also members of larger groups from which many of their ideas derive. The ideas from this cultural inheritance have a bearing on the choices the individual makes when they exercise their freedom, because a part of the understanding that the individual has of himself or herself is as a member of those different groups.

We shall be concerned with the freedom of not merely the individual but the individual as a member of the nation along with other members of the nation. Here, too, freedom means little apart from the ability to control the fate of what those individuals understand to be their nation. The freedom of the nation, not only to exist but also to act in the world so as to safeguard its existence, conveys the requirement that the nation must be more than a cultural community organized around a recognized territory with other distinguishing factors, for example, a common language or religion. In order to be free to act in the world, the nation must also have independent sovereignty as a national state. During the nineteenth and twentieth centuries, this freedom of the nation to act in the world has been known as the 'right of self-determination'—a right ensconced in 1945 in the Charter of the United Nations (reaffirmed in 1960 in General Assembly Resolution 1514) and implied earlier in 1920 in the Covenant of the League of Nations (Article 22).

Of course, the assertion of national sovereignty has a much longer history. The cultural and historical processes of the formation of earlier nations, for example, twelfth century England, thirteenth century Poland and sixteenth century Netherlands, and their further consolidation into national states were rarely, if ever, an entirely new innovation. Like the individual, these nations, in the on-going processes of their development, drew upon, and thereby reinterpreted, their cultural inheritance. In so doing, there was also a combination of restoration and innovation, as nations sought their freedom against empire, for example, the English and Dutch wars against Spain in the latter half of the sixteenth century.

It is precisely here where we come upon an enormous tension in the cultural heritage of the West. On the one hand, the religion of the West is monotheistic which, as such, asserts that all human beings, irrespective of their national origin, are, as children of the one and only God, equal. On the other hand, as previously noted, the individual is never merely an individual; for the individual understands himself or herself to be a member of a nation, thereby recognizing not equality among all humans but distinction between them, between an individual who is a member of the nation and an individual who is a foreigner. To navigate between these two, simultaneously held orientations—what scholars have characterized as the sacred universality of monotheism and the primordial attachments of nationality—an inherited cultural resource was often drawn upon.[2] It was turned to because it recognized national freedom and sovereignty as a legitimate ideal within an otherwise universal monotheism. As the accomplished scholar of nationalism Anthony Smith rightly argued, that cultural resource was the biblical image of the nation of ancient Israel and its struggle for freedom against empire.[3]

That pursuit of freedom combined both innovation and restoration. The innovation was national sovereignty, established during the reigns of Saul, David and Solomon (approximately 1000 to 920 BCE) and later during the period of the Maccabees or Hasmoneans (approximately 167 to 63 BCE). The restoration was the returning to, and safeguarding of, the religious tradition and customs of the ancient Israelites, as expressed by the initial plea of the Israelites to the Egyptian pharaoh: to worship the LORD (Exodus 3:18; see also 5:1-3), the God of their ancestors (3:13), the God of Abraham, Isaac, and Jacob (3:16; see also 6:2-3).

The tension of simultaneously recognizing both a monotheistic God whose jurisdiction is the entire world and the legitimacy of a distinctive nation is sanctioned in the Old Testament with the succinct assertion of Exodus 19:6, even though the whole world belongs to God, Israel is set apart as a holy nation.[4] As a result, the image of ancient Israel became the prototypical symbol within the monotheistic, cultural heritage of the West for national independence and sovereignty, often in opposition to empire. That image was appealed to in the development of, for example, the nations of England, both well before and especially throughout the sixteenth and seventeenth centuries, late medieval France, Bohemia, Scotland, and The Netherlands.

The paradigmatic expression of the monotheistic God recognizing the nation of Israel as being in some way chosen to become his own and free to become so is the liberation of Israel from the Egyptian house of slavery (Exodus 13:3; see also 3:8 and 3:17), where God 'makes a distinction between Egypt and Israel' (Exodus 11:7). Seven times we find the phrase 'Let my people go' (Exodus 5:1, 7:16, 8:1, 8:20, 9:1, 9:13, 10:13) and five additional, similar formulations such as 'I am the LORD, and I will free you from the burdens of the Egyptians and deliver you from slavery to them' (Exodus 6:6, 6:11, 6:13, 6:26, 7:2). The repetition of these twelve verses in the span of only six chapters of Exodus underscores the significance of the image of the liberation of ancient Israel from Egyptian bondage as a paradigmatic expression for the freedom of the nation.

But in the ancient Israelites' pursuit of freedom from Egyptian slavery, is there a military battle between them and the Egyptians? Here, there is, perhaps surprisingly, some ambiguity in the biblical narrative. Exodus 13:18 states, 'the Israelites went out of the land of Egypt prepared for battle [with the Egyptians]'. However, whatever suggestion of an armed conflict between Israel and Egypt might have been introduced into the account by this reference to the Israelites' preparation for battle, and, as we shall see, however much the idea of an Israelite battle against imperial bondage was subsequently appealed to in European history, that suggestion and appeal are severely compromised by the biblical narrative in Exodus. It is not the Israelites but God who is described as having destroyed in battle the Egyptians. It is God who is described as 'stretching out his hand

and striking Egypt with all his wonders' (Exodus 3:20). It is God who is described as having 'brought Israel out from Egypt by the strength of his hand' (Exodus 13:3), having sent the ten plagues against Egypt. And it is the LORD and not Israel who drowns the Egyptian army in the sea, as the Song of Moses makes clear, 'the Lord is a warrior; the LORD is his name. Pharaoh's chariots and his army he [the LORD] cast into the sea' (Exodus 15:3-4).

Because God, and not the Israelites, is described as having vanquished the Egyptians through the ten plagues and the drowning of the Pharaoh's army, the account of the battle may be characterized as myth. The justification for this characterization is abundantly clear from the description of the miraculous events of the ten plagues and the parting of the Red Sea. Furthermore, we have today no historical or archaeological evidence that would confirm the biblical account of the Israelite exodus from Egypt.[5]

This mythical quality of the description of the liberation of Israel from Egyptian slavery by the hands of the divine warrior has not prevented the biblical account of the exodus from being brought from the past into the present as a further justification for a nation's military rebellion against empire, for example, the Dutch struggle for freedom and sovereignty against the Spanish during the sixteenth and early seventeenth centuries. The mythical quality may have even contributed to the attractiveness of the account's adapted reception as it allowed the ideas of freedom and national sovereignty to be understood as being inseparable from the nature of the universe, that is, as the providence of God on whose behalf the battle for national freedom was waged. The attractiveness of this adapted retrieval is confirmed by the fact that one finds the story of the Israelite exodus everywhere during the sixteenth and seventeenth centuries, for example, in the numerous pamphlets, songs, dramas for the stage, engravings and paintings of early modern Dutch culture.[6]

The appeal to ancient Israel as a prototype of national freedom which, as a prototype, was believed to be applicable to the present became a commonplace during the sixteenth, seventeenth and eighteenth centuries. It is found in the art, music and political writings throughout early modern European culture. The depiction of Israel's liberation from Egypt at the crossing of the Red Sea can be seen in many of the paintings of the time, for example, by the German Lucas Cranach the Elder, 1530 (Fig. 5.1). The power of the image of the liberation of Israel from Egyptian bondage in European culture is confirmed by observing its continual exploitation, for example, as in the seventeenth century paintings of the crossing of the

Red Sea by the Flemish Martin Pepijn and the French Nicolas Poussin and Charles Le Brun.

Subsequently, many other paintings portraying the exodus appear, for example, by the early eighteenth century British painters Francis Danby and Benjamin West; and they continue to do so. The question worthy of being pondered is, why this persistence? The cultural significance of these pictorial depictions is that they convey an understanding by the members of several European nations that they, like the ancient Israelites, had also been chosen by God; they like, Israel, achieved the freedom to restore what they understood to be their ancient liberties through national sovereignty and independence against the empires of their time, the Holy Roman Empire and Spain.[7] They had become, and the members of these nations, for example, the French of the early thirteenth century, the Czech-speaking Bohemians of the fifteenth century, the Scottish and Dutch Calvinists of the sixteenth century, and the English and American Puritans of the seventeenth century, understood themselves as having become, 'new Israels'.[8]

And so, too, it would be with poetry and music. One finds use of the biblical account of the exodus in Milton's poetry, for example, his Psalm 81 and sonnets, both to convey England as a 'new Israel', and to liken its deliverance from King Charles I as a deliverance from another 'pharaoh'.[9] In 1738, George Frederic Handel composed his oratorio, *Israel in Egypt*, the most significant part of which revolves around the drowning of the Egyptian army in the Red Sea. In 1841, Giuseppe Verdi composed the opera that launched his career, *Nabucco*. While not about the exodus from Egypt, Verdi's opera also deals with Israel's bondage—the historically later bondage following the Babylonian King Nebuchadnezzar II's destruction of the Jerusalem temple (586 BCE) and exile of the leading sections of the Jewish population to Babylon. The opera conveys the thirst for national sovereignty and independence, nowhere more clearly than in the famous so-called 'Chorus of the Hebrew Slaves' (*Va, pensiero, sull'ali dorate*). In Act III, Scene II, we hear the slaves' lament,

> Fly, thought, on wings of gold;
> go settle upon the slopes and the hills,
> where, soft and mild, the sweet airs
> of our native land smell fragrant!
> Greet the banks of the Jordan
> and Zion's toppled towers.

Oh, my country so lovely and lost!
Oh, remembrance so dear and so fraught with despair!
… Rekindle our bosom's memories,
and speak of times gone by!

It is probable that some of the enthusiastic Italian response to Verdi's *Nabucco* had to do with the desire of the Italians for their own sovereignty and independence from, at that time, Austria.

This retrieval of the image of ancient Israel into the culture of early modern Europe can also be seen in legal and political writings. The late sixteenth and early seventeenth century Anglican theologian Richard Hooker, Dutch jurist Hugo Grotius and especially the English historian of law John Selden turned to ancient Israelite and rabbinic law as relevant to the law of their own time. During this same period, there appeared a proliferation of works on the so-called 'republic of the Hebrews', for example, by the Calvinist Corneille Bertram, the Catholic Carlo Sigonio, the Dutch Arminian Petrus Cunaeus and the Lutheran Wilhelm Schickard.[10] That these and many other writers of the sixteenth and seventeenth centuries looked past Greek and Roman history to the biblical account of the exodus and subsequent history of Israel for a political model of how national societies should be organized for their own times is nowhere more obvious than in Johannes Althusius' *Politica* (1603 CE). Whatever the differences among these many authors about how they understood the history of ancient Israel and its applicability to the politics of their times (differences ranging from a sympathy with centralized monarchy to federated republic), they, as were those previously mentioned legal scholars, were all in agreement with the necessity of the freedom of the nation and its sovereignty against empire. As Israel was victorious in its 'battle' with Egypt, so, too, would their respective nations be victorious against the Egypts of their own times.

No one wishes to be commanded to do what he or she resents doing. No one wants his or her traditions persecuted, because to do so is to undermine that person's existence by demeaning his or her self-understanding. To be free to live one's life, including pursuing how one understands that life through cultivating one's traditions, is part of what is conveyed by the biblical account of the liberating exodus of Israel from Egyptian slavery. That this freedom is not accidental but rooted in the meaning of human existence because it is accomplished through the acts of the creator of the world is also conveyed by the biblical narrative.

These are the reasons for the potency and resiliency of the portrayal of God's battle against those who enslave.

There are, however, other Jewish wars against imperial servitude which have been appealed to, and by so doing brought forth into the present as a model for action, in the course of European history. One was the Jewish war ostensibly against the Assyrians, the decisive battle of which was waged by the heroine Judith. Another was the war of the Maccabees against the Seleucid Empire.

These other wars were fully in accord with the earlier Israel of the exodus as the historical prototype of national freedom, because the biblical covenants, both before and subsequent to the exodus, had firmly established, as constitutive of Judaism, the goal of the sovereign independence of Israel through the promises that God had made to Israel: numerous descendants of Abraham, Isaac and Jacob who will dwell in the clearly demarcated land meant only for them.[11] The difference between, on the one hand, the decisive battles of these two later Jewish wars against imperial oppression and, on the other, the biblical description of the exodus is that those former battles were described in the Bible as having been waged by human beings and not by God. They, therefore, lack the mythical quality of the account of the exodus.

The Battle of Judith against the imperial army of Nebuchadnezzar—a battle which, as we shall see, is certainly fictional—is described in *Judith*, a book found in the Roman Catholic and Orthodox Bibles but not held to be canonical in the Jewish and Protestant traditions. The setting, as laid out in the first chapter, is the defence of the Israelites against the invading Assyrian army. Already the reader faces complications that call into question the historical reality of the events portrayed in the book, as Nebuchadnezzar is described as the ruler over the Assyrians in the capital of Nineveh, when, in fact, he was king of Babylon after Nineveh had been destroyed in 612 BCE. The account is further confused by two references in chapter four: to the second temple, even though the temple was rebuilt a century or two later; and to the Jewish high priest who appears to have had not only religious authority but also military responsibilities—a combination contrary to Jewish tradition but which would nonetheless appear in the second century BCE during the period of the Maccabees. Thus, it seems that the narrative combines details that actually span a period of six centuries, from the seventh to the second century BCE, the latter being the probable date of its composition.

Doubt about the historical accuracy of the book arising from these details is only further compounded by the description of the extraordinary actions of the remarkable heroine, after whom the book is named, Judith. As Judith enters into the narrative in chapter eight of this sixteen-chapter long book, her city Bethulia, about which we have no historical evidence, has been surrounded for thirty-four days by the Assyrian army led by Nebuchadnezzar's general, Holofernes. Their water supply cut off and facing starvation, the inhabitants of the town propose to surrender to the Assyrians so that they will not witness their children dying before their eyes. Believing themselves to have been abandoned by God, they prefer slavery to death. At this point, the widow Judith, who was 'beautiful in appearance and very lovely to behold' and 'feared God with great devotion' (Judith 8:7-8), steps forward, reprimanding the Jews of Bethulia for thinking that they understood the ways of God. They did not understand, as Judith did, that the Jews' faith in God was being tested. Judith, with unwavering faith, understood that God would 'deliver Israel by her hand' (Judith 8:33). She then prays to God, saying

> the Assyrians do not know that you are the Lord who crushes wars ... break their (the Assyrian) strength by your might, and bring down their power in your anger; for they intend to defile your sanctuary, and to pollute the tabernacle.[12] Give to me, a widow, the strong hand to do what I plan. By the deceit of my lips strike down the prince ... Crush their arrogance by the hand of a woman ...Make my deceitful words bring wound and bruise on those who have planned cruel things against your covenant ... Let your whole nation ... understand that you are God ...and that there is no other who protects the people of Israel but you alone. (Judith 9:7-14)

The reader soon discovers the deceit referred to in Judith's prayer. 'Having made herself very beautiful to entice the eyes of all the men who might see her' (Judith 10:4), Judith and her maid leave Bethulia and arrange to be captured by an Assyrian patrol for the purpose of revealing to Holofernes how to capture the town. The deceit, however, does not consist in her putative betrayal of the Jews of Bethulia; rather, her plan, having seduced Holofernes with her beauty, is to murder him, thereby saving Israel from Assyrian servitude. And so it comes to pass. Holofernes tells his eunuch to invite Judith to a private banquet, saying to him that 'it would be a disgrace if we let such a woman go without having intercourse with her. If we do not seduce her, she will laugh at us' (Judith 12:12). Of course, the ironic reversal here is that Judith is the successful seducer: Holofernes, 'having drunk at the banquet more than he had ever done in any one day since he was born' (Judith 12:20), passes out on the bed and is decapitated by Judith.

Paintings of Judith's decapitation of Holofernes were common during the fifteenth, sixteenth and seventeenth centuries. One of the more famous of those many paintings was done by the Italian female Artemisia Gentileschi in 1612 (Fig. 5.2). Judith and her maid, who has put Holofernes' head in a bag, leave the Assyrian camp, return to Bethulia, reveal the head to the astonished Israelites and have it placed on the parapet of the town's wall for all to see. The following day, the Assyrians, having discovered the headless body of their general and, hence, are 'overcome with fear and trembling' (Judith 15:2), flee, whereupon they are slaughtered by the Israelites.

The Book of Judith concludes with a song that conveys the independence of the nation against imperial oppression. 'The Assyrian boasted that he would burn up my territory, and kill my young men with the sword, and dash my infants to the ground, and seize my children as booty, and take my virgins as spoil'(Judith 16:4). The ambiguity of 'my' in this verse, that is, the 'my' may refer to God, Judith or the Israelites, reinforces the patriotic intention of the song. It continues by connecting the plan of God with the plan of Judith,

> But the Lord Almighty has foiled them by the hand of a woman ... For she put away her widow's clothing to exalt the oppressed in Israel. She anointed her face with perfume; she fastened her hair with a tiara and put on a linen gown to beguile him. Her sandal ravished his eyes, her beauty captured his mind, and the sword severed his neck ...Woe to the nations that rise up against my people. The Lord Almighty will take vengeance on them in the day of judgement. (Judith 16:5,7-9,17)

The concluding lines of the song reveal clearly why the figure of Judith has often been appealed to in European sculpture, painting and music as a symbol for patriotism, for courage in defence of the freedom of one's people.[13] Here, too, to be free is to defend, and thereby restore, one's traditions: in the case of the Israelites, to defend the Temple against Assyrian (or Seleucid or Roman) desecration, to defend the Israelite covenant with God. While not mythical as the biblical account of the Israelite exodus from Egypt, the obviously fictional portrayal of the female heroine likely only contributed to both the call for moral courage and the idea of the unity of the nation, as it is a woman whose extraordinary actions save her people.

Those people, male and female, gazing at depictions of Judith could be Florentines (so Donatello's bronze sculpture of 1455, Fig. 5.3, of Judith as a symbol for defence of Florentine liberty),[14] other Italians (so paintings by Gentileschi, Giorgione, Titian and Caravaggio among others), Dutch (paintings by Rembrandt and Rubens) and English (for example, William Etty).

All could have sung the song or variations of the song that concludes the Book of Judith, including the French. In 1873, Charles-Édouard Lefebvre's three-act lyrical drama, *Judith*, was performed in Paris, with its probable intention of rallying the French in the aftermath of the 1871 Prussian victory over France.

The problems of historical accuracy, whether mythical or fictional, as represented respectively in the account of the exodus and the story of Judith, do not appear in another example of Jewish wars appealed to throughout European history, the fight of the Maccabees for the freedom of Israel against the Seleucid Empire. In 1 Maccabees, like the Book of Judith found in the Roman Catholic and Orthodox Bibles but not in the Jewish and Protestant Bibles, there is no description of God waging a decisive battle. There are no miracles. There is no young David, having slain the Philistine Goliath with his slingshot (1 Samuel 17:49), displaying the head of the giant, as depicted so magnificently by the Italian painter Caravaggio in 1607 (Fig. 5.4). There is no alluring Judith, with a sword to decapitate the Assyrian Holofernes. The military battles of the Maccabees stand in contrast to these examples of solitary individuals who single-handedly achieve military victory for the Israelites.

In 167 BCE, the Seleucid King Antiochus IV undertook a program of religious persecution of the Jews, having decreed a ban on circumcision and observance of the Sabbath (1 Maccabees 1:43-50). Armed opposition erupted in response, led by the five Maccabee brothers and their father Mattathias. The Jewish war against the Seleucids to restore the laws and customs of the Jews lasted for twenty-five years, culminating in the re-establishment of Jewish sovereignty in 141 BCE under Simon, the remaining survivor of the five brothers (1 Maccabees 13-14).

The descriptions in 1 Maccabees of the battles during this war are historically believable. The Jews often engage in tactically shrewd, guerilla warfare against the Seleucid army. When large battles take place, their descriptions are realistic, as the armies often number from several hundred to several thousand. We are told of realistic debates over military strategy, for example, the decision of the Jews to fight on the Sabbath, thereby avoiding certain defeat (1 Maccabees 2:40-41). When the temple is captured, purified and re-dedicated (*Hannukah* in Hebrew), there is no miracle involved. The story of the small amount of oil miraculously burning for eight days appears nowhere in 1 Maccabees, as it is a much later, rabbinic addition found in the Babylonian Talmud Shabbat 21b. Victories are described, but so, too, are defeats, for example, in 162 BCE, the death in battle of Judas Maccabeus (1 Maccabees 9:17). Here, with the Maccabees, was a realistic example of human initiative to wage war in defence of religion and for freedom of the nation. It would be an example appealed to time and time again in medieval and early modern Europe as a model for action.

The reliance on allegory in the tradition of Christian, Patristic exegesis of the Old Testament allowed for Christians to reinterpret what might otherwise be doctrinally difficult in ways that would be more or less consonant with the Christian tradition. For example, Abraham's sacrifice of Isaac, as described in Genesis 22, became an allegory for the crucifixion of Jesus; and the figure described as 'the son' of the LORD in Psalm 2, or on the 'side' of the LORD as his 'right hand' in Psalm 118, is interpreted as reference not to David or Solomon but to Jesus (so Acts 13:33). It was this allegorical imagination, if you will, which made it possible and plausible for the French, Dutch, English and Puritans of America to understand themselves as 'new Israels', albeit, and however paradoxical, Christian 'new Israels'.

As we shall see, one clearly observes the same imagination used earlier in medieval Europe with the interpretative retrieval of the Maccabees. However, with the Maccabees, an exegetical shift occurs. The Maccabees are not allegorically reinterpreted to represent individuals other than the Maccabees; rather, the latter remain actual historical figures, serving as a prototype to be emulated—a prototype for the Christian Crusaders. Thus, during the Middle Ages, the Christian Europeans waging war to free Jerusalem and the Holy Land were understood to be Christ's Maccabeans. The conquest of the Kingdom of Jerusalem during the Crusades was understood to be a continuation of the Jewish wars of the Old Testament.[15]

Numerous examples of retrieving the example of the Maccabees from the past into the present of medieval Europe are found. According to Guibert of Nogent, Pope Urban II at the Council of Clermont (1095 CE) proclaimed, 'If in older times the Maccabees attained the highest praise of piety because they fought for the ceremonies and the Temple, it is also justly granted you, Christian soldiers [the Crusaders], to defend the liberty of your country by armed endeavor'.[16] Later, the crusading Christian military orders, the Knights Templars and the Teutonic Knights, were described as the 'new Maccabees' or 'successors of the Maccabees' by respectively Pope Celestine II (1143-44 CE) and Pope Honorius III (1221 CE).[17] The Crusades had become, in the words of Pope Innocent III, 'a new time of the Maccabees'.[18]

This retrieval of the Maccabees into the life of European culture would continue. In 1746, Handel composed the oratorio *Judas Maccabaeus*, the purpose of which was to commemorate the victory of the English Maccabean army of the Duke of Cumberland against the Scottish Jacobite uprising at the Battle of Culloden. The significance of the meaning of the memory of the Maccabees for national freedom is abundantly clear with the opening Israelite chorus' lament over the death of Mattathias, father of the Maccabean sons, when the Jews were still under Seleucid occupation. 'Mourn, ye afflicted children, the remains of captive Judah, mourn in solemn strains; your sanguine hopes of liberty give o'er; your hero, friend and father, is no more'. Judas Maccabaeus' recitative, later in the first Act of the oratorio, highlights how the Maccabees were understood in the 'new Israel' of the England of that time.

> So will'd my father now at rest
> In the eternal mansions of the blest:
> "Can ye behold," said he "the miseries,
> In which the long-insulted Judah lies?
> Can ye behold their dire distress,
> And not, at least, attempt redress?"
> Then, faintly, with expiring breath,
> "Resolve, my sons, on liberty, or death!"
> We come! Oh see, thy sons prepare
> The rough habiliments of war;
> With hearts intrepid, and revengeful hands,
> To execute, O sire, thy dread commands.

The first Act of Handel's oratorio points in two different directions: one, the mourning of the death of Mattathias, who, according to 1 Maccabees, began the defence of the Jewish religion against Seleucid persecution; and two, the choice of 'liberty or death' in pursuit of freedom for the long-insulted nation of Judah, but now also England, from its miseries. Both directions were depicted earlier in 'The Triumph of Judas Maccabeus'

(1635) by the Dutch painter Paul Rubens, where Judas, in victory, prays for the fallen Jewish soldiers (Fig. 5.5). For the Dutch of that time, to gaze upon Rubens' painting of Judas Maccabeus no doubt represented to them William of Orange and his son, Maurice, mourning the death of those who had fought for the freedom of the Netherlands against the Spanish.

While the wars of Israel, as portrayed in the biblical accounts of the exodus, Judith and the Maccabees, have repeatedly been drawn upon throughout European history in order to justify the military actions of subsequent Europeans, their retrieval from the past into the present conveys a conceptual tension in the cultural heritage of the West. In fact, it not only conveys but also exemplifies that tension. The crusaders may have been understood to have been 'Christ's crusaders' or 'Christ's Maccabeans'; but, as soldiers preparing for, or engaged in, war they were not in the tradition of Jesus' apostles following the commandments of the Sermon on the Mount (Matthew 5-7). The descriptions of the Israelites preparing for battle at the Red Sea or Judith's beheading of the Assyrian general Holofernes or the Maccabees' war against the Seleucids were not exemplars of spiritual struggle for the eternal salvation of the soul. These wars were certainly not prototypes of *imitatio Christi*. Rather, the appeal to the traditions of these Jewish wars was in the service of the emergence of a 'new time of the Maccabees', of 'new Israels'. In so doing, we witness a peculiar but significant cultural phenomenon having to do with the reception, and thereby transformation, of tradition, thus, the relation between the past and the present.

The partial emptying of the original content of cultural symbols and the introduction into them of a new content reveals how different meanings may co-exist within symbols in the constitution of new traditions. This partial emptying and new introduction is an expression of a conceptual combination of restoration and innovation. In the instances examined in this chapter, the original biblical contents of those earlier Jewish cultural symbols were co-mingled with the new interests, demands and problems of medieval and early modern Europe, representing the emergence of a paradoxical 'Christian Hebraism'.[19] This conceptual co-mingling of content was possible because the Christian Bible contains those earlier Jewish accounts. This possibility was made actual by Christians turning to those accounts, thereby reviving them in their lives, as they understood that content to be prototypes or paradigms for their self-understanding and actions in their own and quite different contexts. Thus, the Battle of the Exodus and the accounts of Judith and the Maccabees became Christian prototypes for the struggle for religious and political freedom, often combined in pursuit of national sovereignty in early modern Europe.

The conceptual difficulty for Christianity is that the nation and the freedom of the national state through sovereignty have very little, if any, doctrinal legitimacy in the New Testament. For that legitimacy, medieval and early modern Christian Europe looked past the heaven of the New Testament, turning to one of its cultural legacies, the national sovereignty of Israel in its Old Testament.[20] That this turn clearly took place leaves us with further questions for our consideration. Might the significance of this turn exist beyond its particular historical occurrence in medieval and early modern Europe? Certainly freedom requires the exercise of power to determine one's fate, to govern oneself. Since this is so, to be free entails the political exercise of self-government, of sovereignty. And if this is so, and if to be free is a fundamental disposition of the human heart, might the Israelites' wars for national freedom and sovereignty against the oppression of empire—Egyptian, Assyrian, and Seleucid—not merely be a part of our cultural legacy but also represent an image for how we should live today if we wish to be free? If the answer to these questions is affirmative, as the varied and frequent appeals to the image of ancient Israel throughout European history indicate, the cultural significance of those appeals is that the memory of ancient Israel, that is, the freedom of national sovereignty, is a continuing component of European culture, even though it may, depending upon shifting circumstances, exist in tension with other components.

Chapter 6

The Battle of the Teutoburg Forest Commemorated: from the Arch of Germanicus to the Arminius Monument

Matthew Nicholls

The Battle of the Teutoburg Forest had long echoes. It became an event whose afterlife was reshaped by successive contexts, in its immediate commemoration at Rome, in the way that later generations of Roman writers thought about it, and then in widely differing historical contexts up until the present day.

The battle happened in 9 CE. The events were generally known by the names of the protagonists rather than by the toponym we now use: the *clades Variana* (Varus' disaster) for the Romans, and the *Hermannschlacht* (Arminius'/Hermann's Battle) for later German writers. The outline of events is fairly well known, and was dramatically retold by Roman writers, from contemporaries Strabo and Velleius Paterculus to Suetonius and Tacitus around 100 years later, to Dio Cassius whose relatively detailed account is a century later again.[1] Three Roman legions under Publius Quinctilius Varus were wiped out in an ambush by German tribesmen led by Arminius, a prince of the Germanic Cherusci tribe, who had received a Roman education and served with the Roman army and was a trusted adviser to Varus. Elements of the story were repeated in successive retellings until they came to have the feel of legend at least as much as solid historical fact: the greed and complacency of Varus, who ignored warnings and whose troops and baggage train were hopelessly strung out in country he wrongly believed to be friendly; the dank, wooded German landscape and climate, fatal to the Romans, too cramped to manoeuvre and with weapons saturated by the rain, but helpful to the native Germans who knew the trackless forest ways; Arminius' guile in building a coalition among the Germanic tribes and deceiving Varus with false reports of an uprising; the drama of Arminius' subsequent conflicts with fellow Germans including his own family, most notably his brother Flavus (with whom Tacitus stages a set-piece debate on the advantages and disadvantages of collaborating with Rome, improbably shouted by the brothers across the Weser river from the positions of their opposing armies);[2] and the emperor Augustus' theatrical devastation on hearing the news of the massacre:

> In fact, they say that he was so distressed that for several months his beard and hair were left uncut, and sometimes he would occasionally dash his head against a door, crying out aloud: "Quinctilius Varus, give me back my legions!" And every year he observed the day of the disaster as one of sorrow and mourning. (Suetonius *Augustus* 23)

The aftermath of the battle was also famous. The dashing prince Germanicus, who earned enormous popularity for a series of campaigns avenging the defeat, piously returned to the site of the slaughter in 15 CE to bury the Roman dead. Tacitus describes his battlefield tour with grim relish:

> ... they visited the mournful sites, ghastly in their appearance and associations ... In the centre of the field were whitening bones, scattered or gathered together as men had fled or stood to resist. Nearby fragments of weapons and limbs of horses were lying about, and also, nailed to trunks of trees, were heads. In the adjacent groves were the barbarous altars, on which they had sacrificed the tribunes and first-rank centurions ... here the legates fell, there the eagles were captured; where Varus was first wounded, where he found his end by the blow of his own ill-fated right hand... (Tacitus *Annals* 1.61)

The aim of this chapter is not to retell the story of the battle, compelling as it is, but to look at its aftermath and reception, both at Rome and later. Already we have seen that Roman authors of the early second century CE, Tacitus and Suetonius, viewed this disaster as important enough to dwell on in accounts they wrote a century or so later, and to invest them with vivid drama. The Varian disaster came to be viewed not only as important in itself, but also as a turning point in Roman expansionism, a defeat so terrible that it became in time a familiar marker in the historical landscape, like the Somme or Gallipoli during the twentieth century.

Roman Dynastic Politics and the Arch of Germanicus

I propose here two contexts for this later Roman evaluation of the battle: the geo-political aftermath, as it seemed to Roman writers of the second and third centuries CE, and the dynastic context. Since for Roman writers the history of their times was in large part the history of the Roman imperial family – particularly so for the biographer Suetonius – the two were closely connected. There was a strong biographical element in Roman historical thought, and a tendency to portray events and individuals through a moralising lens; both, as well will see, coloured later interpretations of Varus' defeat by Arminius.

In geo-political terms, the battle seems to have contributed to a change in attitudes towards the German frontier towards the end of the reign of Rome's first emperor Augustus. Rome had won much new territory during the last decades of the republic (including Gaul under Caesar), and the forty-five years of Augustus' reign had been marked, for the most part, by the largest continuous period of expansion in the history of the empire, with territory added or consolidated in Spain, the Alps, the Balkans, Africa, and the near east – and in Germany. The coming generation of Julio-Claudian princes was directed by Augustus in the last decades of the first century BCE towards the reduction of the German tribes in an apparent continuation of this momentum. Drusus, the brother of Augustus' stepson and eventual successor Tiberius and the father of Germanicus, had crossed the Rhine and won a series of battles, displacing German tribes and forcing them into submission or into alliance with one another.[3] Drusus died in 9 BCE, but for these campaigns he was posthumously awarded the honorific name 'Germanicus' which passed to his infant son. Other Roman generals carried on the process of conquest. The future emperor Tiberius subjugated further tribes and crossed the Weser, establishing a substantial Roman presence as far the Elbe.[4] For much of Augustus' reign the goal, or at least the rhetoric articulated in Augustan poetry and art, was *imperium sine fine* - empire without end.[5]

In 6 CE a rebellion in the Balkans meant that Roman legionary manpower was diverted there,[6] but the process of converting Germany into a Roman province continued, and formed the background to the disaster that helped to reshape Roman attitudes to the German frontier: Publius Quinctilius Varus, an experienced provincial governor and a friend of the imperial family, was sent out with three legions in 9 CE, and took steps to organise taxation in the newly invaded area as a Roman province.[7]

The terrible consequences of Varus' failure in this mission – the loss of well over 10% of the empire's entire complement of legions[8] – seem to have precipitated a radical change of direction. Near the end of his life Augustus produced a series of political testamentary documents which he entrusted to the Vestal Virgins for safekeeping. These included a public testimony of his achievements, the *Res Gestae*, displayed in Rome and all over the empire (our surviving copies come from Turkey). There was a second document specifying Augustus' own funeral arrangements, and a third listing all the military forces and revenues in the empire. This third document, written in Augustus' own hand, included a postscript instructing his successor Tiberius 'that the empire should be kept within its existing boundaries.'[9] Tacitus, who tells us about this instruction, gives a typically cynical reason: Augustus was either afraid, or jealous of any achievements of his successors that might diminish his own reputation. But why should Augustus feel threatened on either score after over four decades of military and political supremacy?

The Varian disaster, five years before Augustus' death, must have been in his mind as he wrote these testamentary instructions. At this date Gaul and the Iberian peninsula to the west had long been reduced to Roman control; to the east, Rome's relations with the Parthians had been marked by an uneasy détente since the Battle of Carrhae in 53 BCE, and would remain unsettled for decades to come with little prospect of permanent conquest. The German frontier seems to be what Augustus had in mind – it was in fact the focus of military activity immediately after his death – and his caution, if we rule out the base motive of jealousy, must have been prompted in part by the loss of Varus' legions. His instructions were followed. The Elbe and Weser were abandoned as frontiers, and Roman troops retreated to the west bank of the Rhine; in the 80s CE the frontier was formalised in the Domitianic *limes Germanicus*, a network of fortifications that stretched from the mouth of the Rhine to Regensburg on the Danube. Although eastward forays were made, including as we will see under Germanicus, greater Germany remained unconquered. Later emperors chose other targets for expansion: in 43 CE Claudius invaded Britain, whose consolidation as a province took several decades; the Flavian emperors wrestled with Jewish revolt and war in Dacia (Romania) in the late 60s to 90s CE; Trajan at the start of the second century completed the latter conquest and made a short-lived invasion of Parthia. The permanent conquest of trans-Rhine Germany was not attempted. Although it is possible, and perhaps correct, to see the abandonment of the ambition to conquer Germany as the product of a decades-long process of entrenchment, military reorganisation, and changing attitudes to frontiers,[10] it is still the case that the Varian disaster was seen by Roman writers as a turning point – and it may well have been so, as well as a symptom of a more systemic change.

The dynastic legacy of the disaster comes from the involvement of Germanicus in shaping its aftermath. Germanicus was 24 in 9 CE and already acclaimed as a significant military leader. He was also, importantly, marked out as an heir to imperial power. Augustus, who was 72 by this time, had chosen one heir after another to try to settle his succession: his son-in-law Agrippa, his nephew Marcellus, his grandsons Gaius and Lucius. He eventually adopted his stepson Tiberius in 4 CE as these promising candidates successively died and, even though Tiberius had a son of his own (the younger Drusus), Augustus required him to adopt Germanicus, a descendant (through his mother) of Augustus' own family line. Augustus' intention was to unite two branches of the family into the succession and to secure two generations of potential heirs. But Germanicus' popularity, and his family lineage – he married the emperor's granddaughter and had numerous children by her – in fact made him a threat to Tiberius and his own son.

Germanicus had entered public life early, and campaigned in Germany from 11 CE in the immediate aftermath of the Varian disaster. After holding the consulship in Rome (12 CE), he returned to Germany as commander and successfully put down a mutiny of the Rhine legions on Augustus' death in 14 CE. He diverted the energy of the would-be mutinous legions by crossing the Rhine, mounting a very successful set of punitive expeditions that recovered the lost legionary eagles, and buried (as we saw) the Roman dead of the Teutoburg Forest, winning enormous popular affection.

At this point, so the story goes, Germanicus was poised to sweep through the German tribes and restore Roman power up to the Elbe. But the emperor Tiberius recalled him to Rome in 17 CE, gave him the honour of a triumph, and packed him off to a special command in the eastern empire. Tacitus claims that Tiberius acted out of jealousy of Germanicus' successes, and particularly of his popularity with the people and the troops.[11] We have already expressed some caution over this jealousy motif in Tacitus; we might note that he says exactly the same of his father-in-law Agricola's recall from Britain by an anxious Domitian,[12] and that there is no certainty that Germanicus could have completed the reduction of Germany more successfully than Varus. But we can at least be confident that the leadership of the Roman forces in the aftermath of the Varian disaster and the death of Augustus was closely bound up with dynastic power politics on the home front, and that this played a part in making the disaster a permanent turning point rather than a temporary set-back.

Tiberius was now faced with a dilemma: how to honour the success of a dashing and popular man increasingly regarded as his rival? The question was all the more acute after Germanicus died in suspicious circumstances in Syria on 10 October 19 CE. The Roman people reacted with violent grief[13] and Tiberius was accused of mourning insufficiently, or even of complicity in the death of his dashing young rival via the agency of his Syrian governor Gnaeus Calpurnius Piso; a complex and murky trial resulted in Piso's suicide and left a cloud over Tiberius.[14] There was a universal public demand for the commemoration of Germanicus from a reluctant imperial house, calling to mind the aftermath of the death of Diana, Princess of Wales.[15] What sort of commemoration would strike the right note?

Rome had, of course, a long tradition of commemorative victory architecture. Much of this was associated with the route and nature of the triumph, the victory procession that was the ultimate accolade to a conquering general.[16] Germanicus had been awarded this honour in 17 CE. The triumph, however glorious, was an ephemeral honour, and a more permanent form of commemoration through architecture soon grew up to mark a triumphant general's achievements permanently in the fabric of the city. In the republic victory temples had clustered along the triumphal route; the last generation of republican politician-generals had diversified into more crowd-pleasing and less obviously pious structures like Pompey's Theatre of 55 BCE, and Augustus had added one or more gateway arches celebrating his triumphs to the Forum.

Could some sort of posthumous triumphal monument to Germanicus be added to this catalogue of victory monuments? This was a difficult matter, whose solution sheds some interesting light on the developing genre of triumphal architecture at Rome. Even if Tiberius had not had a hand in Germanicus' death, he was widely seen as a beneficiary from it in dynastic terms. Moreover, Germanicus' record of success, though no doubt due to personal brilliance, had serious limits. His victories in Germany were not decisive conquests, but mopping-up exercises carried out at least in part to burn off the energies of mutinous troops, undertaken in response to one of the greatest disasters in Roman military history, and called off by a jealous commander-in-chief before they could come to complete fruition.

As it happens we do have some evidence of how this problem of commemoration was tackled. The Senate and other bodies approved a range of posthumous honours. Tacitus gave a short list, which included commemorative arches in Rome, on the Rhine, and in Syria, 'with an inscription recording his achievements, and how he had died in the public service'.[17] Remarkably, a series of bronze inscriptions has been found which

Fig 1.1: Composition A
Piet Mondrian (1872-1944)
(Alinari/Art Resource, NY)

Fig 1.2: The Massacres at Chios
Painted in 1824 by Eugene Delacroix (1798-1863)
(Scala/Art Resource, NY)

Fig 1.3: The Oath of the Horatii
Painted c.1784 by Jacques-Louis David
(1748-1825)
(RMN-Grand Palais/Art Resource, NY)

Fig 1.4: Masada
Side view of Masada.
(*Balage Balogh/Art Resource, NY*)

Fig 2.1: Derniere & miserable ruyne, bruslement & saccagement de Troye la grand, par les Grecs
Anon (1583)

Fig 2.2: Troy
Remainders of the ancient city of Troy showing the palace walls on the North side. Wood engraving, c. 1875.
(*Art Resource, NY*)

Fig 2.3:
Trojan Horse in Çanakkale, Turkey.

Above Fig 3.1: Marathon
Man runs first marathon to bring news of the Greek victory over Persia.
(*NGS Image Collection/The Art Archive at Art Resource, NY*)

Below **Fig 3.2: Tumulus of Marathon**
Tumulus of Marathon, in Attica, Greece. The ashes of 192 Athenian soldiers killed in the Battle of Marathon (490 BCE) are buried here.
(*Gianni Dagli Orti/The Art Archive at Art Resource, NY*)

Fig 3.3: Idealised view of the Acropolis and Areopagus in Athens
Painted in1846 by Leo von Klenze (1784-1864)
(*bpk Bildagentur/Art Resource, NY*)

Fig 3.4: Parthenon Frieze
Horsemen from the west frieze of the Parthenon at the Acropolis, Athens, c.438-432 BCE.
(*The Trustees of the British Museum/Art Resource, NY*)

Fig 3.5: George III coin
Gold sovereign of George III, Great Britain, 1817. One of the most secure coins in international trade in the nineteenth century. Designed and engraved by the Italian artist Benedetto Pistrucci (1783-1855), it shows St George and the Dragon – a design which is still used on sovereigns struck at the Royal Mint for collectors.
(*The Trustees of the British Museum/Art Resource, NY*)

Fig 4.1: Leonidas at Thermopylae
Painted in 1814 by Jacques-Louis David (1748-1812)
(*RMN-Grand Palais/Art Resource, NY*)

Fig 4.2: Leonidas monument, Thermopalae
This monument, celebrating the heroism of Leonidas and the Spartans, was commissioned in 1955 by Paul, King of Greece.
(*Vanni Archive/Art Resource, NY*)

Fig 5.1: The Passage through the Red Sea
Lucas Cranach the Elder (1472-1553)
(*State Gallery, Aschaffenburg*)

Fig 5.2: Judith beheading Holofernes
Artemisia Gentileschi (1593-1653)
(*Museo nazionale di Capodimonte, Naples*)

Fig 5.3: Judith decapitating Holofernes
Donatello (1386-1466)
(*Palazzo Vecchio, Florence*)

Fig 5.4: David with the head of Goliath
Caravaggio (1571-1610)
(*Kunsthistorisches Museum, Vienna*)

Fig 5.5: The Triumph of Judas Maccabeus
Peter Paul Rubens (1577-1640)
(*Musée des Beaux Arts, Nantes*)

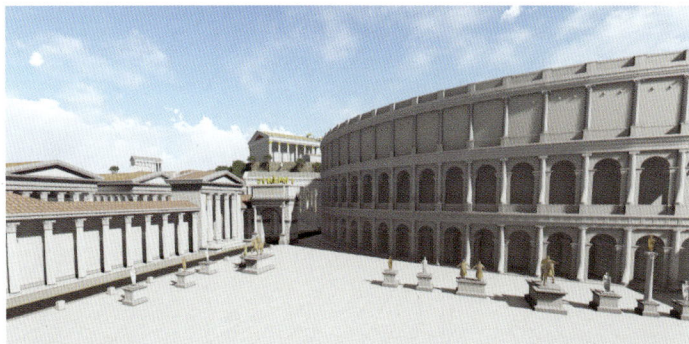

Fig 6.1:
The Arch of Germanicus and southern Circus Flaminius from Matthew Nicholls' digital model of ancient Rome.
(*Matthew Nicholls*)

Fig 6.2:
The Arch of Germanicus from Matthew Nicholls' digital model of ancient Rome.
(*Matthew Nicholls*)

Fig 6.3: Hermann Monument
Inauguration celebration of the Hermann Monument in the Teutoburg Forest, 16 August 1875. Engraving after a drawing by Hermann Lüders.
(*bpl Bildagentur/Art Resource, NY*)

Fig 7.1:
Harold is crowned King of England on 6 January 1066, on the same day as King Edward's funeral. A scene from the Victorian copy of the original eleventh-century Bayeux Tapestry (more accurately, an embroidery), completed in c.1886, kept in Reading Museum, England. (*Reading Museum*)

Fig 7.2:
The Normans building ships to invade England. (*Reading Museum*)

Fig 7.3:
The Battle of Hastings.
(*Reading Museum*)

Fig 7.4:
The death of King Harold (the Normans are seen killing the King).
(*Reading Museum*)

Fig 7.5:
Hasting Hill, with the ruins of the abbey in the top left-hand corner.
(*Roy Boss*)

Massacre de Béziers.

Fig 8.1: Béziers
A nineteenth-century history book
illustration of the Massacre of Béziers.
(*Editors' Collection*)

Fig 8.2: Le Dernier cathare, vol. 1: Tuez-les tous!
Arnaud Delalande and Eric Lambert
(*Les Editions 12 bis, Pairs, 2010*)

Fig 9.1: The Battle of Courtrai
Nicaise de Keyser
(*Museum Groeningeabdij, Courtrai*)

Fig 9.2: Bruges Monument
(*Eric Sangar*)

Fig 10.1:
Alcobaça Monastery,
commemorating the
Portuguese Victory at
Ourique.
(*B. Heuser*)

Fig 10.2:
Tombs of the King John I Aviz and Queen Philippa of Lancaster, at the Abbey of Our Lady of
Victory at Batalha, Portugal.
(*B. Heuser*)

Fig 10.3: The Battle of Poltava 1709
Eighteenth-century etching
(B. Heuser)

Fig 10.4:
Bumper sticker of the Lega
Nord, Lega Lombarda.

corroborate and extend Tacitus' account, recording the legal instruments which established these honours. These texts were themselves displayed around the empire, extending the act of commemoration beyond Rome itself as proof of their universal importance. The longest surviving such document is the Tabula Siarensis, discovered in 1982 at ancient Siarum in Spain.[18] This consists of two large inscribed bronze fragments, the first of which reports that the Senate passed the decree in late 19 CE after consulting the emperor and the imperial family. The text then lists the funerary honours to Germanicus: the erection of an arch in Rome and monuments in provinces; annual commemorations; the rescheduling of the Ludi Augusti (a set of games); the acknowledgment of honours by the plebeians; and the proposal to inscribe the eulogies pronounced by Tiberius and Drusus before the Senate.

The description of the arch at Rome is of particular interest here. It stipulates with some precision what it should look like, where in Rome it should stand, and what text and images it should carry (Roman arches were typically platforms for the display of both):

> The Senate determined that a marble arch should be erected in the Circus Flaminius . . . placed near [or "facing"] statues to Divus Augustus and to the Augustan house . . . with figures of defeated nations . . . on the face of this arch, "The Senate and Roman people have dedicated this monument... to the memory of Germanicus Caesar, since he, having defeated the Germans in war, having repulsed from Gaul . . . having recovered the military standards, having avenged a treacherous defeat of an army of the Roman people, having put the status of the Gauls in order, as proconsul sent to the overseas provinces to organize them and the kingdoms of the region in accordance with the instructions of Tiberius Caesar Augustus . . . sparing himself no effort ... he died serving the *res publica*." And on top of this arch a statue of Germanicus Caesar should be placed, in a triumphal chariot, and, beside this, statues of Drusus Germanicus, his father and the brother by birth of Tiberius Caesar Augustus, and of Antonia, his mother, . . . and of Livia, his sister, and of Tiberius Germanicus, his brother, and of his sons and daughters ... (Tabula Siarensis, 9-21)

This inscription makes a case for Germanicus that starts to establish an 'official' reception of the events in the Teutoburg Forest. It links his campaigns in Germany to the 'avenging' of a 'treacherous defeat'. This projects responsibility for the events of 9 CE and Germanicus' expeditions across the Rhine squarely onto the treacherous Germans, and elides the other factors that we have already seen in Tacitus and elsewhere - the mutinous state of the Rhine legions, the rebellion in the Balkans, Augustus' own instructions not to expand the empire any further, the rapacity of Varus. It also implies that Germanicus' recovery of lost legionary standards marked a sufficient victory (a tactic already used by Augustus in his expiation of the defeat of Carrhae), and avoids establishing any official ambition for the further conquest of Germany.

The text also makes every attempt to connect Germanicus' lustre tightly to the whole imperial household – the arch is near other statues of the imperial family, and carries a total of eleven statues as well as that of Germanicus: his father who, we are reminded, was the emperor Tiberius' brother, and of other members of his family – his mother, his brother and sister, his children.

Since the text also gives us a location for the arch, we can think about the visual impression it would have made and the significance of where it was set up. The inscription names the Circus Flaminus, an area in the southern campus Martius that had been completely overhauled under Augustus and which therefore had an appropriately monumental and imperial visual flavour. Although there are no standing remains, the foundations of an arch there are shown on the Forma Urbis, a third century CE marble map of ancient Rome,[19] giving us the probable location, size, and ground plan of the monument to Germanicus. It is possible to use this information, along with that in the inscription, to create a visual reconstruction of the arch and a proposal of its inscribed text, as shown in Fig. 6.1 and Fig. 6.2.

Noting that the inscription calls it a *ianus* (gateway), not an *arcus* or *fornix*, we can see that it does indeed serve as a gateway into or out of the Augustan Circus Flaminius area with its piazza, temple porticoes, theatre, and the existing Augustan family statue programme named in the inscription. The arch effectively closes off one end of the Circus Flaminius, as Augustus' arch(es) closed off the Forum (Tiberius had in fact also already decreed a separate arch for Germanicus, celebrating his imposition of a king on the Armenians, which similarly formed an entrance to the Forum of Augustus).[20] Any movement through this area now has to negotiate, pass through, or at least see the arch. In particular, it is a gateway on the triumphal route, serving as a waymarker for future triumphs (we know that some elements of triumphal processions, presumably constrained by this narrow pinch point, also passed through the adjacent theatre).[21] The Capitoline, the eventual destination of the triumph, is visible right ahead; this arch stands at the point of transition from the commemorative architectural world of the Campus Martius to the centre of the city.

The Arch of Germanicus is therefore in a prominent position, but I think we can say more than that about the character of the spot chosen for it. It stands between two other imperial family monuments. One is the Theatre of Marcellus, named for a nephew of Augustus, son of his sister Octavia, who had been marked out as heir, died prematurely in 23 BCE, and was widely mourned: the Germanicus of his day. This theatre was named in his honour and dedicated in 12 BCE.[22] The other, to the left in these images, is the Porticus Octaviae, a porticoed square enclosing two older temples, built by Augustus some time after 27 BCE and named after his sister, who then dedicated a library within it in honour of her son Marcellus.[23] Octavia was dynastically unlucky – Augustus' lack of children put some pressure on her to provide heirs, but Marcellus, the son of her first marriage, died, and the children of her second marriage to Marc Antony (one of whom was Germanicus' mother) were sidelined from the succession when Marc Antony broke with Augustus, abandoned her, and took up with Cleopatra. This corner of Rome, with its statues of the imperial family and monuments dedicated to the troubled line of Augustus' sister, might be thought to have developed a particular resonance of sadness, of abandonment, of failed attempts to extend the family line - of early promise snuffed out.

If so, the choice of this location for Germanicus' arch, sandwiched between earlier monuments to his antecedents and situated in a liminal position between the pleasure grounds of the Campus Martius and the centre of Rome, is an eloquent one. Though certainly prominent and honourable, close to other Augustan statue groups and monuments, it also subtly marks Germanicus as an also-ran, cut off in his prime, kept just outside the true centre of power. The inscription associates his successes with the greatest military failure of the age, and begins to characterise them as an end point rather than a beginning – which, as we have seen, was a view of the Roman presence in Germany that had become entrenched by the time Tacitus, Suetonius, and Dio wrote their accounts.

The Invention of Germany and the Arminius Monument

The story of the Teutoburg Forest enjoyed a second life long after its treatment by contemporary monuments and ancient writers. Apart from a reference by Paulus Orosius, a Spanish historiographer and theologian who died in 1418, we hear little of the battle until the sixteenth century when the peripatetic Hessian humanist Ulrich von Hutten wrote a Latin dialogue, the *Arminius*, published posthumously in 1529.[24] By this date Tacitus had become relatively widely available; the first printed edition of his whole surviving corpus was printed in 1515. A manuscript of Velleius Paterculus was discovered in a monastery library in the same year, and an *editio princeps* was published shortly afterwards. Suetonius had a long manuscript tradition in the monastery libraries of the middle age, and a first printed edition was made around 1470. The growing circulation of these authors brought the story of the Teutoburg Forest back into the consciousness of a Europe that was increasingly aware of the legacy of the Classical world, and increasingly predisposed to find ancient parallels, allegories, or explanations for modern phenomena.

The battle, or at least its depiction by later Roman writers, began to take on a new resonance in early modern Europe. Hutten's dialogue was prefaced by his friend Eobanus Hessus with a remark that it was a 'special monument to his *patria*', but the work seems to have been concerned less with German proto-nationalism than with viewing the Roman empire as a metaphor for sixteenth-century Germany's relationship with the Catholic church.[25]

In the following two centuries further writers found new uses for Arminius, now sometimes known as Hermann (claimed as the Germanic equivalent of the Latin name by the Suabian chronicler Johannes Cario).[26] He sustained a usefully wide variety of interpretations or emphases; he could be read as proto-patriot or as traitor (doubly so – to his own people, family, and culture, and then to Rome), underhand guerrilla or clever freedom fighter, barbarian or 'noble savage', battlefield warrior or player in a domestic drama.

These ambiguities are there in Tacitus, who tended to locate a primitive virtue in the motives and conduct of the tribes opposed to Rome, painting them in favourable contrast to the squalor and flattery of the imperial court and holding up their leaders as foils to degenerate emperors like Nero. Boudicca and Calgacus, Britons who also took up doomed arms against Rome, are good examples: Tacitus gives both of them rousing speeches in defence of their liberty,[27] and includes famous aphorisms about the degradation and slavery inherent in conquest by his own, supposedly civilised, Roman Empire:

> If their enemy is rich, [the Romans] are greedy; if he is poor, they
> are eager for conquest; neither the east nor the west can satisfy
> them: alone of all men that crave wealth and poverty with the

same avidity. To robbery, massacre and plunder they give the name of empire, and where they make a wilderness, they call it peace. (Tacitus, *Agricola* 30)

Those who dared stand up to the Roman imperial machine were crushed, but Tacitus allows them to go down fighting and is surprisingly even-handed in his treatment of their virtues and flaws (it is worth remembering that Tacitus had already written a *Germania*, an ethnographical account of the German tribes which suggests a familiarity and a sort of respect for the peoples of the region). Tacitus' Arminius is a hero in this mould: a barbarian, but also a resourceful and bold military leader who outwits a rapacious Roman force under poor leadership, and in doing so offers a moral lesson:

Without doubt the liberator of Germany [*Germania*], and one who challenged the Roman people not in their infancy, like other kings and leaders, but at the highest point of their empire. (Tacitus, *Annals* 2.88)

With the invention of pan-German nationalism, Arminius indeed began to be seen as liberator of Germany [*Deutschland*], which of course had never existed as a state but in the form of many states, most but not all of them members of the Holy Roman Empire. In the eighteenth century several authors dedicated novels to Hermann, but his fame surged when events in the early nineteenth century created an opening for an even more acutely politicised Hermann. In the most famous of the plays then written about Hermann, the *Hermannschlacht* (Hermann's Battle), completed by the ardent pan-German patriot Heinrich von Kleist in 1808 during the Napoleonic occupation of several among the German states, Hermann tries to unite the Germanic tribes against Rome (an analogy for France). Meanwhile Hermann's wife, the blonde Thusnelda (who in reality was taken to Rome in captivity by Germanicus) is attracted and nearly seduced by the Roman Vintidius, who clearly stands for the lure of refined French culture vs. Hermann's robust German(ic)ness.

A trickle of further plays on Hermann followed, until there was a new burst of interest around the time of the creation of the Second German Empire (1871), the first time a *Deutschland* came into existence as a state. This spurred the completion of the *Hermannsdenkmal* or Arminius-monument near Detmold, at a place in the Teutoburg Forest traditionally held to be the site of the battle. The sculptor Ernst von Baudel had started collecting money by popular subscription as early as 1836 for a monument to be built to commemorate the German hero. The product, a hilltop statue of Hermann on a large stone base, remained uncompleted until victory in the Franco-Prussian war in 1871 unleashed a surge of patriotic feeling which found a suitably impressive archetype in Arminius. It was finally inaugurated in 1875 (Fig. 6.3). The monument, and Hermann/Arminius, carried a range of associations, including anti-Catholic feeling and patriotic pride during the First World War. The monument became a popular site of nationalist pilgrimage, for school and staff outings, not only from the region but much further afield. After the First World War, the *Hermannsdenkmal* was co-opted by the militarist right in the Weimar period as a nationalist symbol; still people flocked to it on week-end outings, taking amateur photographs.

There is much in this legacy that was problematic in post-war Germany, and the nationalistic elemets of the Arminius story were understandably played down. The parallel British patriotic fervour for Boudicca might now seem similarly dated and chauvinistic; she still stands in her bronze chariot on Victoria embankment opposite the Houses of Parliament, a Victorian symbol of British imperial valour in a city she had in fact burned to the ground as an act of resistance to empire. But the *Hermannsdenkmal* continues to be a popular visitor attraction and the story is too good to let go, even though archaeological finds seem to have proved beyond reasonable doubt that it was constructed on a site that is nowhere near the actual battlefield.

The latter, situated near Kalkriese, has since been excavated and a state-of-the art museum built in situ. It is not conceived as a *lieu de mémoire* for German national identity, but as an introduction to archaeology, the Romans, and the Germanic tribes. Its website, however, contains an excellent short section on the Myth of Arminius, surveying art and literature that dealt with the subject 'between scholarship, artistic licence and political calculations' [28] - a fitting summary with which to end this brief survey of the afterlives of this significant battle.

Chapter 7

The Battle of Hastings:
Military History, Myth and Memory

Matthew Bennett

The battle which took place between King Harold II of England and an invasion force led by William, Duke of Normandy, on 14 October 1066 is probably the best known event in British history. Also, considering that the battle took place almost a millennium ago, it is surprisingly well recorded in contemporary (or near-contemporary) written sources, in that extraordinary survival, a 70 m long embroidery known as the Bayeux Tapestry, and memorialised by a large, if now much ruined, Benedictine Abbey. Furthermore, the event has been mythologized in succeeding centuries in such a way as to give it political purchase even today. Hastings is generally seen by the British population as a battle in which *They* (greedy Continentals) overcame *Us* (noble patriots) and led to centuries of foreign dominance from which *We* eventually emerged via the Protestant Reformation to reach *Our* place in the sun as the creators of the British Empire. One day does not a conquest make; yet the defeat of the English (actually Anglo-Danish) army and the death of Harold Godwinneson has been turned from the conclusion of a succession dispute into a cultural icon.

Sources

History is written by the victors, so the majority of the information available comes from Norman sources. The collection of annals written in the Old English vernacular known as the Anglo-Saxon Chronicle(s) does provide information about the impact of the Norman Conquest in the generation after 1066; but it has little in detail to say about the battle itself (although these annals say almost nothing about all such brief encounters at any stage). The *Gesta Normannorum Ducum* of William of Jumiéges, a survey of Norman history from its origins until 1070, provides us with only three brief chapters on 1066 and a bare four sentences on the fighting and its outcome.[1] In contrast, the most detailed information comes from the *Gesta Guillelmi* of William of Poitiers (a former knight, later ordained and chaplain to Duke William) a classically inspired panegyric, but with genuine insights from its military author.[2] The *Carmen de Hastingae Proelio* is exactly what it says, an 800-line poem, with some additional insights, but somewhat limited by its genre. The so-called Bayeux Tapestry provides a unique visual representation of the history of the succession dispute and for almost half of its length, lovingly depicts men, horses, arms and armour, military and naval equipment, and the fighting, in vivid scenes.[3] There is enough congruence with Poitiers' account to make historians confident about describing the course of events.

Myth of the 'Bayeux Tapestry'

It would be difficult to find a more misnamed artefact than the Bayeux Tapestry. It is true that it was held in the treasury of the cathedral of Bayeux, recorded in the mid-fifteenth century, and was famously rescued from destruction at the time of the Revolution by a history conscious local lawyer. However, all recent studies show that what is in fact an embroidery, was made at the instruction of Odo, bishop of Bayeux, also duke of Kent, the Conqueror's half-brother. Art historical investigations have demonstrated that its iconographic sources are to be found in English manuscripts, mostly associated with the abbey of St Augustine's Canterbury. Hence my contention that the textile should be renamed: The Canterbury Embroidery, and along the lines of the Elgin Marbles, proceedings should be launched to recover it for the nation! Also, it was known in the nineteenth century as *La tapisserie de la reine Mathilde*, the tapestry of Queen Matilda, and seen as product of William's queen and the ladies of her household, not least because embroidery was seen as a genteel activity for Victorian ladies. In truth, although the artist who created it is unknown, it certainly was the product of several workshops, employing men as well as women and the greatest triumph of the *opus anglicanum*, which is otherwise represented by small items, such as borders to ecclesiastical robes. Even the orthography of Latin rubric accompanying the powerful images, is strongly marked as English in origin.[4] (Fig 7.1)

To return to the other sources, the Anglo-Norman historians of the twelfth century: Orderic Vitalis, Henry of Huntingdon and William of

Malmesbury are important enough to be called a school of history, and their insights into the impact of the conquest and subsequent events are of a very high standard of interpretation, although they only add to our knowledge of the battle in a limited way.[5] My own favourite source is Wace's *Roman de Rou*, a poem in Insular French of some 12,000 lines, of which about one third are devoted to 1066, which although it was composed a century after the events it describes, captures both the spirit and some of the detail of warfare which is absent from the Latin sources.[6]

The campaigns of 1066

Crucial to the outcome of *Hastings* were the other two battles fought that year against the invasion of King Harald II of Norway, supported by Harold of England's rival brother Tostig, Earl of Northumbria. Some historians (including the author of the Ladybird book) claim that these were co-ordinated with William's plan; but there is no real evidence for this supposition (a mini-myth). In the autumn of 1065, there was a rebellion against Tostig, which, the *Vita Edwardi Regis* makes clear, if not engineered by Harold, was at least exploited by him, resulting in Tostig's exile to Flanders.[7] This enabled Harold to seize the throne on King Edward's death in January 1066, by having himself crowned the next day, without having consulted the English nobility. I do not think that the significance of a coup of this nature, which must have provoked a great deal of resentment amongst the Anglo-Danish aristocracy, for the events of the rest of the year has really been fully appreciated.

Certainly Harold expected to be challenged, and he was: first by his brother Tostig who attempted landings in the Isle of Wight and Kent in the spring; but he failed to rally anyone to his standard and instead sailed north, seeking refuge at the Scottish court. His later alliance with Harald of Norway looks to me more like opportunism than a pre-arranged alliance. Meanwhile, William was preparing an invasion fleet in order to make his challenge. We do not need to believe the Tapestry's representation of ship construction proves William had no other source of vessels; but in any event, creating an invasion force was bound to take time. The long delay in operations on all sides was to be expected given the logistic difficulties of maritime invasion. At some point, possibly not until the summer, King Harold called out his fleet and army to defend the south coast; but these had to be stood down on 8 September, after completing their term of service and in preparation for the harvest. (Fig 7.2)

Myth of Bad Weather

It used to be thought that William, having prepared his forces, was prevented from setting off any earlier by contrary winds. However, it is most unlikely over a period of several months that the prevailing south-westerlies would have failed. Marjory Chibnall has pointed out that William was waiting until the coast was clear (literally) until setting out a couple of days later. Unfortunately, at that point, a great gale got up and scattered his fleet (just as it had done 30 years earlier for to his father's attempt).[8] Running for cover up the Channel, the Norman ships took shelter in the mouth of the River Somme. It would have taken several days to reorganize, by which time it was mid-September. This is the moment when the winds were unfavourable, delaying the fleet for another two weeks until Michaelmas Day (29 September). By a stroke of luck, Harold had already set off to deal with the Norwegian invasion in the North. King Harald and Tostig had landed and defeated a northern force under the Mercian earls Edwine and Morkere at York's Fulford Gate on the 20th. The English king made a forced march and surprised the victorious Vikings still celebrating on the 25th at Stamford Bridge, killing both Harald of Norway and Tostig, and slaughtering their men.

Harold's own fleet had been blown to the four winds by the same storm which had scattered the first Norman attempt at a crossing, so there was nothing to interfere with William's landing in the broad marshlands of Pevensey Bay. The duke then mustered his men and advanced to what was at the time a peninsula site at Hastings, which he fortified with a castle, and established as a base for supply. He then sent out his troops to ravage the surrounding countryside. Not only did this provide supplies of food and fodder, but since Harold's lands lay in the area, it was a direct challenge to the English king. Moving with the same celerity as when he had marched north, Harold was back in London by the first week in October. Instead of waiting there, and possibly hoping to surprise William as he had Harald, King Harold pushed south to within a few miles north of Hastings, to a mustering point known as the 'Old Apple Tree'. This was on the London road through The Weald (ancient forest) along a hammerhead ridge some 6 miles (10 km) north of Hastings. Two English sources say that he did not have his full force (ASC, D), perhaps only a third of his army (John of Worcester). Also, he seemed to expect that the Normans would remain within their defences. But instead, early on the morning of 14 October, William launched a pre-emptive attack. The English had not yet drawn up in battle array when their opponents arrived on Telham Hill, opposite what is now the town of Battle.[9]

Myth of the Battle site

Another myth is that the battle did not take place on the site now dominated by the abbey ruins. Alternative sites have been put forward. The first is Caldebec Hill, which lies a little to the north, which was suggested twenty years ago by Jim Bradbury - a well-respected medieval military historian – who points out that the hill is steeper, with woods closer to it and a pond – possibly Sand Lake or Senlac (a name chosen by Orderic Vitalis) close by.[10] This proposal has been taken up by John Grehan, who is demanding archaeological excavations to find the 'thousands of bodies' [sic] which he believes must still remain at the 'real' site. The problem is that nothing relating to the battle has been found on the accepted site; but this does not surprise me because it is rare to find anything on pre-modern battlefields (as opposed to siege sites) for the event – a few hours fighting – is ephemeral and there are many reasons why potential finds may have disappeared, not least after an interval of almost a millennium.

There was also an attempt by a resident of Crowthorne in Sussex to prove that the battle was fought there. A website entitled Secrets of the Norman Conquest provided some very interesting insights into the differing nature of the coastline in 1066. Its author, Nick Austin, suggested that William's fleet was too large to have landed only at Pevensey, and furthermore that Bulverhythe, an inlet further east, would have been a far better anchorage. So far, so good, but unfortunately a *Time Team* programme in 2014, in a closer examination of his additional claims undermined his thesis, by disproving his archaeological finds. Perhaps the last word should be left to Roy Porter of English Heritage who wrote a scholarly article in that organisation's *Historical Review* (2012), proving by weight of near contemporary written evidence that the site of Battle Abbey is the correct one.[11]

Back to 1066...

Up until this point details about the campaign have been pretty sketchy, but the narrative thickens out, although we must be careful in interpreting the various sources. First, it is necessary to examine the composition of both armies. Harold's English, or rather Anglo-Danish force was made up of the hearth troops of the aristocracy, supported by a wider levy. The toughest troops were the *huscarls*, the word is Scandinavian, and meant the bodyguard and household of the King, his brothers Gyrth and Leofwine, and other nobles, both clerical and lay. As shown on the Tapestry, they wore helmets and long mail coats, bore round or tear-drop shields, and carried either spears and javelins or the long-handled and two-handed Danish 'bearded axe'. The Bayeux Tapestry seems to show they fought in teams for mutual support, the spearmen covering with their shields the axe bearers who were capable of inflicting enormous damage on both men and horses. They fought in a shield-wall which is well recorded in both Latin (*scutorum testudo*) and OE (*scild burh*) sources, and depicted on the Bayeux Tapestry. This might, but need not, involve overlapping shields for greater solidity of formation and protection for individuals. In addition there were more lightly armed men. Warren Hollister's research in the 1960s have created a picture of the Select Fyrd of armoured men and a more general levy of more lightly protected or even unarmoured men.[12] This interpretation can be drawn both from documentary sources and the illustrations of the Bayeux Tapestry; but whether it properly represents the English army is not certain. The existence of the Lesser Fyrd is not proven, and certainly authorities such as Eric John, who see warriors serving in a vassalic relationship with their lords, much like the 'Feudal' Continent, would deny it.[13] (Fig 7.3)

Either way, however, there can be no doubt that the English fought on foot. Both the *Gesta Guillelmi* and the *Carmen* remark on this as an unusual practice, for in northern France, the aristocracy practised cavalry warfare. It may be that the English military did fight on horseback on occasion; but they did not at Hastings; their role was to fight on the defensive and exhaust the Norman attacks by the solidity of their formation. Nor do they seem to have had many archers, and the description of the missiles thrown is suggestive of many improvised weapons. They seem to have been drawn up in single dense line, with knots of the best warriors beneath the standards of Harold and his brothers. Overall numbers are unknown, although they are usually taken to be some 7-8,000 strong (a total based on the guesswork number for the size of their opponents forces!).

In contrast, William's army was much more diverse in composition. For a start, it was drawn not only from his Norman lands, but composed of French, Bretons and Flemings and mercenaries from other parts of Europe. Half-a-century later the knight service of Normandy was about 500 men; this would have been an insufficient force to attempt the conquest of such a large country as England. It is generally accepted (although with uncertain evidence) that William led some 2,000 cavalry. The number of his foot soldiers is unknown, although there may have been 5,000. In the initial attack the archers and crossbowmen led the way. William of Poitiers describes the presence of armoured spearmen in the second line (although these do not appear on the Tapestry), with the cavalry in reserve. The army was divided into three divisions (known as *batailles*), on the left the Bretons under Count Alan the Red, the French in the centre and the Normans on the right flank under William's old companion in arms, Roger of Montgomery.

The Myth of the Gallant Jongleur

Descriptions of the battle a century ago, would certainly have contained a reference to a minstrel, mounted and armed as a knight, riding between the battle lines, even singing the Song of Roland to encourage the invaders (see below). Known as Taillefer, he appears in several sources: he strikes the first blow, killing an Englishman.[14] Perhaps this kind of romantic chivalry sits ill with modern scholars, or maybe the experience of the First World War made this behaviour seem inappropriate; but he has generally fallen out of the narrative today.

The course of the battle now falls into a number of phases and can be reconstructed by combining the *Gesta Guillelmi*, the Tapestry and other sources, in support of one another. The initial archery barrage does not seem to have inflicted many casualties on the well-protected shield wall. Then the spearmen advanced but were unable to make any headway against the English line. Supporting cavalry charges rescued them but also made no impact. In fact, the Breton left wing found itself bundled back down the hill and turned in flight. They were pursued by the English in that sector who rushed forward and established themselves on hillock a couple of hundred yards in front of their main line (as the Tapestry may also portray). This was the first crisis of the battle, for in the rout the cry went up that William had been killed, which could have led to a general retreat.

William of Poitiers, with a nod to his classical models, describes this moment vividly:

> Baring his head and lifting his helmet, he cried: "Look at me. I am alive, and with God's help I will conquer. What madness is persuading you to flee? What way is open to escape? You could slaughter like cattle the men who are pursuing and killing you. You

are abandoning victory and imperishable fame, and hurrying to disaster and perpetual ignominy. Not one of you will escape death by flight." At these words they recovered their courage. He rushed forward at their head, brandishing his sword, and mowed down the hostile people who deserved death for rebelling against him, their king. Full of zeal the Normans surrounded some thousands who had pursued them and destroyed them in a moment, so that no single one survived.[15]

This scene from the Bayeux Tapestry captures the moment perfectly. It adds the role of Odo, bishop of Bayeux rallying the inexperienced knights with his baton and Eustace, count of Boulogne, bearing the Papal banner and pointing out the still living William to the deserters.

When the Normans and the troops allied to them saw that they could not conquer such a solidly massed enemy force without heavy loss, they wheeled about and deliberately feigned flight. They remembered how, a little while before, their flight had brought about the result they desired. There was jubilation amongst the barbarians [i.e. Anglo-Saxons], who hoped for a great victory. Encouraging each other with joyful shouts, they heaped curses upon our men and threatened to destroy them all forthwith. As before, some thousands of them dared to rush, almost as if they were winged in pursuit of those they believed to be fleeing. The Normans, suddenly wheeling round their horses, checked and encircled them, slaughtering them to the last man.[16]

Some commentators have doubted the feasibility of this manoeuvre; but there is every reason to believe it would have worked. In the twelfth century it was known as the 'tor Franceis' - the French turn - which was particularly useful for a jouster in tournament. Wace's further interpretation of the Norman cavalry luring out the English bit-by-bit, adds further credibility. William of Poitiers tells us that the trick was used twice more, before the Normans returned to the attack. This led to the English line shortening and thinning. At the same time the missilemen began shooting anew, this time into the air. The exhausted defenders could no longer hold up their shields and the falling arrows began to inflict casualties. This is how their impact is shown on both the Tapestry and by Wace.

Myth: the arrow in Harold's Eye

This rendering of events ties in well with the story of King Harold being wounded in the eye by an arrow, which first appears in Henry of Huntingdon, writing two generations later and is expanded by Wace. There seems to be support for this story on the Tapestry, although there is much scholarly argument on the matter. (Fig 7.4)

The first reference to King Harold's wounding in this way is found in Henry of Huntingdon, writing two generations after the battle. Once again, it was embroidered by Wace. The earliest written source, the *Carmen de Hastingae Proelio*, describes Harold being cut down and dismembered by four named knights in gory detail, but does not mention the arrow.[17] However, the scene on the Bayeux Tapestry, has been interpreted as showing Harold first wounded and then hacked down with a blow to the thigh which matches the poem in one regard. Some scholars have drawn attention to vestigial marks of the needle suggesting that the falling figure did have an arrow in the face, while others believe this to be a later (possibly nineteenth century) addition justifiably removed. It is noticeable that the Latin text informing us that it is Harold who is being killed, has been broken to focus on the falling figure. Iconographically speaking, it is possible that the identically-dressed standing figure is also Harold, in the same way as figures are duplicated in *bande dessinée*, or strip cartoons of modern comic art.

All the sources agree that the English, weakened by their losses and the death of Harold and his brothers Gyrth and Leofwine began to flee. Wace has an important insight into the value of the cavalry, as he describes the knights using the weight of their horses to break into the enemy ranks.[18] This was the point at which Harold was attacked and hacked down by a group of knights and the rout became general. There seems to have been a reverse at a defended ditch (later called the *Malfosse*, although Wace connects this story to the Breton collapse earlier in the battle) which checked the pursuers for a while; but otherwise the outcome of the day was decided. Only a few notable Normans are described as dying, while the bulk of the English commanders were killed and the rest of their force scattered. Harold's body was too mutilated to be properly identified, although various legends grew around his possible after-life.

The Myth of the Battle

This kind of myth-making began almost as soon as the battle was over. William of Poitiers deliberately created myths around the figure of Duke

William. As well as describing his superhuman activities in the battle, and having three horses killed under him (an old trope), he associated him with heroes of classical history and legend. William's fleet is described as larger than Agamemnon's at the siege of Troy; his bravery is greater than Achilles. He is particularly likened to Aeneas as they share 'a destiny marked out for them by the will of Heaven', they seek out their perjured rival for personal combat. Just as Aeneas was the originator of the Romans, William's Normans founded a new nation in England. The duke is also shown to be greater than Caesar, through a variety of comparisons, especially in relation to the conquest of Britain. The duke-king is also attributed Caesar's desire for clemency and forgiveness although: 'the underlying ruthlessness of both is deliberately glossed over...'.[19]

The Anglo-Norman chroniclers are much less in love with William the Conqueror as they balance their praise with criticism of his brutality, especially in relation to the later stages of the conquest of England. For example, Orderic Vitalis writes feelingly of the suffering brought about by the 'Harrying of the North' during the winter of 1069-70.[20] This is inspired both by his sense of being born of a Norman father and English mother, and also the fearsome king being long dead when he wrote. In contrast, Wace is much more positive. This is because, as I have suggested elsewhere, he is addressing a Norman aristocratic audience of the mid-twelfth century, and wishes to emphasise their value to the then monarch, Henry II. Without the loyal support which his ancestor received, Wace argues, Henry would not enjoy such a wealthy inheritance. He presents the earliest version of a list of the members of Norman families who fought at the battle which won the Crown of England. This list continued to grow throughout the medieval period from the two dozen of the *Roman de Rou* to several hundred by around 1500, as families attempted to raise their status by citing noble ancestors.

In the seventeenth century the Conquest took on a more negative aspect in the dispute between King and Parliament. Instead of the Conqueror being seen as an inspirational creator, the relationship of the Crown to the people was represented as the Norman Yoke. This idea continued into later disputes connected to the development of universal suffrage in the nineteenth century. Also, in the Victorian era, from the Queen down, there was the conscious creation of a nostalgic link to King Alfred (creator of the first 'English' fleet) and Old English state as the natural ancestors of the British Empire (ruling courtesy of the Royal Navy.) During this period, historians such as E. A. Freeman talked up 'Anglo-Saxon' England as superior to the 'Feudal' Normans; a movement later challenged by J. H.

Round, the first true Normanist who worked in French archives, an ancestor to the current experts in Anglo-Norman history.

Eighteenth- and nineteenth-century views on Hastings

Edward Gibbon provides his usual balanced view of the Norman Conquest, although this is rarely followed in Victorian popular histories.

> In the decisive battle of Hastings, the valour of the English was unable to withstand the flower of Europe's chivalry, led by an experienced general and supported by the thunder of papal excommunication.

Subsequently

> Sixty thousand knights were bound by duty and interest to support the throne of the benefactor. The government was military; and a military government tends to despotism. The only compensation which England received for so many calamities, was a system of manners somewhat more polished and a more extensive influence on the Continent.[21]

It was common to record the anniversary of the battle, for example at the end of the nineteenth century, in the *Bristol Mercury:* 'Red Letter Days: October 13th 1066 Battle of Senlac, or Hastings, death of Harold, the last of the Saxons. Victory of William, the Norman Conqueror. One of the decisive battles of the world.'[22] Or, in the *Blackburn Standard*: 14 October, Battle of Hastings 'more than 30,000 were slain in the battle'.[23]

From *The Ladies Cabinet of Fashion, Music and Romance,* comes Taillefer singing the Song of Roland 'throwing his lance in the air... catching it by the point... and repeating the same operation with his sword... a conjuror', compared with the 'evolutions of the military bandmasters are in the habit of performing with their tall, gilded and tasselled staffs of office when in marching at the head of their regiments' 'archaeologically considered' to derive from that![24] While *The Boys Own Magazine*, 1862, describes an imagined 'intrenched [sic] position' of the English.

> Driving in his outposts, Harold concentrated his whole force within his intrenchments, and drew his army up along the entire force on the

hill, which, sloping with a gradual inclination to the plan, enabled him to present an imposing front to the enemy; at the same time he protected his flanks from the assault of the Norman cavalry by an abbatis of felled trees on his left and a succession of deep trenches, which, artfully covered over with sods and concealed by rushes and smaller branches of trees effectively protected his right.[25]

Then there is the story of King Harold's possible survival in *The Morning Post* of 1831, headed 'Did Harold escape after the Battle of Hastings?', which records that Editha [sic] Swan Neck, took a 'ghastly decomposed and mutilated corpse' back to Waltham Abbey'. But apparently there was:

> a decrepit anchorite, who inhabited a cell near the abbey of St John at Chester. This recluse, deeply scarred, and blinded in his left eye, lived in strict penitence and seclusion. Henry I once visited the aged Hermit, and had a long and private discourse with him; and, on his deathbed confirmed to the attendant Monks that he was Harold.[26]

Contemporary Interpretations

In the twentieth century, especially associated with the 900th anniversary in 1966, there began to be re-enactments of the great events. These included a walk from York to Battle in imitation of Harold's march south. Over the last thirty years there have been regular battle re-enactments below the remains of the abbey. The one of 2006 (which I attended), there were some 200 cavalry and 2,000 foot soldiers involved. These were sponsored, until recently, by *English Heritage*, with a public address system producing very pro-English commentaries (although this tone has moderated over time); they are currently suspended (although there was small revival for the 950th anniversary) owing to the possible damage to the site by large numbers of both actors and spectators. (Fig 7.5)

Just how much Hastings represents a part of our modern identity is shown by the recent work of Siobhan Brownlie published as *Memory and Myths of the Norman Conquest.* [27] Even in the first decade of the twenty-first century the register of interest and identity with the King Harold and the English is well represented in the popular Press. It is noticeable that in discussion involving *Hastings* or using the battle to stand for a point of view and common expression is: 'We lost'.[28] Such attitudes tend to promote nationalism and isolationism from a wider European community which has important political implications for the future of Great Britain.[29] So, for example, there is a surprising continuity of interest from 1848 (Bulwer-Lytton) to 2008 of the idea of Harold as the 'Last Anglo-Saxon King'. Television documentaries still tend to present antagonism between Norman and Saxon (beloved of Sir Walter Scott's *Ivanhoe* and other romantic novels) for a century or more after 1066. There is still a strong pro-Saxon strain in popular understanding in which members of the British population understand themselves as linked to a golden age of Old English liberty, with the Saxons as our true ancestors. This theme even appears in a 2008 documentary on Domesday Book introduced by Stephen Baxter, an Oxford don prominent in the field of medieval studies.[30] The Channel 4 factional documentary *1066*, produced in 2009, represents the Normans as brutish invaders, called Orkish by the sympathetically represented Saxons. In the light of J. R. R. Tolkien's professed dislike for the Normans, this choice of word carries extra weight. Interestingly, also, the *Battle of Hastings* still retains its status as the most important battle in British history, even for such a sophisticated observer as Robert Bartlett, when he was fronting a series on the Normans for the BBC in 2010.[31]

Myth of the 'English Resistance'

This is not to say that there was no resistance to William's rule in the years following 1066; quite the opposite. A single battle does not a conquest make.[32] The new king needed to fight campaigns in all corners of his kingdom, in order to establish his authority. Initially the greatest problem was in the south-west, sponsored by Harold's mother Gytha, at Exeter, and later by his surviving sons raiding from Ireland (1068-69).

There were also challenges in the North: at Durham where the new earl and his garrison were massacred, and at York, where the ruling elite were equally troublesome and were also joined by a Danish fleet in a manner reminiscent of Aethelred's disastrous reign over half a century earlier. Both these attacks were dealt with firmly, but especially so in the winter of 1069-70 when, frustrated by his failure to impress his will on the region, William launched a campaign of devastation – fire and sword – which destroyed and depopulated the northern shires. As a mark of his determination he held his Christmas Crown-wearing at York, transferring his court and royal regalia there, as a demonstration that, unlike his English predecessors, he would not tolerate a semi-independent sub-kingdom in Northumbria.

The Mercian earls Edwine and Morkere also rebelled against him, although it is debatable as to whether the initiative was for national independence or as a result of William pressurising the native aristocracy by redistributing their lands to the incomers who had won the crown for him. The last serious rebellion was that of Hereward the Wake, based at the abbey of Ely in the Fens, which required a huge effort and extensive amphibious siege operations to put down (1071). The crucial moment came in the spring of 1070, when William used Archbishop Lanfranc to bring the English church to heel, replacing almost all the pre-Conquest bishops and abbots, with loyal men. The king was only too aware that the abbeys' treasuries had been used by rebels all over the country to fund their insurgencies; so that the ecclesiastical and governmental reform both enabled and reinforced military success.

Peter Rex has even argued that William's regime was so oppressive and genocidal that it bears comparison with Nazi Germany led by Adolf Hitler. He calls the crowned Christian king 'Der Führer' at one point and characterises those English who did not rebel as 'collaborators'.[33] This is clearly an anachronistic and unhelpful interpretation. Another, ironic, take on the situation might be to point out that the three main protagonists in 1066: King Harald, King Harold Godwinnesson and Duke William, were all of Viking descent. In the twelfth century a Norman aristocracy was introduced in to Scotland, leaving a descendant of this immigration – Robert the Bruce (Old French: Brus) - to fight for independence from the English Crown almost two centuries later. It is almost as if the history of medieval Britain remained that of Northmen falling out with each other.[34]

Finally, though, the Conquest can be positively remembered, and in the most sensitive of environments. Here I can draw on my personal experience. The British war cemetery at Bayeux in western Normandy features a solemn colonnade bearing the inscription: *Nos a Guillelmo victi victoris patriam liberavimus* (We who were conquered by William have liberated the homeland of the conqueror). There lie the two other captains of the company of the Durham Light Infantry in which my late father-in-law served (and was also wounded) in 1944, and which we visited together in 1989. There can be no clearer linkage of past events: myth and history creating a common understanding of the significance of military conquest and its implications of oppression or liberation.

Chapter 8

Béziers, 22 July 1209

Catherine Léglu

'Kill them all, because God knows who belongs to Him.'[1]

Memorial culture that focuses on battles tends to overlook the histories of regions.[2] This is particularly problematic for the process of coming to terms with the European collective past, because a conflict between regions can often become a war of conquest, signalling the growth of one emerging nation at the expense of another. The Massacre of Béziers was the first major act of war of a conflict known as the Albigensian Crusade, a war that led to the absorption of the lands of the counts of Toulouse into the kingdom of France, creating what is now known as Southern France.[3] The crusade was begun because the count of Toulouse and his vassals were accused of harbouring and protecting heretics, specifically the dualist sect known as the Cathars. Hostilities only ended in 1249, and the county of Toulouse, a territory embracing much of the region that spoke *langue d'oc* or Occitan, definitively entered the French king's territories in 1271. 'Occitanie' became a concept and a cause until it was adopted after a series of public consultations on 30 September 2016 as the name of the administrative region of central Southern France, encompassing 13 *départements*, with Toulouse as its capital.[4]

Most accounts of the crusade commonly follow a narrative arc from its first act, the slaughter and burning of an innocent civilian population at Béziers, to its tragic last act, the martyrdom of dozens of Cathars, who it is said leapt willingly into the flames of a vast pyre at Montségur in 1244. The subject is a powerful myth up to the present day. On 16 October 2016, an apology for the persecution of the Cathars was held at Montségur by the Catholic community of the Ariège.[5] One of the priests who launched this campaign stressed the relevance of the apology: 'We wish to avoid repeating those moments in History when religion became a tool of coercion against peoples (…) Burning in the name of Love, that's a paradox, isn't it?'[6] This chapter's focus will be on the controversial first act of the crusade, the siege and massacre of the city of Béziers.

The events

A crusade against the Albigensians was called by Pope Innocent III (1198-1216) in the year 1208, after the murder of his papal legate Pierre de Castelnau. Its ostensible target initially was Count Raymond VI of Toulouse (1156-1222), who was suspected of having ordered the legate's death out of a desire to protect a heretical movement that was gaining ground in his lands. The first campaign of the war was led by a group of prelates and ended as soon as the traditional forty days of required military service were over. The second campaign was led by noblemen from the Ile-de-France (the king of France would not join the conflict until 1226). Many of these men had fought together in the Fourth Crusade (1202-05). This army assembled at Lyon and travelled south, under the leadership of the papal legate and abbot of Cîteaux, Arnaud Amaury (d.1225). The Count of Toulouse quickly did penance, joined the crusade, and deflected the conflict towards his nephew and rival, Raymond Roger Trencavel, viscount of Béziers and Carcassonne (1185-1209). Béziers was the most prestigious of the six titles that were held by the young viscount. Another of his lands was the city of Albi.

In medieval Europe, warfare was usually a series of short campaigns waged in springtime, when there was less heat and less chance of snow. Pitched battles were avoided, because they were more costly in men, horses and equipment. Armies set up sieges around fortified towns and waited until the inhabitants surrendered.[7] A siege offered richer pickings if the target location surrendered without too much damage. The city of Béziers was strategically less important than the cities of Montpellier and Toulouse, which surrendered without a siege. The viscount fled with his Jewish community to his stronghold at Carcassonne. Plunder was the only advantage that capturing the city could give the crusaders. The bishop of Béziers failed in his attempt to persuade the population to surrender, and he gave the crusaders the message that the city would not give up without a fight.

The crusaders pillaged the city and slaughtered the population. Civilians and clergy sought refuge inside the cathedral of Saint-Nazaire. The clergy put on their vestments and rang the bells, signalling that they were Christians under the bishop's protection. Others assembled inside the church of St Mary Magdalene, which was the consuls' church. Both buildings were set alight and all those inside them were killed. Written nearly a decade later, the short narrative by the Cistercian monk Caesarius of Heisterbach claims that Arnaud Amaury was asked how the men were to tell who was a heretic and who was a Christian. Caesarius says that he replied with those infamous words, 'Kill them all', then cited from Scripture: 'for God knows who belongs to Him'.[8] Carcassonne fell within a month and the young viscount died in prison the following Autumn.

A few days after Béziers fell, the papal legates reported to the Pope that nearly 20,000 people had been killed. Over the centuries, the numbers have fluctuated from 7000 in the church of the Magdalene alone, to 60,000.[9] There is no doubt that the massacre took place. Around 1242, the king of France restored property and money that had been confiscated from families of individuals who had been massacred in 1209.[10]

Nevertheless, contemporary historians still debate some key aspects of this conflict.[11] Notably, well before the Albigensian crusade was called, the Cistercian order of monks identified and named the dualist heresy that is now known as Catharism. Possibly they distorted the evidence in order to depict their mission against heresy as a struggle between the true Church and a unified rival.[12] *Cathari*, from the Greek *katharoi* ('the pure') were a short-lived early Christian movement. The term reappeared in the 1160s to describe a heresy that believed that the material world had been created by a bad divinity, and that the good divinity had created heavenly realms as well as souls. These 'dualist' principles were identified by churchmen with another religious movement of late antiquity known as Manicheism. Europe's scattered communities of dualists had no knowledge of either Manichees or *katharoi*, and we do not know what they called themselves. This new religion shared many features with Bogomilism, an established heretical church in the Balkans since the tenth century.[13]

There was a second heresy spreading fast across Western Europe at the time. This was a Christian evangelical movement founded in Lyon by a certain Waldo around the year 1170. Waldensians were Christians who rejected the organized priesthood and the clerical hierarchy. They preached and they translated the Bible into everyday language. Known colloquially as 'clog-wearers' or 'bearded men', these wandering preachers who refused to swear oaths were often lumped together with Cathars, and the two movements would continue to be confused for several centuries.

For the past twenty years, academics have reviewed and debated the key documents concerning the crusade and the inquisition that was founded in 1229. It has been suggested that the size of the Cathar community in the Languedoc was exaggerated by the Cistercian order.[14] It does not mean that there were no heretics. Béziers was a centre for Waldensians, and a century later, it would be a centre again for a similar movement, that of the Spiritual Franciscans.[15] An indiscriminate massacre might be explicable if the crusaders truly did not know how to identify heretics in the region. This debate is limited to academics but it draws attention to two important points. The first of these is the unusual passion that is roused by this conflict. The atrocities committed in the Albigensian crusade were shocking, even to those who perpetrated them.[16] However, they look small next to other crusades and wars of the Middle Ages. The second point is that despite the vast bibliography that is dedicated to this subject, some of the key evidence remains flimsy, because it is viewed through the prism of the myths that surround both the conflict and the heresy.

Myth 1: A massacre with divine sanction

The first myth constructed on these events came into being soon after they occurred: this was a narrative of well-deserved punishment. In his analysis of the historical disputes concerning the Albigensian crusade, Philippe Martel classifies the perspectives of historians and other writers as a debate between the 'indignant', those who condemn the atrocities in this conflict on moral grounds, and those who are burdened by the task of justifying them.[17] Arnaud Amaury was the first of the 'burdened' writers. He and his fellow legate Milon wrote to the Pope that while they were negotiating the terms of freeing those of the town who seemed to be Catholics, the army's *ribauds* (thuggish mercenaries) and other low-born and unarmed men, launched an attack without the permission of their officers. 'To our amazement', they crossed the ditches and scaled the walls 'within two to three hours'. Thereupon, 'our men' slaughtered every man, woman and child before pillaging the city. They conclude that it was a miraculous act of divine vengeance.[18] The apologists give the impression that the crusaders' military and spiritual leaders simply failed to stop a frenzied action by their lowest-ranking men. They present the massacre as unfortunate, unless the Pope believed that the ultimate command responsibility lay with God.

One such key apologist was Pierre des Vaux-de-Cernay, a Cistercian monk who joined the crusaders in 1212. His chronicle draws on eye-witness reports. He provides a lot of reasons for this 'miraculous' slaughter, and the mercenaries' insubordination is only one of them. Béziers was a very noble city, but it was full of heretics. Its people were also rapists, adulterers and thieves.[19] Some men had once injured a priest who was carrying his chalice to Mass and urinated onto the consecrated host. The date of the massacre, the feast-day of St Mary Magdalene, was significant because the heretics said that the Magdalene had been the concubine of Jesus. Furthermore, the massacre came forty-two years after they murdered their viscount in the church of the Magdalene, just as Jerusalem was sacked by the Romans forty-two years after the Passion of Christ.[20] The last claim is strange, given the crusaders' claims that the viscounts had protected heretics, but it serves its rhetorical purpose: the city had deserved its fate many times over.

The other key narrative source is a poem composed in Occitan by a cleric from Navarre called Guillem de Tudela. He sided with the crusaders, but he did not present the massacre as a miracle. In his version of events, the crusaders had already decided to use slaughter as a strategy to ensure the quick surrender of the region. The viscount left with the city's Jews, and he told the townspeople to defend themselves while he went to Carcassonne to gather an army.[21] The bishop then announced that there would be no mercy unless the citizens surrendered.[22] For Guillem, the crusaders (or rather, 15,000 of their mercenaries) committed a crime 'worthy of pagans'. The townspeople who gathered in the church of the Magdalene saw their clergy put on their vestments and ring the bells that were traditionally rung for masses for the dead. The beautiful church broke in two as it burned. For him, Béziers was like Troy, fallen to the avenging Greeks because of a petty story of adultery, or even like a convent burned down by a berserk baron.[23]

In the kingdom of Arles, some 150 km east of Béziers, Gervase of Tilbury wrote some entertaining stories for the court for the young emperor Otto of Brunswick. He says that in 1211, a murdered young man came back as a ghost that was willing to answer questions from visitors. The bishop of Orange (a Cistercian) took the opportunity to enquire if God was pleased with the slaughter of heretics. The ghost replied that God was delighted, as His aim at the Last Judgement was to distinguish the good from the wicked.[24] The ghost's answer implies that the crusaders were not sifting the 'good' from the 'wicked' souls before they killed them. Caesarius of Heisterbach's short anecdote, also written in these years, praised Arnaud Amaury's order to 'Kill them all' as a miracle. Were those words from Scripture, 'God knows who belongs to him', being used in sermons to justify a policy of slaughter?[25] One hundred years on, the inquisitor and historian Bernard Gui's comment on the Massacre of Béziers is an uneasy assertion that it was 'quite just'. As a man of the Occitan-speaking regions as much as an officer of the inquisition that had been founded in 1229 to pursue the work of the crusaders, he does not condemn the population of the Languedoc.[26]

Myth 2: Cathars as early Protestants

Four centuries later, we see the rise of a second myth: France's Wars of Religion catalysed a reinterpretation of history depicting the Cathars along with the Waldensians as precursors of Protestantism. Catholic writers equated them with heresy and Protestants made them part of a long tradition of dissent.[27] A new translation of the chronicle of Pierre des Vaux-de-Cernay went through three editions in 1569.[28] Its author, Arnaud Sorbin (1532-1606) was at that time preacher to King Charles IX of France (1550-1574). He also published in 1569 some legislation passed in Languedoc against the Albigensians, and a pamphlet celebrating a military victory 'against the rebellious Calvinists'.[29] Sorbin's translation is peppered with marginal notes, on the lines of 'a heretical thought, more than ridiculous', and 'Calvinist opinion'. So where the chronicle reports that a priest was assaulted by men of Béziers and his chalice defiled, Sorbin adds a note, 'And what more would a Calvinist do?'[30] In 1572, the French crown orchestrated a series of massacres of Protestants across France. This is known as the 'St Bartholomew's Day Massacre' (24 August 1574). Sorbin praised it as the greatest military achievement of his king.[31]

Waldensians and Cathars were conflated, notably in the Calvinist pastor Jean-Paul Perrin's sympathetic account of the 'Albigensian Christians', which was published in Geneva in 1618, commissioned by synod.[32] Perrin's text pits 'Romanists' against' 'Albigensians'. He depicts Raymond VI as a man torn with remorse at the thought of destroying both the city of Béziers and his own nephew.[33] The bishop begs the legate to spare those in the population who have continued to adhere to the Roman church, on the grounds that the church 'takes no pleasure in blood'. Arnaud Amaury disagrees:

> The legate grew angry with horrible threats, and, swearing, he declared that if all those who lived in the city did not recognise their sin, and did not align themselves with the Roman church, then they would all be put to the sword, with no regard for any Catholic, of any sex or age.[34]

Perrin narrates a further atrocity and claims that it has been covered up by propagandists. When the crusaders took the city, a procession of priests and monks emerged from the cathedral, singing in celebration. The crusaders, 'who had had from their Legate the order to kill everyone, threw themselves at this procession, sending flying the heads and limbs of priests to the best of their ability; such that they were cut to pieces'.[35]

Perrin's grisly narrative aligns the conflict with the tit-for-tat atrocities of the Wars of Religion. The 'purified' *Cathari* reappeared in texts that applied the pejorative term 'Puritan' to the strictest of Protestants.[36] In the eighteenth century, Calvinist peasant insurrection was feared, and pastors were executed as late as 1762. Voltaire's campaigns against religious intolerance included polemics concerning the 'Albigensians'.[37] Protestants (especially but not exclusively those of Southern France) continued to claim descent from the Cathars and Waldensians well beyond the French Revolution. A Protestant pastor of the nineteenth century was to produce a more enduring myth for the conflict. Napoléon Peyrat's three-volume *Histoire des Albigeois*, published in 1870-1872, followed his studies of clandestine French Protestantism.[38]

Peyrat's extraordinarily influential work set the historical narrative within a frame of Grail legends and Wagnerian fantasy.[39] His ideas stem from best-selling books by free-thinking Republican historians. For example, Henri Martin's histories were immensely successful, rewarded with prizes, re-edited and reprinted until the end of the nineteenth century. In 1867-85, he published an illustrated *Popular History of France* (*Histoire de France populaire*).[40] He traced the union of Church and State (which Republicans rejected) back to the conquest of Druidic Gaul by Rome, and its conversion to 'Roman' Catholicism. In line with ideas current since the 1820s, Martin says that the Midi had a superior civilisation to the North, and that its greater wealth and sophistication made it more tolerant. The Albigensian crusade destroyed a 'civilisation', and introduced the 'perversion' of religious intolerance to France.[41] Martin calls Arnaud Amaury, 'an Attila in monastic robes'.[42] An illustration to Martin's *Histoire populaire* depicts a mother and child amidst the massacred population inside Béziers cathedral, clearly designating the atrocity as a massacre of the innocent 'Southerners' by fanatical barbarians from the North (Fig.8.1).

Martin's histories were attacked for promoting evolutionary theory, paganism and heresy, notably by the medieval specialist Henri de L'Epinois (1831-1890).[43] By 1872, France was recovering from its defeat in the Franco-Prussian War. Accordingly, L'Epinois (along with others) dismissed the words 'Kill them all!' as 'slander' written by a German monk, ignoring the fact that the monk in question was a member of Arnaud Amaury's order and was intending to praise him.[44] Peyrat (an eye-witness of the siege of Paris) echoed Martin in suggesting that the Albigensian crusade marked a clash between militaristic 'Northerners' and peaceful 'Southerners'.[45] L'Epinois' writings sketch out the emerging concern of right-wing historians, which is that the memory of this conflict undermined the idea of France's preordained unity as a nation. He warned that pitting 'North' against 'South' was tantamount to claiming a racial difference between the two regions.[46]

Myth 3: Popular culture - Literary myths

The Peyrat school became dominant after 1900. It produced a theory that the Cathars held the Grail, popularized by the Nazi Otto Rahn, then dismissed in 1942 by Pierre Belperron, whose history of the Albigensian crusade (carefully written despite its pro-Vichy preface) criticises Peyrat as a fantasist and describes Rahn's work as 'blighted by ignorance and insincerity'.[47] Nevertheless, English-language and French popular media and children's literature repeat key elements of the Peyrat-Rahn narrative. The story goes that the Albigensian war is triggered by the arrival in the Languedoc of a knight who has brought the Grail. Cathars are persecuted by wicked churchmen and Northerners either because they are liberal, gentle folk who threaten the church's power, or because they are involved in protecting a secret treasure that may or may not be the Grail. Reincarnation (a dualist belief) or an inherited mission are involved. In parallel, the 'freedom' of a nation called 'Occitania' is invoked.

The romantic novel *A Wheel of Stars* (1990), presents the reunion in modern England and France of a couple from medieval Languedoc, who find themselves embroiled in a hunt for the Grail. A similar story is recounted in the first volume of Kate Mosse's 'Languedoc Trilogy', *Labyrinth* (2005).[48] These stem from the same mixture of cultural and historical sources that produced Dan Brown's 'conspiracy thriller', *The Da Vinci Code* (2003).[49] They share a common source, according to which the Albigensian crusade is a traumatic conflict that haunts the consciousness of modern Christianity, surfacing in dreams or in hallucinations. In *A Wheel of Stars*, one of the reincarnated Cathars comments that the fall of Montségur, 'the freedom of the individual was dealt a blow from which it has never recovered, even now'.[50] These books insist on the global significance of the conflict. Their shared sources include the writings of Arthur Guirdham (1905-1992), who published a series of books in the 1970s which claimed to report English men and women's recovered memories of their lives as persecuted Cathars.[51] Guirdham invoked the work of René Nelli (1906-1982), who wrote the postace to the French translation of his *Cathars and Reincarnation* in 1972 (Lawrence Durrell contributed the preface).[52] Nelli, a champion of neo-Catharism, combined serious scholarship with an appeal to the burgeoning sexual revolution. He was the author of a popular history of the everyday life of Cathars.[53] An earlier source available to the wider public in both France and in England was the historical novelist Zoé Oldenbourg's *Le Bûcher de Montségur* (1959), published in a series dedicated to narrating 'thirty days that made France'.[54] A stinging review by Etienne Delaruelle, Catholic historian and founder of the major annual conferences devoted to medieval Occitania at Fanjeaux, noted that Oldenbourg's book had put scholarship back by a century.[55] The book is still in print.

Oldenbourg's book was a key source for a dramatic reconstruction of the Albigensian crusade and its aftermath, broadcast over two episodes on French television in 1966, which ends as the Cathars process to the fire at Montségur.[56] These were in fact the last scenes broadcast of the prime-time television series *La caméra explore le temps,* just as President Charles de Gaulle's government had it cancelled. The series' producer, Stillio Lorenzi, was a socialist and union activist. One of its presenters later stated that the government put an end to the series because of Lorenzi's involvement in strike action, but the legend grew that the show was stopped because it tended to privilege divisive themes in French history.[57] The Gaullist government was sensitive to topics that challenged the unity of France in the period immediately following a tumultuous and violent period of decolonisation.

Episode 46 opens with Decaux narrating with gentle irony the French king's desire to assert himself when his kingdom is encircled by 'the English' and 'the Germans'. To the south, however, there is a territory that is 'free' of the French king's ambitions, that of the Count of Toulouse. The drama begins with a flashback. A troubadour laments the destruction of the civilized society that was 'l'Occitanie'. We then see the troubadour as he attends the deathbed of a leading Cathar, just as Montségur falls in 1244. The dying man orders the troubadour to take away 'the Cathar treasure' and to recount the story in Occitan for 'all the Occitans of the future'. Thus the Albigensian crusade is presented as a war of French colonisation, and the Peyrat legend of a Cathar Grail endures.

Like Oldenbourg before him, the journalist Michel Roquebert came to the Cathars via popular culture. He spent over thirty years producing a reliable history. Also, in 1975-76, he worked with the artist Gérald Forton on a two-part graphic novel. It developed from a cartoon strip in a regional daily newspaper, at a time when Larousse's history of France in comic strips (1976-77) did not mention the Albigensian crusade.[58] Concern for defending French national unity while acknowledging the impact of the crusade also appears in the children's novel, *Le Trésor de Montségur*, by Renée Aurembou, which provides its young readers with maps and historical notes. Here, a boy from Paris called Philippe develops a tense friendship with a boy from Toulouse called Raymond. They join forces to find the lost treasure of Montségur. In the end, they decide to abandon their quest. Yes, mass suffering in the past should be remembered, but the aggressors suffered too, and what they have discovered is that they are both French: 'That is the essential thing!'[59]

Recent decades have reintroduced young adult readers to the subject via heroic fantasy, notably in the ten-volume BD series *Memory of Ashes* by the Belgian Philippe Jarbinet, starring a half-English Cathar warrior girl.[60] Alain Delalande's four-volume BD series *The Last Cathar* (based on his bestselling novel, *The Church of Satan),* devotes its first volume (*Kill them All!*) to the Massacre of Béziers.[61] Its protagonist Escartille is a young nobleman and troubadour, and like the troubadour of the TV drama of 1966, he appears first as an older man, writing his memoirs for posterity after the fall of Montségur. The secret-bearing, fugitive knight from the East is his own long-lost father. The mercenaries who kill the population of the city are in hot pursuit of the knight. Here, the Massacre of Béziers is prompted by Occitan resistance to the Church. At the siege encampment, the remorseful Raymond VI marches into Arnaud Amaury's tent to announce that he will not surrender Toulouse, nor indeed any other city of Occitania, to the crusaders. The legate replies that he will conquer Toulouse forthwith, and orders his men to 'Kill them all'. The destruction of Béziers is then recounted through a series of dramatic images, with the caption 'Kill them all' inserted. (The same dramatic confrontation between the Count and Arnaut Amaury occurs in *La caméra explore le temps*. The order 'Kill them all!' is repeated several times by Raymond VI as he remembers the massacre on his deathbed). Delalande's protagonist finds himself trapped inside the burning cathedral of Saint-Nazaire and escapes by jumping down from the bell tower. He then confronts the gloating 'king' (leader) of the mercenaries, whose words are then placed over a cataclysmic scene of Béziers in flames: 'Welcome to Hell, Cathar!' (Fig.8.2). Delalande's novel (not the BD adaptation) opens with a letter claiming to have rescued Escartille's manuscript from the 'Hell' (the legendary holdings of forbidden books) of Paris's Bibliothèque nationale in the year 2000. The idea that this well-known history is somehow forbidden by forces of repression, be they in Paris or the Vatican, endures in popular literature.

Myth 4 : 'Intolerable tolerance'

In 2009, a commemorative plaque marking 800 years since the massacre was unveiled on the outside wall of Béziers' centre for Occitan language and culture.[62] The plaque is in Occitan and reads, 'On 22 July 1209, the great massacre punished the intolerable tolerance of the people of Oc'. It is unlikely that Occitan regions were any less intolerant than their counterparts in the kingdom of France, but the stated aims of the crusade were to prevent the tolerance of heresy by the region's powers.[63]

Tourism is now an important factor in commemorating this conflict. Heinzen cites battlefield tourism as a phenomenon that draws together notions of pilgrimage, sight-seeing, and voyeurism. He notes that visitors are drawn by a queasy combination of 'the timeless allure of the past, which was often fuelled by regret for lives, traditions and empires lost', and 'uncanny excitement upon confrontation with the aftermath of mass death'.[64] We see this clearly in some contributions to the website *Tripadvisor*.[65] The Cathedral of Saint-Nazaire attracts a range of comments. Out of nearly 300 reviews, a small number in French and in English report an emotional response to the site's history:

> The Cathedral represents the holocaust unleashed on the people of Languedoc by the Inquisition when the whole population was massacred on orders of the Catholic Church in 1209.Very depressing could not listen to the mass, so gave our money to the beggars at the door. The overbearing architecture and decoration only added to the dismal experience. (rusanjos, 24/07/2015)

One of the twenty-four published reviews of the church of la Madeleine highlights the siege and sack of Béziers as part of the church's appeal:

> 20,000 inhabitants of Beziers were put to death in the Catholic crusades against the Cathars in 1209. Many were burnt alive in this Church Saint Madelaine. I was thinking about this today whilst sitting in the square next to this impressive 4th Century building. Even if you do not enter into the historic church (which is open 3 times a week), I can highly recommend eating; drinking

or bargaining in the adjacent lively square & breathing in the history of this sacred place.' (sugarandspice2', 20/08/2014).

The visitor wishes to experience the city of 2014, but she strives to imagine the same site in the process of being destroyed. Her comments coincide with the reconstruction of the church as it had been on the eve of its destruction in 1209. In 2016, the city of Béziers' tourism information site informed potential visitors that the church is now part of the topography of 'Cathar country': 'the church has regained its Romanesque purity'.[66] The restoration of the medieval structure had been a factor in obtaining the full classification of the church as a historic monument in 1986, as a 'symbol of the urban community (former consular church) and of regional resistance (Albigensian crusade)'.[67] The restoration of the medieval church reflects the importance to the local economy since the 1980s of creating a tourist attraction. Béziers has been in economic decline since its wine industry collapsed in the 1980s. It has struggled to attract French tourists who flock to the nearby coast for sun and sea. The massacre's commemoration is a means of adding the town to the lucrative Cathar tourist circuit.

Conclusion

Associating the Occitania of 1209 with tolerance has its own power. Occitan identity politics can be adapted to non-nationalist and non-regionalist claims. For example, a demonstration in Toulouse in 2012 included French citizens of Maghrebi Berber heritage, who were using Occitan claims to further their own claims about the non-recognition of Berber identity in Morocco.[68] There is more to the crusade than domestic tourism and a tendency to reduce complex socio-economic history to a matter of 'Northern' (Parisian) encroachment on the South. The journalist Stephen O'Shea has commented:

> The Cathars of Languedoc defy obscurity because their story has become legend, a tale which belongs to everyone. The story of their defeat has given rise to a collective, international narrative, its various strands picked up and rewoven by a succession of 'alternative' movements for more than 100 years.[69]

Nor is it only of interest to O'Shea's 'alternative' communities. Cathar country tourism is big business in France. The creation in 2016 of a region

118

modelled on the county of Toulouse, and the apology for persecution of Cathars launched the same month tell their own story about the political relevance of this very old conflict. The Massacre of Béziers attracts a cluster of incompatible but powerful cultural associations. Some of them reflect obsolete political disputes, but others are still live. It remains a difficult and complex moment in history, casting a long shadow over popular culture too.

Chapter 9

Courtrai, the Battle of the
Golden Spurs 1302[1]

Eric Sangar

'And over all the battle-field raged the Butchers, their arms, their bosoms, and their axes smeared with gore, their hair streaming wildly, their features rendered undiscernible by mire and blood and sweat, yet fixed in a grim expression of bitterest hatred of the French and intense enjoyment of the conflict.'

Hendrik Conscience:
The Lion of Flanders, vol. III ch. VI.

One of the latest accounts of the Battle of Courtrai of 1302, the so-called Battle of the Golden Spurs, was published in 2009 in the series *Les Batailles Oubliées* (the forgotten battles). Indeed, during the research conducted for this chapter, I was surprised by the almost complete lack of knowledge about this battle that I encountered when talking to both Francophone and Flemish-speaking colleagues and citizens in Belgium.

So why does it make sense to include this battle in the volume? The history of the myths around the Battle of Courtrai illustrates well two larger insights: on the one hand, myths are historically contingent, they serve specific purposes pursued by political entrepreneurs. The structure and 'ownership' of myths can therefore change depending on their perceived political utility as well as the timely mobilisation of artistic production and popular mobilization. On the other hand, despite their constructed nature, myths cannot be purely 'invented' in the complete absence of links to actual historical events. Manufacturers of identity discourses will need some sort of references to 'available pasts'[2] in order to make a myth plausible and legitimate. Therefore, understanding the evolution of historiographic discourse is crucial not only for assessing the 'truth' of a myth but also for appreciating the conditions of its emergence.

Courtrai 1302: why was the battle so singular?

Seven-hundred years after the event, the Battle of Courtrai continues to be a topic for military historians. The reason for this ongoing interest resides in the fact that the battle can be considered the first successful asymmetrical victory of an infantry army against the dominating weapon of the time, armoured cavalry. How was such a victory, achieved against the then dominating land army in Europe, possible? The following account draws mainly on one recent account of the battle by Xavier Hélary,[3] whose quality resides not only in its reliance on both French and Flemish sources, but also on the critical discussion of their respective reliability and their underlying moral and political agendas.

At the end of the thirteenth century, the French King annexed and occupied the lands of Guy of Dampierre, the Count of Flanders. Eager to increase the political and economic autonomy of his fiefdom, the count's political manoeuvres between the French King Philip IV the Fair as his feudal overlord, the English King Edward I as the ruler of the county's main trading partners, and local patrician elites that firmly defended their privileges in local administration, had eventually made him a weak target for King Philip's ambition to expand and consolidate the direct rule of the royal court.

In Spring 1301, the French king's visit to several cities in the newly acquired Flemish territories eventually results in tensions between patricians and artisans in Bruges. A weaver named Pieter de Coninck takes the lead of a protest movement, which initially contests the unequal contribution among the town's social classes to finance costs caused by the reception of the King's visit. Jacques de Châtillon, the royal governor that replaced Guy of Dampierre, supports the Patricians in the oppression of the protesters but fails to undermine growing popular support in Bruges for de Coninck. The charismatic artisan even attempts to extend his leadership over a similar protest movement in Ghent. However, his attempt to organise a regional uprising against the Patricians seems doomed as the royal governor demonstrates his willingness to use military force to suppress any attempt to challenge the patricians' rule in the Flemish cities. Having expelled Pieter de Coninck from their city, the citizens of Bruges assert their fidelity to the governor and allow him to enter the city, accompanied by a heavily armed garrison of 800 armoured men. However, some of the insurgents make a clandestine return into the city and commit what will be subsequently known as the *Bruges Matins*: about 120 French troops are killed in the night of 17 to 18 May 1302, while governor Jacques de Châtillon and other French leaders manage to escape.[4]

Already before this event, Philip the Fair had prepared a large-scale military intervention to restore the authority of French rule in the Flemish territories by starting to raise a royal army. After the killings in Bruges, the calls to arms are sent to a broader audience of vassals.[5] Eventually, this army moves into Flemish territories and arrives at Courtrai on 8 July 1302. In this town, a small garrison French is already under siege by the main insurrection forces, led by Guy of Namur and William of Jülich. The two leaders are respectively son and grandson of Guy of Dampierre, by then held in a French prison.

Soon after the arrival of the French army, on 11 July 1302, the two armies engage in the Battle of Courtrai. The essential 'asymmetrical' character of the battle in terms of opposing force structures is undisputed. The French army, whose leader Robert II of Artois had decades of experience in campaigns in North Africa and Italy, comprises predominantly a cavalry force of 2,000 to 3,000 men-at-arms (including up to 500 knights), which is supplemented by a small infantry force.[6] The 'Flemish' army, although led by two noble-men, is in fact a heterogeneous coalition of local town militias. Its core force is the militia of Bruges, which includes a small professional force of about 500 crossbowmen as well as between 2,000 and 3,000 volunteer craftsmen, organised by the individual guilds. Two other militias of similar size, one from the Bruges countryside, another composed of volunteers from all over Eastern Flanders, make the Flemish therefore numerically superior to the French contingent.[7] This quantitative advantage is, however, made up by a qualitative handicap: although the Flemish units are, thanks to the wealth of the Flemish cities, relatively well trained and equipped, they suffer from a lack of warfare practice and do not have cavalry at their disposal. The only Flemish leader with considerable warfare experience is the Zealand knight John of Renesse, who acts as the effective tactical commander during the battle.[8]

Despite these limitations, the Flemish forces achieve a decisive victory in Courtrai, killing at least half of the French soldiers, including its leader Robert d'Artois and most of the nobles of his entourage. 500 golden spurs, one of the privileges of knights, are claimed to have been collected on the battlefield, some of which are later suspended at the ceiling of Courtrai's *Church of Our Lady.*

Such a decisive defeat sends a shockwave to the French king, who now has serious concerns for the stability of his authority well beyond the territory of Flanders. In turn, the Flemish forces seize the initiative and successfully take control of cities until then controlled by elites loyal to the authority of the French king, including Ghent, Lille, and Douai.[9] According to Véronique Lambert, the battle produces also a collective 'Flemish' identity through the very experience of an improbable victory against the dominating military power of that time. Rather than mobilizing already existing 'national' feelings, the very military deed appears to have galvanised the spirits of all participants and stimulated a feeling of shared destiny of struggle in support of the Count of Flanders.[10]

Although Philip the Fair managed few years later to restore royal control over Flanders, the Battle of Courtrai and its result had the durable effect of puzzling contemporary and later observers about the deeper reasons of one of the first defeats of a mighty cavalry by an inexperienced infantry force. This puzzle proved to be a fertile ground for the subsequent construction of myths both in the immediate aftermath of the battle, and during the nineteenth and twentieth centuries.

A battle decided by immoral treachery or noble arrogance?

At the outset, the Battle of Courtrai was less a source of myth in itself but rather a threat to an existing myth: the myth of the military but also moral superiority of noble cavalry in wartime. Indeed, not only the military system but the social and political order of medieval feudalism depended on the assumed inherent superiority of cavalry, led by (noble) knights. The very perception that knights, who claimed a range of monetary and non-monetary services from their feudal subjects in exchange for protection, could be defeated by a militia of common men might challenge the legitimacy of this order. If this event could not be framed as 'exceptional' and/or 'immoral', the victory of the Flemish insurrection might incite other territories to call for greater financial or political autonomy from the rule of the French King and his local vassals.

Consequently, Philip the Fair sought to put his spin on the interpretation of the battle as early as possible. Immediately, royal messengers were sent to all royal territories to establish an official narrative of the defeat. At the core of this version was the idea that the French Army was not sent to oppress a popular uprising but rather as an intervening force serving to restore peace among the Flemish. The Flemish insurgents were successful only because of immoral acts of treachery, which enabled them to lead the brave and peace-seeking French into destruction. The historical 'facts' found to support this version were, of course, the *Bruges Matins*, but also the way in which the French cavalry supposedly succumbed to the Flemish infantry during the battle.[11]

Until today, there is a historiographic consent regarding the tactical cause of the defeat: trenches in the battlefield effectively denied the French mounted units their mobility to manoeuvre and as a result made them vulnerable to attacks by the Flemish infantry using their *Goedendag* (a spiked club that facilitated bringing down horses and their riders). But it was the nature of these trenches that became the target of myth-making of French official history: according to the royal instructions to the messengers, 'these enemies made hidden holes and ditches out of treachery.'[12]

This official history, and its underlying myth according to which the French Army's defeat was only possible because of the immoral treachery of the Flemish insurgents, remained of course not uncontested. Interestingly, in the aftermath of the battle, the contemporary observers' position depended less on their 'national' perspective (an unknown concept at the time) but rather on the individual authors' moral intention. Thus, many of the available accounts, including Francophone sources, blame the French knights for carelessness and contempt for ordinary foot soldiers. Especially their leader Robert d'Artois is criticized for severely underestimating the fighting capabilities of the Flemish artisans. Certain of the superiority of his men-at-arms, he is portrayed by some medieval observers to launch the full cavalry attack early in the battle, despite knowing the risks posed by the trenches – out of fear his knights would have to share the glory of victory with the small French infantry force.[13]

By contrast, especially the accounts written in the Flemish territories soon after the battle emphasised 'the courage of a few rebels and the wise advice of their brave leaders who fought in their midst, [which] made possible this splendid victory against the finest French noblemen.'[14] Neither the unfavourable terrain, nor the Flemish military virtue becomes the decisive factor in the defeat of the French army, but the arrogance and self-confidence of their leaders, which provoked God's interference in favour of their modest and humble opponents.[15] In this narrative, the French defeat in Courtrai therefore serves to stabilise an already established myth according to which a lack of humility is the safest way into defeat.

A battle decided by an outburst of Belgian spirit of freedom?

To a certain extent, these first myths about the Battle of Courtrai fell into relative irrelevance for almost five centuries, as Flanders lost gradually its political autonomy. After its restoration as an autonomous feudal territory under the authority of the French crown, the territories of the County of Flanders become subsequently part of the Duchy of Burgundy, of the Spanish and Austrian Netherlands, and eventually of the independent United Kingdom of the Netherlands, which was formed after the Congress of Vienna in 1815. In 1830, any remaining autonomy was dissolved as Flanders became part of the independent kingdom of Belgium.

Across Europe, the aftermath of the French Revolution was accompanied by attempts to transform the witnessed power of popular mobilisation in favour of a sovereign and democratic nation into a resource of legitimacy and military strength for the restored or newly formed monarchies. The Kingdom of Belgium was no exception, as the new state had to find ways to increase its internal legitimacy and external strength by integrating a population that was economically, linguistically, and culturally heterogeneous.

This can explain the impetus of 'inventing' a national historiography, resulting in an intense scholarly debate around the question of how to demonstrate that 'the Belgians' – despite their mentioned differences – had a shared history, whose virtues were represented by the contemporary nation-state.[16] Interestingly, since the early conceptions of Belgian national history emphasised a cultural-biological understanding of Belgian identity, in which the concepts of 'race' and 'nation' became mutually interchangeable, the absence of political independence was not perceived as an obstacle per se for the evolution of the Belgian nation. Rather, independently from their actual political constitution, the Belgians were portrayed as sharing a 'national spirit', characterised by a love for freedom and a heterogeneous but harmonious mix of the 'Germanic' and 'Celtic' races, whose distinctive origin can be traced back to Pre-Roman periods.[17] Thus, Belgian history is 'invented' as a continuous narrative of a people in a permanent struggle for freedom and independence: 'Precisely the lack of self-determination and the postulated permanent antagonism between foreign rulers and the indigenous population was interpreted as evidence for the desire of freedom rooted in the Belgian national spirit.'[18]

In this context, the Battle of Courtrai was re-mobilised by historians, but only as an episode *inter alia* in this continuous narrative, spanning two millennia, and not as a singular event that might have sparked the first outburst of a Belgian sense of national belonging. Even the creation of the new Belgian state in 1830 did not result in a fundamentally different, more politicised historiography of the events of 1302, let alone the invention of a thorough founding myth. Although there was an increase in historiographical publications on the Battle of Courtrai between 1830 and 1850, these followed largely the medieval narrative structures and frames of interpretation.[19]

Only some historiographers, such as Théodore Juste, writer of several popular national histories, explicitly frame the cause of the conflict in terms of an outburst of a 'national spirit' among the lower classes. But even this last account still subscribed to the larger view of a people united over millennia through a common desire for freedom, of which the Battle of Courtrai only constituted one among other episodes, and which had essentially the function of a warning against any foreign power not to threaten the independence of the young Belgian state.[20] This was especially relevant for the perceived threat by France, which had annexed Belgian territories few decades earlier after the French Revolution: For the political elites of 1830, 'France was the ancestral enemy, and the recollection of "1302" was intended to contribute to vigilance with regard to that powerful neighbour. It was a matter of national integrity.'[21]

The decisive impulse for the last – and this time thorough – re-invention of the myth of the Battle of Courtrai did not originate in the diligent efforts of academics to invent a uniting national history for the new Belgian state. Instead, it was the Courtrai industrialist and part-time local historian Jacques Goethals-Vercruysse that *nolens volens* paved the way for a thorough re-interpretation of the battle, which had lasting consequences for intra-Belgian politics until the late twentieth century.

A battle decided by a contest of will between the Flemish and French nations?

Since the end of the eighteenth century, Goethals-Vercruysse worked on a meticulous historical chronology for his hometown Courtrai, whose first volume (published in 1814) dedicated more than twenty pages to the description of the events during the battle of 11 July 1302. However, it is not the length of the analysis but the basic interpretation of the tactical reasons for the French defeat that represents a profound innovation compared to the established accounts of historiography since the fifteenth century. Citing the description by the early fourteenth-century Flemish clergyman Lodewijk van Velthem, he rejects the until then even by Belgian historians accepted claim according to which the French defeat was caused by the ruse of previously dug and then covered trenches. Instead, in his narrative, the trenches are part of *natural* terrain obstacles, which only have a subordinate role in a battle decided by the robustness and strength of the Flemish troops against a quantitatively and qualitatively superior but arrogant French force.[22]

Systematically lacking specific references for his claims, Goethals-Vercruysse's research does not meet even the contemporary standards for historiographical works. Nevertheless, his interpretation became soon so influential that it grew into the backbone of the myth, bolstering Flemish nationalist movement of the late nineteenth century. How did this happen?

Lacking professional credentials, Goethals-Vercruysse did not have access to the wider scientific community of Belgian historian. His version of the Battle of Courtrai only gained widespread attention thanks to the friendship to Auguste Voisin, teacher of rhetoric and holder of a doctorate in philosophy. In 1834, Voisin and Goethals-Vercruysse published a condensed narrative of the battle in the *Messager des Sciences et des Arts de la Belgique*, a leading Belgian scientific journal. Surfing on the lively discussion on Belgian national history after 1830, this publication gained widespread popularity. More importantly, it became the source of two artistic works, the historical painting *La Bataille de Courtrai* by Nicaise de Keyser, displayed first in 1836, and the three volume historical novel *De Leeuw van Vlaanderen* by Hendrik Conscience, published in 1838. Only the popular impact of these two works, whose artistic transformation resulted in a simplified and dramatized narrative of the battle that would become the essence of the subsequent myth, made it possible that Goethals-Vercruysse's version of the battle suddenly turned into the mainstream interpretation not only in public but even in historiographical discourse.[23]

Especially *De Leeuw van Vlaanderen* played an essential bridging function between a historical narrative that was still rooted in the debates around the possibility of a *Belgian* national history, and the legitimacy needs of the nascent *Flemish* national movement. Indeed, Henrik Conscience's artistic biography symbolises this symbolic bridge: working as a translator in the municipal administration of Antwerp, since 1836 he systematically published his work in Flemish, despite French being his own mother language and the dominant administrative and cultural idiom of the new Belgian state. In 1838, he even declared that all Belgians that spoke French were dishonouring their forefathers' heritage.[24] Nevertheless, the Francophone elites seemed to perceive this work as perfectly compatible with the dominant discourse of Belgian national identity emphasising unity through a common national spirit despite linguistic and political diversity.[25] (Fig 9.1)

The novel's utility for the subsequent politicisation by the Flemish national movement resides in Conscience's romanticised and idealised re-framing of Goethals-Vercruysse's account. The novel reinterprets the Battle of Courtrai as a struggle between Good – incorporated by a united Flemish community fighting for their freedom – and Evil – incorporated by the French bloodthirsty and scheming oppressors. The Flemish determination to kill the French without mercy, first during the *Bruges Matins* and then on the battlefield, was a legitimate and necessary means to defend the *Flemish* nation. As a result, the novel adopts the form of a full-scale national epic, portraying the battle as an apocalyptic battle that conveys to the present "the no-holds-barred obliteration of the enemy threat and the firm moral lesson that this feisty stance of the ancestors ought to be an example to modem-day readers."[26]

To bolster the myth of a union of Flemish nobles and lower classes in the struggle against the French enemy, Conscience even chose to present Robert of Béthune, the oldest son of Guy of Dampierre, as the military leader of the Flemish troops, although the nicknamed 'Lion of Flanders' was in reality held in a French prison until 1305. This – literally invented – *union sacrée* between the Flemish population and their 'indigenous' noble leaders and their determination to extinguish their French enemy is what makes Battle of Courtrai such a singular event in the nascent Flemish narrative.[27] Whereas both the medieval and the early nineteenth-century Belgian historiography allowed for the differentiated – although of course not neutral – assessment of the personalities of participating individuals and their social interests, in Conscience's narrative the behaviour of both heroes and villains seem to be exclusively determined by their national origin.[28] This becomes clear in the novel's explication of the question why the French Army did not take into account the trenches on the battlefield:

> The French general, Robert d'Artois, was a brave and experienced soldier; but, like many others of his fellow-countrymen, he was too rash and self-confident. [...] The space which separated them [the Flemish troops] from the French army was a succession of meadows, which lay very low, and were watered by the Mosscher brook, which converted them into a kind of marsh. [...] The French

general took no account of this; he made his plans as though the field of battle were firm and hard ground.[29]

But the most profound rupture with established accounts of Belgian historiography resides in the Battle of Courtrai's political lessons for the present, which is barely disguised in the following quotation:

> We Flemish have a history, a past as a country and as a people. [...] And now they want us to become Walloons, to sacrify our old glory, our language, our glorious history, and everything we inherited from our forefathers.[30]

Of course, given the fragmented cultural, social and political history of the territories that once formed the historical county of Flanders, it is easy to dismiss any claims about historically rooted, persisting 'national' differences between 'the Flemish' and 'the Walloons' (with the latter term originating only in the fifteenth century, and therefore lacking any reference to the political conditions of 1302). But the reasons of the novel's success can be found in the way the work fulfilled a latent political need of part of the population in the new Belgian state: by re-framing the Battle of Courtrai as the moment in which the collective, trans-social uprising against the French gave birth to a Flemish national identity, Conscience was able to transform an objective marker of social hierarchy in nineteenth century Belgium – namely the use of the French language – into a symbolic resource for collective political mobilisation.

The Flemish-national version of the myth of Courtrai rapidly become dominant as a result of the overwhelming impact of *De Leeuw van Vlaanderen*, which was re-printed in twenty-four editions between 1838 and 1914, and inspired dozens of poems, theatre plays, and visual artwork.[31] The dual nature of the novel – its apparent faithful orientation on historical 'facts', and its popular appeal thanks to elaborate descriptions of romance and violence – made it an attractive reading for the Flemish-speaking intelligentsia, the (petty) bourgeoisie, and the working classes. Nörtemann thus concludes that Conscience's work can be considered to a certain extent the maker of modern Flemish collective identity: 'the *Leeuw* is the canonical version of the Flemish foundational myth [...]. The *Leeuw* has added to the identity reference of language [...] the second basic element of Flemish ideology – the shared memory and the appeal to a glorious past'.[32]

Indeed, in the novel, the linguistic difference defines the protagonists' membership in one of the opposing communities and therefore their mutual perceptions,[33] thereby ignoring that French was already at that time the dominant language used by local political and social elites, including the Count and his sons. The invention of a historical discriminatory effect of language enabled, however, Flemish-speaking readers to make sense of a very familiar contemporary reality: like other regional languages in nineteenth-century nation-states, the Flemish language was seen as vernacular relics and obstacles to the cultural and educational modernisation and homogenisation of the Belgian state. As a result, most inhabitants of traditionally Flemish-speaking territories, especially the local elites, more often than not used French in their daily lives. Only the imagination of the Battle of Courtrai as an event which had forged a 'Flemish people' in the past made it possible for these populations to view themselves as a distinct political community, whose collective political power only had to be 'rediscovered'.

It was exactly this line of argumentation that the early Flemish national movement, the so-called *Flamingants*, used from its beginnings in the late 1830s. The leaders of this movement – and this may illustrate further to what extent the idea of a historically continuous Flemish political identity was a myth – were local intellectuals, who initially pursued the recognition of Flemish as equal second national language. They were probably motivated by their individual desire of gaining the same social recognition as intellectuals publishing in French language,[34] less by a perception of popular demands for linguistic equality. After all, 'when many Flemish in Brussels decided to give their children a French education, they were not doing so out of obligation, but rather out of disdain for their own language, as indicated by the saying "French in the parlor, Flemish dialect in the kitchen."'[35]

The populations that spoke Flemish in the kitchen also had in common an experience of discrimination by the Belgian central state, especially in terms of economic and educational opportunities. According to the Belgian constitution, the right to vote was reserved to wealthy male property-owners. These were in the early days of the Belgian state almost exclusively Francophones originating from the industrialised, southern areas of the country. Since French was also the only spoken language at courts, universities, and administrations, Flemish-speaking citizens had a structural disadvantage accessing and making careers in state institutions.[36] At the same time, the poorer educational infrastructure in Flemish-speaking areas represented an effective obstacle to thorough language assimilation. As a result, 'policy choices made at the time of the founding [...] imposed upon the two major linguistic segments differential costs of membership in Belgian society [...]. It was not a matter of "mere symbols" since institutional arrangements discriminated against members of the Flemish language group and concretely affected their life-chances in comparison with members of the other group.'[37]

The *Flamingant* movement successfully transformed these experiences of discrimination into the perception of a binary, century-old conflict between two distinct communities, the 'Flemish' nation, defined by its language, and the 'Walloons', whose linguistic and cultural proximity with the French denied them the status of a nation of their own. Rather than the culmination of a millennia-old story of a people united in diversity, the Belgian state was portrayed as yet another scheme in the tradition of Francophone attempts to dominate the Flemish nation.[38] As in 1302, 'French' oppression could only be overcome by the reconstitution of the political unity of the Flemish community.

The institutionalisation of the Flemish foundational myth

In the absence of greater recognition of the Flemish-speaking population, the myth of 1302 became the central symbolic reference of the *Flamingant* movement, which gradually shifted its demands towards the full autonomy of the 'Flemish nation' within Belgium. Ten years after the publication of Conscience's novel, a local *Flamingant* society organized the first public commemoration of the Battle of Courtrai in Brussels.[39] Subsequently, 'the commemoration of 11 July (the day of the Battle of the Golden Spurs) was beginning to be an annual consciousness-raiser in various Flemish cities. The sixth centenary of the battle, in 1902, was considered a nationally Flemish event.'[40] And even in Francophone Belgian discourse, 'the term "Flandre" [sic] was used more and more to designate the Dutch-speaking part of Belgium, rather than the old medieval county'.[41] The increasing ownership of the Flemish national movement over the myth of the Battle of Courtrai and its institutionalization can be illustrated specifically by two examples: the debate on and subsequent construction of a monument to the battle in Bruges, and the institutionalisation of the 11 July as a day of national commemoration. (Fig 9.2)

Nineteenth-century Bruges was dominated by petty bourgeoisie citizens who struggled to keep their economic status. This milieu was, for the reasons stated above, especially sensitive to the idea of a Flemish nation in quest for recognition by the Belgian state. In the 1860s, several petty bourgeois associations launched an initiative to build a monument to the – supposed – organisers of the *Bruges Matins*, Pieter de Coninck and the butcher Jan Breydel, and thus to link the Flemish national movement to local Bruges patriotism. The poor financial situation of the city and its inhabitants might explain why it took more than twenty years until the inauguration of this monument. But this lack of means ensured that the commemoration of the battle was increasingly perceived as an integrative movement across social classes as the initiators of the monument project organised a number of mass celebrations and gatherings as fundraising events. However, the question of how to organise the inauguration ceremony in 1887 brought persisting and new lines of tension: by inviting the Belgian King and other 'non-Flemish' officials, the 'Catholic' city administration expressed its preference for a link between Flemish nationalism and Belgian state patriotism, while the 'Liberal' monument initiative organised an alternative ceremony that was exclusively reserved to members of 'Flemish' associations and intellectuals.[42]

The 1890s can be considered the period in which the movement for the commemoration of the Battle of Courtrai became truly 'national' in the sense that numerous local initiatives with partially differing political and social agendas increasingly evolved into nationally organised interest groups, such as the *Nationaal Vlaamsch Verbond,* the *Vlaamsche Wacht,* and the *Algemeen Nederlandsch Verbond*. The latter association sought to introduce the celebration of the 11 July 1302 in all Flemish-speaking municipalities, an objective that was supported by the West-Flanders provincial government that decide in 1892 to close all provincial buildings on that day.[43] In the following years, marches, fairs, and art festivals proliferated in many cities and towns, and were supported by civil society representatives and politicians across the spectrum, even those that were part of local Francophone elites. These two evolutions – the 11 July commemoration's increasing mass popularity as well as its institutionalisation – enabled the national movement to present itself as the only legitimate political representative of the Flemish-speaking populations, who were increasingly demanding recognition and equal political participation in the Belgian state.[44] Until 1914, the issue of the political and cultural rights of the 'Flemish nation' became a profound cleavage in Belgian politics, and the national movement accomplished first political successes, such as the recognition of bilingualism in legislation and administration in 1898 or the right of children to schooling in their mother tongue.[45]

Conclusion: a 'forgotten' myth with a lasting impact on Belgian politics

By the end of the nineteenth century, thanks to the impact of Conscience's novel that successfully remixed historical 'facts' with romantic national ideas, the plurality of myths associated with the Battle of Courtrai was replaced by the dominant myth of the forging of a united Flemish nation through a courageous battle of French-speaking oppressors.[46] How successful the Flemish movement was in its attempt to change the collective representation of the Battle of Courtrai from an episode in Belgian history into the exclusive foundational myth of the Flemish nation demonstrates King Albert's troop address on the beginning of the First World War. Instead of referring to a shared Belgian memory, Albert asks his soldiers: 'Flemings, remember the Battle of the Golden Spurs, Walloons, remember the 600 Franchimontois!'[47]

After the two World Wars, the successful division of the collective memory of the Belgian state paved the way to a thorough reorganisation of power that exceeded the hopes of even the most radical elements of the early Flemish national movement. Despite the damaged reputation of parts of the Flemish movement that had collaborated with German occupiers during the Second World War, the commemoration of 11 July 1302 regained strength after 1952, the 650th anniversary of the battle. In 1973, the Flemish-speaking territories achieved the status of an autonomous political entity, the 'Flemish cultural community', which obtained considerable cultural and educational competences. This first step towards the federalised Belgian constitution of today marks the eventual institutionalisation of an identity conflict whose lasting consequences continue to put question marks behind the continuous existence of the Belgian state – despite the reversal in the distribution of economic and political power that happened during the twentieth century. The identity narrative that had emerged from a romanticised reformulation of answers to a puzzle of medieval military history is today 'used to legitimise Flemish demands to set the federated entities of Belgium on a teleological path towards independence…[T]he symbolic reproduction of the causes that led to the mobilisation of the

Flemish movement in the nineteenth century still contributes to a sense of grievance felt by the Flemish against the francophones.'[48]

At the same time, with its durable political institutionalisation, the Flemish identity narrative (such as other national identity narratives) seems no longer require the continuous reference to historical myths in order to sustain and legitimise its existence. Having declared the 11 July a public holiday in 1973, the Flemish community government re-qualified it a working day again few years ago, thus visibly giving neoliberal austerity greater weight over sustaining the emotional appeal of the battle. The growing 'forgetting' of the myth of 1302 may also be illustrated by the museum 'Kortrijk 1302' that was inaugurated in Courtrai in 2006. The museum is the result of an initiative of a Flemish minister of culture, who thought that just like other nations, the Flemish needed a dedicated museum for 'their' battle.[49] Despite this clear political mandate, the museum has probably become one of the most efficient contributions to 'historicise' the battle. A quotation from a dialogue of the museum's pedagogic film that redraws (and thus deconstructs) the history of the myths of Courtrai may illustrate best this observation and conclude this chapter:

> In 1973, the Dutch cultural commission, the precursor of the Flemish council, chose 11 July as the date for the holiday of the Flemish Community.
>
> Of the historical point of view, this is not correct, because the Battle of Courtrai had nothing to do with national identity, but of course this is logical.[50]

Chapter 10

Famous Battles: A Typology

Beatrice Heuser

In our case studies we have passed review many battles and their myths. According to the British historian, George Schöpflin, we must not confuse historical fact with mythical interpretation: 'myth is about perceptions rather than historically validated truths (in so far as these exist at all)…'.[1] Battles, cast in mythical terms, are drawn upon later to justify policies, and indeed to stir up people to take or support action – often in the context of conflicts centuries later – action, that is interpreted in analogy to those original battles. The sacrifices of the past, commemorated in mourning, are invoked to call for new sacrifices. 'As regards national memories,' said Ernest Renan in his famous lecture, 'mourning is worth more than triumphs; four it imposes duties, it demands a common effort' – to be made to avenge the fallen, to reverse a historic defeat, the reader is left to conclude, or to fight against a new adversary who is cast as the successor of the old enemy of that historic battle.[2] People are called upon to show the same readiness for self-sacrifice as preceding generations, regardless of the outcome then or now. In the context of conflict, such myths can be powerful arms; if brandished skilfully by politicians, they can lead to much renewed antagonism and even war. This makes for the poignancy of our subject.

Battles are central to European national identities, especially as they crystallised in the nineteenth century. The German Historical Museum in Berlin in 1998 organised an exhibition on 'The Myths of Nations'. The conference volume edited by Monika Flacke that accompanied this exhibition covered eighteen countries with five important national myths each, i.e. historical events that have been invoked as catalysts or crucial markers of national identity. Of ninety such myths, fifty concern battles or sieges or wars in general. As contributing authors were not instructed to give battles and war such precedence, there is no reason to think that this predominance of battles as national myths in Flacke's volume is anything but a realistic representation of their predominance in collective memory.[3] They can also be commemorated to strengthen class solidarity, as we shall see below.

In more benign contexts, myths can gently fade away, and leave at best inconsequential, perhaps romantic images, barely recognisably derived from actual historical events, turning themselves into tropes of fiction or legend and fairy-tale. They can end up as little more than kaleidoscopic reconfigurations of all or a number of the following components of epic story lines: heroes (perhaps on both sides even), traitors, an underestimated leader rising to the occasion or a boisterous leader unmasked as a coward, self-sacrifice (sometimes of a leader, sometimes of a lowly soldier or bodyguard to save the master or the standard or banner), a symbol (such as a banner) that is fought over, valiant steeds, magic swords or hunting horns, meteorological miracles (a sudden frost or thaw, a sun standing still, a cross appearing in the heavens…), other divine interventions, sin and redemption or sin and punishment, and so on. This benign passing into legend applies to the (possibly historical) Battle of Badon Hill fought by the Romano-Celts, supposedly under King Arthur, against invading Saxons, in the late fifth or early sixth century, the Battle of Roncevaux in which the mythical Roland was mortally wounded, and the Battle of Culloden (see Volume 2).

But in antagonistic contexts, myths can be hammered and forged into interpretations that give political clout to calls for action, they can consciously or unconsciously contribute to a particular narrative of the past. This may not be shared entirely by all members of the group that it addresses – see for example the divergent myths concerning the Battles of Hastings in 1066, Courtrai in 1302, or of Chatham in 1667 – but it will certainly be recognised by all of them.

Schöpflin's taxonomy of myths has inspired the following one that is focused on the myths attached to historical battles.[4]

In hoc signo: Battles willed by God

Battles as markers of identity can be found not only in Homer's great work, but also in the Hebrew Bible. As Chapter 5 reminded us, the Lord of Hosts sent the Israelites into battle repeatedly, and a Battle of Megiddo is an important marker of the history of the Chosen People. The prophesy of a rerun of this epic battle in contained in the New Testament, referred to as Armageddon (*Revelations* of St John). After some debate among the earliest Christians the Roman Church adopted the Israelite belief that there could be just wars willed by God. As Christians saw themselves as the new Chosen People, they took the Hebrew Bible's stories about war as moral lodestars (see Chapter 5).

The first Roman emperor to have tolerated Christianity and to have embraced it for himself was Constantine I, later canonized by the Church. His conversion is famously attributed to the battle he fought at the Milvian Bridge against his competitor for the rule of the entire Empire, Maxentius, in CE 312. In a dream he is supposed to have seen a cross in the skies, being told that he would win (if he fought) under this sign, '*in hoc signo vinces*'. Constantine and most of his successors would indeed subsequently go into battle carrying a standard or *labarum*, embellished with Christian symbols.[5] This story, told by the Church historian Eusebius, clearly impressed barbarian rulers of European tribes subsequently converted to Christianity: there several legends attributing this to the divine promise of victory in battle in exchange. The earliest of these is probably the Frankish ruler Clovis, who had himself baptised at Reims after he emerged victorious in CE 496 from the Battle of Tolbiac against the invading Allemanni. France thus became 'the oldest daughter of the Church' (at least in Western Europe as the other Christian entities at the time had espoused beliefs condemned as heretical by the Pope), the basis of France's claim to be the protector of Christians throughout the world (explaining both the Crusades and France's engagement in the Middle East from the nineteenth century).

We encounter this motif also in Portuguese history, where in 1139 the Portuguese (Christian) Prince Afonso Henriques saw a crucifix in the sky on the eve of the battle he would win against the Muslim Almoravids at Ourique (a mythical rendering of the story not found in the contemporary sources),[6] and in Danish history, where in 1219 during the Battle of Lyndanisse by the (Christian) Danes against the (heathen) Estonians what is now the Danish flag (the *Danebrog*), a cloth bearing a red cross on white background, fell from heaven; in praying to God, the Danes were victorious.

A derivative of this linking of the Christian cross as a symbol under which to go into battle with a just cause and victory can be seen in the *vexillum Christi*, a standard with an (often red) cross much like the English flag. This seems to have been derived from the late Christian Roman army's standard. Such a flag with a cross, in recognition of the justice of his cause, was requested by William the Bastard of Normandy and graciously given by the Pope before his invasion of England, and it is even depicted on the

Bayeux Tapestry. More typically, a war against heathens or heretics could only be a crusade if it was sanctified by the Pope through the granting of a *vexillum Christi* to the leaders of the host, and they could then claim that 'God wills it,' *Deus lo vult*. Later generations seem to have contented themselves either by harnessing His subordinates to their cause (famously, St George and St Denis respectively in the Hundred Years' War), or by simply claiming that God was on their side, 'With God for King and Fatherland' (*Mit Gott für König und Vaterland*).

Europe saw relatively few battles in the Middle Ages. Battle was seen as a divine ordeal in which God might judge not only the worthiness of the cause itself, but also the sinfulness of the combatants. The Church made men aware of their sinfulness, and thus rulers and their armies feared not only for their lives but also for their souls, if they were defeated and killed. Conscious of their own imperfections, victors presented their victory as a gift of God, as 'wrought by God'. The fifteenth-century Agincourt Carol, commemorating the victory of Henry V against the French in 1415, is most perfect example of this:

> Owre Kynge went forth to Normandy
> With grace and myght of chivalry
> Ther God for hym wrought mervelusly [sic!];
> Wherefore Englonde may call and cry
> Chorus
> Deo gratias!
> Deo gratias Anglia redde pro victoria!
> [Thanks to God!
> England, give thanks to God for the victory!]

Commemoration of the victorious dynasty

While strictly speaking, this meant that a king should not claim merit in victory, indirectly, he would make just that claim: after all, God had chosen *him* over the adversary. Much political mileage could be made out of this. It is a classic Greek, Roman and later Christian tradition to vow to the gods or *the* God or to one of His saints gifts such as battle spoils, candles or *ex voto* objects if an adversity is overcome. But spending several years' income of a state on founding and equipping an abbey to celebrate one's victory is more than that.

Already in the early sixth century, after his famous victory over the Alamanni which led him to convert to Catholicism, Frankish King Clovis founded the church that is today the Pantheon in Paris. Just a little later, his successor King Childebert I founded an abbey in Brittany, later refounded as the Abbey of Relec, to commemorate the fallen in a battle of 555. In 988, William Sanchez of Gascony founded the Abbey of St Sever in gratitude for his victory in nearby Taller against invading Vikings some five years earlier. Similar origins in a battle are attributed to the Abbey of Quimperlé, once again situated in Brittany, founded in 1029 by (Saint) Gurthiern of Cambria with the help of the Duke of Cornwall. Gurthiern is supposed accidentally to have killed his own nephew in a battle fought on British soil over the Cambrian succession, upon which, full of remorse, he became a monk, retiring to Brittany. The religious foundation of Quimperlé is situated far away from the original battle site, and this is also true for the bishopric of Merseburg, created in 968 by Emperor Otto I to give thanks for his victory against the Hungarians at the Battle of Lechfield (near modern day Augsburg in Bavaria), hundreds of miles away, in 955. By contrast, when in 1070, William the Conqueror had an abbey built to commemorate his victory near Hastings, as atonement for the killings that had inevitably gone along with the battle, the battlefield was nearby (see Chapter 7).

Such an abbey was a power base for its founder and his dynasty, with monks praying for them, conscious of their particular dependence on the patronage of the royal family. Travellers calling upon the hospitality of such an abbey would participate in this ritual, and see the abbey itself as a reflection of the greatness and magnanimity of the monarch in question. Little wonder, then, that others emulated this gesture both of self-humbling and of self-promotion.

In 1153 Afonso Henriques – now King Alfonso I of Portugal – founded the Monastery of Alcobaça (Fig. 10.1) to celebrate the large gains he had made against the Moors in his *Reconquista* of land, especially with the above-mentioned Battle of Ourique some fourteen years earlier. (The site of the Battle of Ourique itself has not been identified.) Alcobaça subsequently became one of the mausolea of the Burgundian Portuguese royal dynasty. In 1222, eight years after his resounding victory over the Holy Roman Empire and the English at Bouvines, King Philip-Augustus of France founded the Abbey or Our Lady of Victory at Senlis. Henry II the Pious of Silesia was buried at the battlefield of Legnica (Legnickie Pole), initially in a modest church next to an already existent Benedictine monastery, but his sacrifice was commemorated through nearby monastery of Krzeszów, founded by his widow a year after the battle. A further, Benedictine monastery next to the modest church and the battlefield was in the eighteenth century given a new portal designed around a tropaion and was also designed to commemorate both battle and dynasty.

The most magnificent surviving example in Europe of such a commemorative foundation is the Monastery of our Lady of Victory at Batalha in Portugal, founded by King John I, first of the Aviz dynasty, to commemorate his victory Battle of Aljubarrota over the Castilian pretender to the crown in 1385. This victory would keep Portugal independent from the Spanish crown for two centuries. Like Battle Abbey in England, the Monastery of Alcobaça and the Abbey at Senlis, Batalha Monastery functioned as a hostel (in this case on the much-travelled road between Lisbon and Coïmbra), thus showing royal largesse to all travellers. Moreover, Batalha also housed the tombs of King John, his queen Philippa of Lancaster, and their royal offspring. Like Alcobaça Abbey, Batalha Monastery in its astonishing beauty is a palace for the dead royals, where their magnificent funerary chapels are open to all passers-by to marvel at. (Fig. 10.2)

The Battle of Aljubarrota competes with the earlier Battle of Ourique to be the founding myth of Portugal. Batalha Monastery was chosen in 1924 as the site to commemorate Portugal's soldiers who died in the First World War, fighting against the Central Powers on several fronts. Even though Aljubarrota has been discredited as a site of the actual battle of 1385 by the research of a Portuguese historian (much to the chagrin of the Aljubarrota Association, formed to raise the money to commemorate the battle), a site near Batalha Monastery has won the competition to be presented as Portugal's cradle: the field of St George.[7] Here, an area that might plausibly have been the battlefield has been marked by a visitor centre, built with European Union subsidies in the early 2000s, presumably to stress that French- and Englishmen also fought in this battle (and thus to take the nationalist sting out of it).

Less public is the foundation by King Henry VI of England and the Archbishop of Canterbury, Henry Chichele, of All Souls' College in Oxford to commemorate the souls of all those who had given their lives at the (for Henry's father, victorious) Battle of Agincourt of 1415. Possibly the latest in this series of battle abbey foundations is that of the Escorial, founded by Philip II of Spain after the Battle of St Quentin in 1557 which Spain won against France. What we think of today mainly as a Spanish royal palace was first and foremost a monastery in which the puritan *Rex catholicissimus* chose to live, and which became, like the two Portuguese monasteries, the principal burial site for the royal dynasty.

All these foundations had in common the propagation of the myth of the God-willed victory that favoured the founder and his family. Besides supporting the prayers of the monks for the victor's dynasty, these were propaganda myths of divine favour cast in stone. In each case, these foundations celebrated the ruling dynasty, and were only later appropriated by entire nations as symbols of their collective prowess.

The Death of the Hero-Commander

A pattern that can be traced back to the Greeks is that of one warrior or a group of warriors who sacrifice themselves for the others, and whose sacrifice must be emulated by them. We find this appeal in the commemoration of the sacrifice of the Spartans under Leonidas in the Battle of Thermopylae (see Chapter 4), but also in the funerary oration attributed to Pericles by Thucydides:

> We who remain behind may hope to be spared their fate [of the fallen], but must resolve to keep the same daring spirit against the foe. ... They gave their lives, to [Athens] and to all of us ... It is for you to try to be like them.[8]

The proud resignation of the Celtic tribal chief Vercingetorix in 52 BCE after his defeat by Caesar and his fits this pattern: it was taken, in post-1871 France (otherwise still very keen on her Roman heritage) as emblematic of Gallic valour and of the cruelty of the victorious adversary that treacherously put to death such a noble foe – Vercingetorix was not slain on the battlefield but murdered in a Roman dungeon.

When Christianity came, as sociologist Maurice Halbwachs has noted, 'Christian collective memory in each era adapted its recollection of the details of the life of Christ and of the places to which they are attached to the contemporary needs of Christianity, ... and to its aims.'[9] Christianity took up this meme of Jesus' self-sacrifice so that mankind might be saved, always with the injunction that those saved should 'take up their cross and follow Him'. Jesus himself is the protagonist in the eternal battle of Good against Evil. How not to see an analogy in the death of a Christian king in battle against pagans that would nevertheless ultimately result in the conversion of the pagans! Thus King Olaf of Norway, fallen in 1030 in the

Battle of Stiklestad against pagan war lords is celebrated as St Olaf, and the battle itself is the founding myth of Christian Norway.

The myth of – and the injunction to emulate – the hero who dies in battle but makes his contribution to the metaphysical victory of Good over Evil, or the good side against the evil side, did not depend on victory in the battle itself. In the Battle of Roncevaux of 778 Charlemagne's nephew Roland (later revered as St Roland) and the noble Oliver laid down their lives in defence of Christendom. Silesian Duke Henry II the Pious, revered as the 'Servant of God', was killed in the Battle of Legnica in 1241 which, although a Mongol victory, constituted the point of greatest penetration of the Mongols into Europe, after which they turned back. Serbian Prince Lazar Hrebeljanović fell in the Battle of Kosovo Polje (Blackbird Field) on 28 June 1389 against the Turks, which in this case ended not with the saving of his country, but its subjection to the Ottoman Empire, yet Prince Lazar is revered as hero. Similarly, King Lajos II, the last Jagellonian king of Hungary, was killed by the Ottomans in the Battle of Mohács of 1526, losing Hungary to Ottoman rule, but achieved mythical fame.[10]

Other hero-martyrs of battle include the Bohemian king Přemysl II Ottokar at the Battle of Marchfield in 1278 against Count Rudolf of Habsburg (the first Habsburg ruler of the Holy Roman Empire: the death of King Přemysl is narrated as loss of Bohemian independence vis-à-vis the 'Germans').[11] A rare example of a commoner cast in this role of martyr for the nation is that of the Swiss soldier Arnold Winkelried, who in the Battle of Sempach in 1386 is said to have seized hold of the tips of a number of spears with which the Habsburg army charged the Swiss foot soldiers. He directed them against his own body, thus creating a breach in the horizontal line of enemy spears which allowed his fellow-soldiers to penetrate the body of the attacking army formation, and then to defeat it. Winkelried was pierced by the many spears he deflected from his companions, uttering the famous last words, 'I want to clear the way for freedom'.[12]

Special mention must be made of Gustavus Adolphus, 'the Lion from Midnight', the Swedish King who weighed in on the Protestant side in the Thirty Years' War and then died on the battlefield of Lützen in 1632. Gustavus Adolphus has to this day remained Sweden's saviour-figure, the closest Protestantism gets to a saint-martyr, but also a national symbol of Sweden's imperial age when as a great power it ruled the Baltic Sea and all the territories around it. As such the commemoration of Sweden's successes in the battles of the Thirty Years' War stand in stark contrast with Swedish pacifism and neutrality as developed since the early nineteenth century. The paradox was long glossed over and 'Gustavus Adolphus Day' (6 November) was until late in the twentieth century celebrated as a public holiday when schools were closed. Today the Swedish flag is still hung from public buildings, and bakeries sell special Gustavus Adolphus tartlets on 6 November. While Swedish King Charles XII also died in war (at the Swedish siege of the Norwegian fortress of Fredriksten in 1718 in the Great Northern War against Denmark-Norway), his commemoration in Sweden carries no comparable pride. King Charles was also the military leader in the Battle of Poltava in 1709 in which Sweden was defeated catastrophically by Russia.[13] Poltava is seen as the initiation of the decline of Sweden and the ascent of Russia (Fig. 10.3).

The French see their defeat at Agincourt with understandable indifference as it was no more than a temporary French setback. They felt obliged to do something to commemorate the 600th anniversary of the battle to cater to lucrative English enthusiasm for battlefield tourism. There was one exhibition on warfare from the Battles of Agincourt and Marignan at the Musée de l'Armée at the Invalides in Paris in 2015 (dwelling on the technicalities and tactics of warfare, not on the political origins and political implications of outcomes); an historians' conference; and a *défilé* by the French *gendarmerie* with the tenuous excuse that Le Gallois de Fougières, commander of an early form of the *gendarmerie nationale*, was killed in the Battle of Agincourt, the martyr-death of a hero-commander.

In 1676 of the Dutch admiral Michiel de Ruyter, victor of a string of previous naval engagements against the English, including the Battle of Chatham (See Volume 2), died a hero's death in battle. Ruyter's celebrated example would later inspire the J.C.J. van Speyk, a youth whose ambition to become a sailor, to the deed of blowing up himself, his ship and a bridge in 1831 so as to prevent a Belgian advance against the Dutch.[14]

Britain has two such war heroes, General Wolfe (1727-1759), who fell in the Battle of Quebec, and Lord Nelson (1758-1805), who succumbed at his greatest victory at Trafalgar, both British victories against the French. Trafalgar became the mythical naval battle par excellence, which all the navies of the world yearned to copy.

Significantly several of these deaths were later painted in ways reminiscent of classical renderings of the deposition of Christ from the cross, or the mourning of the dead Christ: see Benjamin West and Arthur Devis depicting Wolfe's and Nelson's deaths,[15] the mourning King Přemsyl II Ottokar after the Battle of Marchfield,[16] and of St Olaf of Norway[17] and

Lajos II after the Battle of Mohács,[18] remarkable illustrations of how much Christian cultures have in common across national boundaries.

'Gloria Victis'[19] or Decadence, Punishment and Redemption

This is also reflected in other ways. In his taxonomy, George Schöpflin has created the category 'Myths of Redemption and Suffering', where people see the history of their nation – much in the tradition of the history of the Israelites – as 'a process of expiating its sins' and subsequent redemption. He found this to be very widespread in Central and Eastern Europe, but it definitely also applies to the history of Western and Northern European countries, and to the commemoration of Socialist setbacks on the path to world Communism. They share the legacy of the Hebrew Bible: following the French example, most Christian nations like to see themselves as the new Israelites. Like them, Christian nations (or Socialist groups) have been tested by God (or History) and found wanting, have been punished (by a humiliating defeat in battle), forcing them to ponder their sins and other shortcomings, to find back to the ways of the Lord (or their national greatness), and finally to be rewarded with victory or liberation from oppression. This narration can be found in its purest form in France. In an age of Catholic revival, France's defeat at the hands of the Prussians and their allies in 1871 was interpreted as just punishments for sinful decadence. A special monumental commemoration of the Franco-Prussian war is the basilica of Sacré-Coeur in Paris, built in reaction to this *defeat* (not victory as in the case of the battle abbeys described above), to atone for the sins of the people on which this defeat was blamed. France's victory in 1918 can thus be interpreted as the reward following contrition and redemption. Similarly, the Russian Revolution is cast as emerging, Phoenix-like, from the defeat of decadent Tsarist Russia.

A peculiar turn can be identified among defeated nations, and this is to cast the defeat not as humiliation but as noble and valiant collective sacrifice, again as admonition to future generations. If the enemies were barbarians or heathen such defeats can be seen as a sacrifice made by one group on behalf of the whole civilisation (e.g. the Spartans on behalf of the Hellenes at Thermopylae) or by one nation on behalf of all of Christendom.

As we will see in Volume 2, Central and Eastern Europeans, and indeed also Spaniards, Portuguese and Frenchmen, and in the North, besides the Poles that Schöpflin mentions, Swedes, Fins and Balts have seen their respective countries as 'last bastion of Christianity' confronted with aggressive Barbarians. With these *antemurale* myths, they claim that their nations 'bled to near extinction precisely so that Europe could flourish.'[20]

It can be quite enough for a battle lost to be interpreted as a sacrifice made for one's defeated nation alone, a sacrifice proving moral stamina and calling upon later generations to resume the fight for national freedom. This is the Dutch interpretation of the bloodily repressed revolt of the Batavians against the Romans in CE 69-70. As the Dutch uprising against Spanish Habsburg rule unfolded in the late sixteenth century, the Dutch scholar Cornelis Aurelius' work on the Batavian Revolt, *Defensorium gloriae Batavinae,* was printed, gaining great popularity: the Dutch identified with the Batavians, and cast the Spanish in the part of the cruel Roman oppressors. After the Eighty-Year War of independence had come to an end, Rembrandt, and after him Jurriaen Ovens were commissioned by the town council of Amsterdam to paint the scene in which the leaders of the Batavian insurgency pledged to rise up together against the Romans, and Jacob Jordaens painted a stirring battle scene of the Batavian revolt.[21]

Glory in defeat is also the Norwegian interpretation of king Harald III Sigurdson known as Hardrada at the Battle of Stamford Bridge in 1066 against his namesake, the Danish ruler of England, Harold Godwinson. It is easier to mourn and glorify one's defeat if the adversary does not make a big deal of celebrating his triumph – thus for example, the Norwegian commemoration of the Battle of Stamford Bridge or the annual commemorations of great Napoleonic battles are not made in a spirit of triumphalism on any side. There are similarities in the Polish interpretation of the unsuccessful Polish uprising against the Russian occupants under Tadeusz Kościuszko and the Battle of Racławice in 1794, an ephemeral Polish victory as the whole episode ended with a re-assertion of Russian dominance. Commemorations of the battle itself and of Kościuszko kept the flame of national consciousness alive, even though it would take over a century until Poland became a sovereign state again. Glory in defeat was celebrated collectively by the Danes after they were crushed by the Prussian-led coalition in 1864, an event transformed into a national rallying myth of collective valour.[22]

Another recurrent myth is that of one's own defeat bringing on a catastrophe and suffering greater than that which any other nation has borne. The first battle of the Thirty Years' War, pitting a coalition of Protestants against the forces of the Catholic League at the White Mountain near Prague in 1620, has been retrospectively interpreted as the loss of

Bohemian independence, as the 'grave of the nation' – notwithstanding the fact that Habsburg rulers, descendants also from Bohemian kings, had already ruled Bohemia since 1526. Moreover, nineteenth-century Czech historians would claim that 'there is hardly any other case where the subjection of a people has had such terrible consequences' as that of the Bohemians after the Battle of the White Mountain – not a conclusion borne out by comparison with the devastation and fatality rates of other areas of Europe during the ensuing Thirty Years' War.[23]

Victory by the Weaker over the Stronger

It may be a particularly European trait that victory in itself is often not enough to make a battle epic. Heroism is seen as lacking if the defeated party is inferior in numbers. A special glow surrounds a battle if it has been won by a weaker party against a stronger party. Hence the delight nineteenth- and twentieth-century German nationalists took in Germanic rebel Arminius and his bands having defeated Roman legions in his ambush laid in the Teutoburg Forest in CE 9, or which the French took in having defeated the coalition between the Holy Roman Empire (a.k.a. 'the Germans', as later historiography would put it) and the English – France's favourite enemies, both – at Bouvines in 1214, the Scots on defeating the English at Bannockburn a century later, and the Poles on defeating the Teutonic Knights at the Battle of Grunwald in 1310 (see below).

Sieges, Civilian Victims, and Military Heroes

Interestingly, it has not always been easy to conceptualise sieges in terms of heroism on the part of the besieged. The Trojans are a rare exception (see Chapter 2). Just as victims of rape in history assumed the status of heroines only if they committed suicide, populations suffering sieges were pitied, but rarely turned collectively into heroes. Thus the fall of Jerusalem in 1099, the conquest of Constantinople by the crusaders in 1204, the final fall of Constantinople in 1453, or the Sack or 'Wedding' of Magdeburg in 1631, or even the Rape of Nanking 1937/38 did not produce heroes among the victims of the ensuing excesses.

The few exceptions include the charming story of the wives of Weinsberg, a town in South-Western Germany. During the Guelf-Ghibelline wars, in 1140 Weinsberg was besieged by the forces of King Conrad III who told the townsfolk sheltering in the castle that the women could leave, taking with them what they could carry upon their backs. The women emerged from the castle carrying their husbands, piggy-back.

On the opposite end of what a siege could be is that of Béziers (see Chapter 8). Among the worst of all was that of Leningrad, the city of the Tsars, the city of the Russian Revolution, the city of Lenin, the martyr-city of the Second World War where 600,000-700,000 civilians died from starvation and cold in that terrible 900-day siege (1941-1944). Like the Trojan War, it has been duly commemorated – by the poet Anna Akhmatova with *Poem without a Hero* (which she considered to be the major work of her life); by Dmitri Shostakovich with his seventh (*Leningradskaya*) Symphony. Nevertheless, even those who elevated the entire population of Leningrad and especially its dead to the status of heroes would curiously refer to the latter as the 'fallen' (implying they were combatants, not merely victims), as the Soviet journalist and writer Ilya Ehrenburg did in 1949.[24] Equally those opposing the mystification of Leningrad into a city of martyrs, the Moscow leadership of the Communist Party of the Soviet Union, wanted to see the Siege of Leningrad redefined as a battle, with the emphasis not on those who starved, but on the *fallen* – the soldiers who had fought to defend it. The siege of Leningrad could thus be stripped of its myth of uniqueness and turned into merely 'one of ten *battles* [sic!] which Stalin's ingenious spirit had planned to go over to the offensive', as another article in the *Leningradskaya Pravda* put it on 27 January 1950.[25]

'Decisive' Battles and Battles which *almost* changed the world

It is a library-filling sport among military historians to argue over the 'decisiveness' of certain battles, after debating what constitutes 'decisive'. Victory in battle may not outlast subsequent diplomatic negotiations; also, many wars have contained multiple battles like sports matches, victory going at times to this side, at times to the other, with the final outcome of the war uncertain even after several encounters in the field.

If 'decisive battle' is defined as having a significant effect on the overall outcome of the war, there are many candidates for this label, and many more that are not. There are battles which have acquired the aura of a big history-changing event while in reality they were not. Such a one is the Battle of Agincourt in 1415 in English folklore. It was clearly not decisive in bringing the Hundred Years' War to an end, it at best prolonged the war and Castillion (1453) – hardly known in England – was the decisive battle in which the English were soundly beaten and English monarchs lost all their French possession bar Calais.

The Battle of Lepanto in 1571 and the defeat of the Spanish Armada in 1588 (see Volume 2) are interesting examples of 'decisive battles'. The former was greatly celebrated as such at the time even though for decades it was uncertain whether the Turks had definitively been driven out of the Western Mediterranean. It was oversold as a turning point, as the sultan's navy continued to conquer Greek islands in the Eastern Mediterranean. The defeat of the Spanish in the English Channel in 1588 by contrast could only be seen as decisive with hindsight: for decades, England stood in fear of the return of such an *armada*, and indeed several further *armadas* sailed against Elizabethan England, and were fended off only by the chance of adverse winds.

Trafalgar also gave birth to the myth of having been the decisive (naval) battle of the Napoleonic Wars, belied by the fact that those continued for another decade after Trafalgar. With the Battle of Waterloo of 1815 (see Volume 2), the opposite argument is often made, that it was less important than the Battle of Nations at Leipzig two years earlier. While Waterloo could have been won by Napoleon, he would have been defeated sooner or later as the odds were finally staked against him.[26]

This leads us to a further category of myths of decisive battles, namely battles which – in the view of historians – stood at a great parting of the ways, that actually taken by History subsequently, and that which History might have taken, with hugely different long-term consequences. The Battle of Culloden has been interpreted in this sense: Ciro Paoletti calls it a 'pivotal battle of history', and examines its 'long-term implications for not just Britain, but for much of the rest of the world as well'. Paoletti thinks 'that it is not unreasonable to argue, for example, that if the battle had been lost by the Hanoverians, the United States probably would not exist today and French would be the primary language spoken in North America.'[27] This is far-fetched, as two centuries after the English Reformation, Marian Counterreformation and Return to Protestantism, and a century after the Puritan Revolution, Hanoverian Britain was firmly in the Protestant camp. The enemy images of Catholic and French were deeply internalised. Even Scots were quite divided on the question of supporting the bonnie prince with his French and Irish Catholic support and his foreign accent. Nevertheless, as Murray Pittock has shown, attempts to make Culloden an epic turning point go back to the very days after the battle.[28] But while it is reasonable to argue that only the defeat of the reactionary Catholic Stuart Party opened the way to the full unfolding of the Scottish Enlightenment, it remains questionable whether the Stuart Pretenders ever stood a chance of prevailing in the long run. 'What if' speculations have their charm, but alternative history can neither prove firmly what short-term consequences of alternative outcomes might have been, nor that the multiple factors, forces, trends, and human decisions that come together to make history would not have reached a similar outcome as that provided by the actual event, only later in time.

Nation-Building Battles

Culloden (See Volume 2) is mourned as a battle after which essential features of Scottishness were wiped out: a nation-destroying battle. Features of Scottishness *were* suppressed for a generation or two, which is undeniable. Yet paradoxically, much of what we identify today as particularly and peculiarly Scottish, especially in terms of music, folk songs, and popular literature, was born at Culloden. As a common memory and point of national reference, Culloden is thus also a nation-building battle, a major building block of Scottish national consciousness.

There are many examples of nation-building battles, that is battles which, in historical perspective, were re-interpreted as pitting one supposedly ethnically homogeneous group (often under a national label not in use at the time of the battle) against another (ditto). Such re-interpretations usually serve to clothe the past in the fashions of the present. While the Battle of the Lechfield in 955 between the Saxon forces of the Holy Roman Emperor Otto I against invading Magyar tribes (won by the Saxons, only one of several Germanic peoples) is cast as the 'birth of the German nation', there is a notable absence of the word '*deutsch*' in the contemporary sources: for Otto himself, the war was one against the '*hostes antiqui Christi*', the ancient enemies of Christ, and he thus saw himself primarily as defender of Christendom against its pagan foes.[29] Nevertheless, German nineteenth-century nationalism made much ado about this battle, along with that of the Teutoburg Forest in 9 CE This was cast as German(ic) self-determination vs. Latin domination (Latin, rendered in Germanic languages as '*Welsch*', Welsh, a word referring to both Celts, as in the English usage, and Latin peoples, i.e. the French and the Italians, as in the German usage). This nicely equated with sixteenth-century calls for the emancipation of the German language from Latin, or in the early nineteenth, from the domination of all things French. The nineteenth-century constructed history of a German 'nation' thus takes as its turning points the Battles of the Teutoburg Forest, of Lechfield (955), and then (fast forward) the 'Battle of Nations' at Leipzig in 1813, where Napoleon was supposedly defeated by a surge of German national consciousness and solidarity. This grand narrative of German national history culminates in the 1871 proclamation of a united (second) German *Reich* or Empire after the German victory in the Franco-Prussian War. The huge gaps in between, however, are glossed over.

Myths of 'nation-building' battles were engendered particularly when the virus of nationalism began to infect a polity, in the nineteenth or early twentieth centuries. Aleksander Nevskij, prince of Novgorod and later also of Kiev and Vladimir did indeed defend Novgorod against the Swedes on the Neva in 1240 (hence the epithet, Nevskij), and two years later against the Teutonic Knights on frozen Lake Peipus. While the legend that the ice broke and that Germans in their heavy armour drowned, not found in the original accounts, seems to have come into being soon after the battle, Aleksander was only canonized by the Russian Orthodox Church in the sixteenth century. The nineteenth century – predictably – elevated him to a national rather than Christian hero, even though until the Russian Revolution, he was strongly linked to Holy War and spiritual purity.[30] Only with Communism was he transformed into a people's hero with the famous film of 1938 by Sergei Eisenstein, in playing prophetically on the new German-Russian confrontation that was in the making.

Again, the successful invention led to copying: The epic Polish film *Krzyżacy* (Crusaders) on the Battle of Grunwald, based on Henryk Sienkievicz's eponymous novel of 1900, directed by American star Henry Ford, took much inspiration from Eisenstein. So did the 2004 movie *King Arthur,* which borrowed the battle-on-the-ice motif from Eisenstein's *Aleksander Nevskij* for the key clash between Saxons and Romano-Britons.

Battles can also be seen as birthplaces not of ethnic nations, but of political nations. An early example is the Battle of Legnano in 1176, of which we have spoken in Chapter 1. Here a League of Lombard cities, formed a few years earlier, organised itself to fend off the army of emperor Frederick I Barbarossa, Guelfs and Ghibellines for once united. The battle pitted (mainly, but not exclusively) local foot soldiers against the (mainly, but not exclusively) cavalry of the imperial army, so that in the nineteenth century it could be interpreted as a battle waged by the common (Italian) man, inspired by patriotic fervour, against upper class (imperial and foreign, in analogy with the fight against Habsburg domination in the nineteenth century) knights.[31] Dear to nineteenth-century Italian patriots, it was turned into an opera by Giuseppe Verdi, *La Battaglia di Legnano,* first performed in 1849. It has thus been celebrated as the crucible in which Italian national consciousness crystallized.

Similarly, other battles won by (mainly, but not exclusively) indigenous foot soldiers against (mainly, but not exclusively) knights who could retrospectively be portrayed as 'foreign' have retrospectively been cast as patriotic myths or even myths of class struggle, promoted by the Left. These include the 1302 Battle of the Golden Spurs, also known as the Battle of Courtrai (see Chapter 9), the Battle of Bannockburn in 1314 by the Scots under their (in fact Norman) leader Robert the Bruce against the (mainly Norman) knights of England under Edward I, several Swiss pikemen's battles against Austrians (e.g. Morgarten 1315 and Sempach 1386), Burgundians (e.g. Morat/Murten 1476) or the French (Marignano 1515), and the Battle of Grunwald/Tannenberg of 1410, pitting Polish-Lithuanian (mainly) infantry against the Teutonic Knights. (The Poles fought in an alliance with the Lithuanians, who in nineteenth-century Polish historiography would feature little or not at all.)[32] All of these would be evoked as marking the birth of the victorious nation concerned.

A particularly good example of a battle as the foundation myth of the *political* nation is the Battle of Valmy (1792) the first battle won by the French Revolutionaries. Goethe made his famous contribution to forging this myth by claiming that a new era in world history had begun there. For French Republicans, the Battle of Valmy was not just a victory for the Revolution, but it symbolised victory in a just war, as this has been a defensive battle on French soil against foreign forces aiming to crush the Revolution and the free choice of the French people, to follow historian Jules Michelet and the Socialist Jean Jaurès.[33]

A wide-spread motif is that of the battle for freedom (or 'self-determination') of a nation against an aggressive or oppressive empire. We encountered this in with Marathon, Thermopylae, and later Legnano and Bannockburn. We have already alluded to a series of tribal uprisings against the Romans, most of them in the first century CE, which served as inspiration for the Dutch resistance to the Spanish, and later for insurgencies against Napoleonic French occupation.

Anti-militarist Narratives, Class Warfare and Class Exploitation

More a twentieth-century than an earlier phenomenon is the narration of battles in an anti-militarist or anti-colonialist vein, or to cast them as example of exploitation of the working classes by cynical upper classes.

Privately financed paintings of the First World War motives largely broke with previous traditions of depicting battles. Over the centuries aesthetically pleasing and elegant poses of suffering by the dead and wounded had gradually yielded to more realistic depictions of maiming and death. The First World War brought a further, radical shift towards a brutal confrontation with the horrors of war, as seen in the paintings of George Grosz, Max Beckmann and Otto Dix in Germany, by John and Paul Nash, William Orpen and Colin Gill in Britain, and Georges Leroux and Henri de Groux in France.[34]

Turning to novel and film, examples of an anti-militarist take is the telling of the First World War from the vantage point of the grunts. Erich Maria Remarque's novel, *All Quiet on the Western Front*[35] (with a film version of 1930 directed by Lewis Milestone) was an important stepping stone in casting the Great War as a great waste of lives. In *Paths of Glory* (1957, dir. Stanley Kubrick), a further important example of this genre, again based on an eponymous novel (by Humphrey Cobb), three soldiers refuse to be sent on a – pointless, it seems to them – suicide mission in the First World War, and are executed for disobedience. Although their commanding officer (played by Kirk Douglas) defends them, the execution is carried out, much to the disgust of the officer who accuses his superiors of sadism.

Pork Chop Hill (1959, dir. Lewis Milestone and Gregory Peck, with Peck also in the main part) deals with a battle of the Korean War. After an utterly wasteful defence of the hill by American soldiers, this film has a surprising gratifying ending in which the (previously apparently unbothered) US military command decides to reinforce the unit of GIs who are defending it – clearly a tagged-on ending that at the last moment prevents the film from being a direct indictment of the US command. The plot was recycled with a film on a similar actual battle in the Vietnam War, *Hamburger Hill* (dir. John Irvin, 1987), about an American assault on the well-fortified and defended Ap Bia Mountain on the Vietnamese-Laotian border. Here there is no soothing ending; instead the film shows the dead who died in vain. *Hamburger Hill* is one of many anti-war films made in reaction to the Vietnam War.

Battles are not only important to evoke national collective identity; they are also evoked as markers of historic *class warfare or regional uprisings* of collective self-assertion to gain liberty from an oppressive exogenous regime, even if that is of the same language and general culture. Examples of the former include commemoration of the Petersfield ('Peterloo') uprising and Massacre in Manchester in 1819, where British cavalry charged a large crowd of protester demanding the vote, or of the Mur des Fédérés at the Père Lachaise Cemetery in Paris where the executed leaders of the Commune uprising of 1871 are commemorated. Examples of the latter include the Battle of Legnano (see below), the Battle of Courtrai (see Chapter 9), the Swiss pikemen's medieval victories over armies of knights, and the Battle of Valmy in 1792 in which for the first time French Revolutionary forces defeated professional armies of the anciens régimes.

In Volume 2 we will discuss the BBC-commissioned docudrama *Culloden* (dir. Peter Watkins, 1964). A similar interpretation suggested that the people, caught in authoritarian social structures, are seduced and betrayed by their betters who lead them to war and death can be found in the recent Danish TV production *1864* (dir. Dan Laustsen, written by Ole Bornedal 2014), concerning the Danish war with Prussia and its allies. The Danish defence and then retreat from the *Danevirk*e, the early medieval wall seen as symbolic of Danish identity, the subsequent campaign, and finally the battle at the defences of Dybbol (*Kampene van Dybbol, Düppeler Schanzen*) form the central military action of this 8-episode mini-series. The link is explicitly made with Danish military engagements of the present, as the events of 1864 are told through the eyes of a teenager living today, who discovers old memoirs written around 1864. Her brother has died in an overseas' operation (Afghanistan post-2001, one might guess) and her family has been devastated by this loss. Past sacrifice and defeat are explained as senseless waste, inflicted by uncaring and stupid governments. Thus the past becomes an admonition *not* to repeat such folly – in the motto of those who fought in the First World War, 'never again!'

Curiously, this is not how the Soviet Union narrated Russia's mythic national battles, such as the afore-mentioned *Aleksaner Nevskij,* or the Soviet-Italian co-production *Waterloo* (dir. Sergei Bondarchuk, 1970, with Rod Steiger as Napoleon and Christopher Plummer as the Duke of Wellington). Instead, the USSR's film industry celebrated past wars and battles as epic and heroic shows of Russian moral strength and military triumph. New Russia continues in this vein with its representation of war in *Stalingrad* (Fëdor Bondarchuk 2013).

Battles reinvented

Battles and battlefields can become powerful instruments of legitimation in political discourses. According to George Schöpflin, 'Mythic and symbolic discourses can ... be employed to assert legitimacy and strengthen authority.

They mobilize emotions and enthusiasm. They are a primary means by which people make sense of the political process, which is understood in a symbolic form.'[36] Battles and battlefields can thus be invoked in political narratives that seek to mobilise communities for a wide range of ends, not only political, but also cultural or economic, or a combination of these. This is of particular interest in the study of the legacy of battles. Particular battles are commemorated (often with considerable financial investment in festivities, memorials and buildings) and redefined through contemporary political agendas, at times to be reinvented and claimed by different political movements to fit their needs.

Thus the medieval Battle of Legnano has become a point of reference in the discourse of the Lega Lombarda-Lega Nord, a political party in Italy which originally aimed to achieve the independence of Northern Italy (the Po region – a.k.a. Padania) and its constitution as a separate state. On the eve of the March 2018 Italian general elections, it transformed itself into an anti-EU party for all of Italy under the new name of la Lega. The badge of the Lega features an image of a statue of Alberto da Giussano, the most famous of the military leaders of the Lombard forces at the Battle of Legnano. (Fig. 10.4) Similarly, the Battle of Courtrai of 1302 (see Chapter 9) was claimed in the nineteenth century as a 'foundation myth' for the Belgians, before being instrumentalised by the Flemings especially in the twentieth century in their attempts to mark their collective identity as against the Francophones (conflating French and Walloon), and thus to break up Belgium.

The Siege of Leningrad also formed multiple myths. 'There are tombs that make man greater. And those who have fallen [!] for Leningrad can expect from the living great feelings, and great actions.' Thus Ilya Ehrenburg, writing in the *Leningradskaya Pravda* on 27 January 1949. The dead inspire great feelings, calling for great actions, and it is of course those who say so who claim the right to define what these actions are. 'Who does not remember the sufferings endured by Leningrad? In crossing the path of a stranger in the crowd [in Leningrad], I sometimes say to myself: that one there has survived the blockade… One recognises them by their look: one not only sees the memory of something bad, but a strong will has taken root.'[37] Indeed, after the Great Fatherland War, emboldened by this heritage, the leaders of the Communist Party of Leningrad challenged Stalin's autocratic rule repeatedly.

Symptomatic of Stalin's virulent hatred of the cachet and prestige which Leningrad (and its local Communist leaders) had acquired was the action of Stalin's henchman, Georgy Maximilianovich Malenkov, Secretary of the Communist Party of the USSR, a few days after Ehrenburg's article was published. Malenkov visited the Leningrad museum dedicated to the commemoration of its war dead - and ordered it to be closed down. He called the museum 'anti-[Communist] Party', and claimed that it had 'created a myth of a special destiny of Leningrad because of the blockade! It minimises the role of Great Stalin!'[38] As we have seen, the Siege of Leningrad was re-invented as a battle testifying to Stalin's supposed military genius. Indeed, Stalin's fury at the Leningrad comrades' challenge to his leadership led to a new wave of great purges which effectively ended only with Stalin's own death in 1953.[39]

Battles as *lieux de mémoire* for Europe

Since the Second World War, the commemoration of some battles has been used for the thoroughly benign political purpose of reconciliation. The European integration movement, born out of the blood of two world wars, has also seized upon battles and battlefields as sites of mourning and celebrations of peace. This applies particularly to the battlefields of the First World War's Western front. Countless school trips have taken adolescents from many European countries to the Somme and to Verdun, and particularly the latter has become a symbol of Franco-German reconciliation, the main driver for European co-operation and integration. In 1984, to commemorate the outbreak of the First World War, French President François Mitterrand and West German Chancellor Helmut Kohl held a famous meeting at Verdun where they made the symbolic gesture of joining hands over the graves of the fallen, a gesture that resonates through much distributed photographs of the occasion. The city of Verdun, disputed for centuries by France and the Holy Roman Empire and then Germany, has transformed its episcopal palace into a 'World Centre of Peace' where significantly an exhibition was opened in 2017 on the benefits of the European Union. The political message, delivered in time for the debates surrounding the EU in the French presidential election of 2017 which returned pro-European Emmanuel Macron, is clear: the EU is the necessary pacific answer to the horrors of the world wars.

The two world wars are thus key foundation myths of what is now the European Union, in a way opposite to that affirming any narrow national identity against an enemy. This seems to have been completely forgotten by the British who, exactly 100 years after the Battles of the Somme and Verdun voted to leave the European Union (on the Somme, see also Volume 2). The British case is evidence that myths can die. Clearly, the narrative of European reconciliation and integration being rooted in the graves of the Somme and Verdun was either never understood by common Britons, or squeezed out completely during the UK's EU membership referendum by the focus on the single market and purely economic cost-benefit calculations.

Not all commemorations of battles in the name of Europe are benign. On the other end of the spectrum of political movements celebrating Europe we find the young right-wing extremists of the *Bloc Identitaire* who are trying to assert a common European identity exclusive of Muslim immigrants. We are told that at an annual summer camp in 2016, lectures on the great battles of Europe to fend back foreign invaders featured on the agenda: Thermopylae against Persia, Poitiers 732 against the Arabs, Vienna 1683 against the Ottoman Turks (for Vienna see also Volume 2).[40]

***

In Chapter 1, we remarked upon the fact that our opinion poll among historians and other historically educated academics turned out a very long list of battles which only one or two individual scholars found important enough to be among *their* top ten. European commonalities across state frontiers have a variable geometry, and national histories are still overwhelmingly important counterpoints to any European historical narrative.

Generally it seemed from our school polls that the parochialism of collective historical memory when we go beyond Antiquity is very pronounced among the pupils. It complements our findings that many experts were the only ones or one of two to deem certain battles very important.

After Antiquity, shared across Europe as a point of reference, cross-European collective memory only re-emerges with the Napoleonic Wars, and the two world wars. This is likely connected with the fact that most emphasis in schools and even universities is on history since Napoleon, or even since 1914.

We have seen that European cultures, reared on the literature of classical Antiquity and the Bible, have in our context of battle myths developed similar patterns in their reactions to adversity. These include the myth of moral victory in defeat, myths of heroic martyr leaders or the few

158

who have sacrificed himself for the many, the myth of the *antemurale Christianitatis*, the myth of decadence and sin punished by defeat in battle. But while European cultures and nations have developed similar myths, they rarely know that other European cultures claim these very myths for themselves, and thus know little or nothing about each other's history and historic myths. This tells us something about the parochial nature – and the emphatically national nature – in which European history is still largely taught. How many Europeans are aware, for example, that not only their own nation sees itself as the Israelites successors as chosen people, but that just about all the others (plus the Americans ...) also see themselves as such? It is difficult not to see a link between this lack of knowledge and the resurgence of nationalism since the end of the Cold War, and especially in the 2010s.

To conclude, battles of the past remain rallying points for confrontational commemorations even today. The ways battles are commemorated – by pure mourning, with the aim of achieving reconciliation, or in triumphalism, or with vindictive agendas – continue to be a force for good or for bad. If it is possible at all to commemorate battles in a 'neutral' fashion, without judgement or taking sides, as for example the National Trust of Scotland attempts to do rather awkwardly with its Disneyfied visitor centre at Bannockburn, this is not often done. Our aim with this book and its sequel is to alert readers to the manifold agendas underlying such commemoration, and their manipulation by casting them into myths with a political mission.

Endnotes

Chapter 1. Famous Battles and their After-Life: A Framework

1. Cicero: *De finibus bonorum et malorum* Liber V.
2. Pierre Nora (ed/director of English translation): *Realms of memory: Rethinking the French Past* (New York; Chichester: Columbia University Press, 1996-1998), 3 vols.
3. Pierre Nora: "Between Memory and History: Les Lieux de Mémoire", *Representations*, No. 26, Special Issue: *Memory and Counter-Memory* (Spring, 1989), p.19.
4. Ibid., p.22.
5. Ibid.
6. Anne Curry: *Agincourt, in the series Great Battles* (Oxford: Oxford University Press, 2015), pp.180-200.
7. Ernest Renan: *Qu'est-ce qu'une nation?* (Paris: Calman Levy, 1882), p.27.
8. John Hutchinson: *Nations as Zones of Conflict* (London: Sage), pp.77-113.
9. Renan: *Qu'est-ce qu'une nation?*
10. Vít Vlnas and Zdeněk Hojda: "Tschechien: Gönnt einem jeden die Wahrheit", in Monika Flacke (ed.): *Mythen der Nationen: ein Europäisches Panorama* (Berlin: Deutsches Historisches Museum, 1998), p.523.
11. Anthony D. Smith: *The Nation Made Real: Art and National Identity in Western Europe, 1600-1850* (Oxford: Oxford University Press, 2013), p.141.
12. A.V. Seaton: "War and Thanatourism: Waterloo 1815-1914", in *Annals of Tourism Research*, Vol. 26, No. 1 (1999), pp. 130-158. This is also sometimes referred to as 'dark tourism'.
13. Nora: "Between Memory and History", p.22
14. Etienne François and Hagen Schulze: "Das emotionale Fundament der Nationen", in Flacke (ed.): *Mythen der Nationen*, p.18f.
15. Isaiah Berlin: *The Crooked Timber of Humanity* (London: Fontana, 1991), p.2.
16. See also Anthony D. Smith's discussion of foundation myths, in *Myths and Memories of the Nation* (Oxford: Oxford University Press, 1999).
17. Joseph de Maistre: *Considerations on France* (Cambridge: Cambridge University Press), ch.3.

18. George Schöpflin: "Functions of Myth", in Geoffrey Hosking and George Schöpflin (eds.): *Myths and Nationhood* (New York: Routledge, 1997), p.39.

19. Anthony D. Smith: *Nationalism: Theory, Ideology, History* (Cambridge: Polity Press, 2010).

20. Anthony D Smith: *National Identity* (London: Penguin, 1991), p.51.

21. Ernest Gellner: *Nations and Nationalism* (Oxford: Blackwell, 1984 [1983]), p.139. Mondriaan's paintings, such as the one shown in Fig. 1.1, illustrate even more clearly Gellner's account of a world of nation-states.

22. Gellner: *Nations and Nationalism*.

23. For an illustration, go to: http://cartelfr.louvre.fr/cartelfr/visite?srv=car_not_frame&idNotice=22745. Accessed 19 March 2017.

24. Woodrow Wilson: "President Woodrow Wilson's Fourteen Points", http://avalon.law.yale.edu/20th_century/wilson14.asp. Accessed 4 July 2017.

25. James Mayall: *Nationalism and International Society* (Cambridge: Cambridge University Press, 1990).

26. Ernest Renan: http://leesmuseum.bibliotheekarnhem.nl/Books/mp-pdf-bestanden/LM05372.pdf. Accessed 6 April 2017. See also, Renan: *Qu'est-ce qu'une nation?*

27. Foreign rule included long-established 'foreign' invader aristocracies, ruling native populations. The French Revolution, for example, was often cast as a movement of liberation of Celtic or Gallo-Roman populations from a Frankish, Germanic aristocracy. See, Anthony D. Smith *The Ethnic Origins of Nations* (1986, Oxford: Blackwell, 1989), pp.90-1; Emmanuel Joseph Sieyès: *Qu'est-ce que le Tiers état?* (1789, Paris: Éditions du Boucher, 2002), pp.7-8.

28. Peter McPhee, *Liberty or Death: The French Revolution* (New Haven: Yale University Press, 2016).

29. Renan: *Qu'est-ce qu'une nation?*

30. Hans Kohn, *The Idea of Nationalism. A Study in its Origins and Background* (1944[1], New Brunswick: Transaction, 2005). See also, Smith's reference to Rousseau and Herder in *Myths and Memories*, p.139.

31. Anthony D. Smith: "Classical Ideals and the Formation of Modern Nations in Europe", in Thorsten Fögen and Richard Warren (eds.): *Graeco-Roman Antiquity and the Idea of Nationalism in the 19th Century* (Berlin: De Gruyter, 2016), p.21.

32. Roger Parker: "Verdi politico: a wounded cliché regroups", *Journal of Modern Italian Studies* Vol. 17 No. 4 (2012), pp.427-436.

33. H.V. Livermore: *A New History of Portugal* (Cambridge: Cambridge University Press, 1966), p.9.

34. A.H. de Oiveira Marques: *History of Portugal* Vol. I *From Lusitania to Empire* (New York: Columbia University Press, 1972), pp.42, 61. By contrast, the Christian liberation of Lisbon in 1147 did make a huge difference, but is not celebrated as the 'birth of independent Portugal'.

35. Wolfgang Schivelbusch: *The Culture of Defeat: On National Trauma, Mourning, and Recovery*, Jefferson Chase trs. (New York: Granta Books, 2004); Steven Mock: *Symbols of Defeat in the Construction of National Identity* (Cambridge: Cambridge University Press, 2011).

36. This tells us something about the divergent ways in which history is taught and narrated in different parts of Europe, and about the lack of a common narrative of European history. That in turn explains much about the limits in the convergence of European views of the reasons for and achievements of European integration.

37. The most popular among them are arguably E.S. Creasy: *Fifteen Decisive Battles of the World: From Marathon to Waterloo* (1852, London: Richard Bentley, 1859); Basil Liddell Hart: The Decisive Wars of History (London: G. Bell & Sons, 1929); J.F.C. Fuller: *Decisive Battles: Their Influence Upon History and Civilisation* 2 vols (s.l.: Eyre & Spottiswolde, 1939).

38. Cathal J. Nolan: *The Allure of Battle* (Oxford: Oxford University Press, 2017).

39. For early examples, see Charles McFarlane: *The Great Battles of the British Army* (London: s.e., 1833); Anon.: *The Twelve Great Battles of England* (London: Sampson Low, Son, & Co., 1861); Stephen Crane et al.: *Great Battles of the World* (London: Chapman & Hall, 1901).

40. Beatrice Heuser & Cyril Buffet: "Introduction", in Cyril Buffet & Beatrice Heuser (eds): *Haunted by History: Myths in International Relations* (Oxford: Berghahn, 1998), p. ix, and see also there for different definitions of 'myth'.

41. Anne-Marie Thiesse: *La Création des Identités Nationales: Europe XVIIIe-XXe Siècle* (Paris: Seuil, 1999), p.11.

42. Creasy: *Fifteen Decisive Battles*, p.xvi.

43. Miles Kington (ed.): *Punch on Scotland* (London: Robson Books, 1977), p. 38f.

44. David Cannadine (ed): *Trafalgar in history: a Battle and its Afterlife* (Basingstoke: Palgrave Macmillan, 2006).

45. W.C. Sellers and R.J. Yeatman: *1066 and All That: A Memorable History of England, comprising all the parts you can remember, including 103 Good Things, 5 Bad Kings and 2 Genuine Dates* (London: Methuen, 1930).

46. Tim Shipman: *All Out War: The Full Story of How Brexit Sank Britain's Political Class* (London: HarperCollins, 2016).

47. John Lewis-Stempel: "Agincourt: The battle that made our nation", *Express* newspaper, (Sunday 25 Oct 2015): http://www.express.co.uk/news/history/614379/agincourt-battle-englishmen-nation-soldiers. Accessed 4 May 2017.
48. Stephen Cooper: "Attitudes to Agincourt", *History Today* Vol. 62 No. 10 (October 2012).
49. Curry: *Agincourt*; Cannadine (ed): *Trafalgar in History*.

Chapter 2. The Siege of Troy

1. Many thanks to Professor Ian Rutherford and Dr Nicoletta Momigliano for sharing with me their expertise in contemporary Bronze Age research and for commenting on drafts of this article, and to Abigail Fielding-Smith and Thomas Marshall for their criticisms of an early draft.
2. Pausanias 9.9.3, citing one Kallinos, who may or may not be identifiable with the seventh-century BCE elegiac poet, Kallinos of Ephesos.
3. See for example Hdt. 2.53 (mid-C5th BCE), who states that Hesiod and Homer are the earliest Greek poets as well as the ones who 'created a theogony [i.e. an account of the gods' generation] for the Greeks, gave the gods their names and their honours and powers, and indicated their forms'.
4. Susan Sherratt, "The Trojan War: History or Bricolage?", *Bulletin of the Institute of Classical Studies* 53.2 (2010), 1-18, p.1.
5. Richard Janko: *Homer, Hesiod and the Hymns: Diachronic Development in Epic Diction* (Cambridge: Cambridge University Press., 1982), & E.S. Sherratt: "'Reading the texts': archaeology and the Homeric question", *Antiquity* 64 (1990), & Susan Sherratt: 'The Trojan War', p.12.
6. See for example Aeschylus' *Oresteia* trilogy, Soph. *Ajax*, Eur. *Troades, Hekabe.*
7. J.M. Foley: "Oral Tradition and Its Implications" in Barry B. Powell and Ian Morris (eds): *A New Companion to Homer* (Leiden: E.J. Brill., 1997).
8. Sherratt: "The Trojan War" pp.5-6, who notes that no Mycenaean palace has yet been found on either Kefalonia or Ithaka, the two main candidates for Odysseus's homeland.
9. For an influential, although hardly uncontested, reconstruction of various historical phases of the oral tradition see M.L. West: "The rise of the Greek Epic", *Journal of Hellenic Studies* 108 (1988).
10. Sherratt: *The Trojan War.* pp.7-9 & Maria Antonaccio: *An Archaeology of Ancestors: Tomb Cult and Hero Cult in Early Greece* (Lanham, MD & London: Rowman and Littlefield, 1994).

11. Hesiod, *Erga*, 159-60, 161-73. All translations of Hesiod from Glenn W. Most (tr) (ed): *Hesiod: Theogony, Works and Days, Testimonia* (Cambridge, MA & London: Harvard University Press, 2007).

12. M.L. West: "Prolegomena" in M.L. West (ed): *Hesiod, Works and Days, Edited with prolegomena and commentary*, (Oxford: Clarendon, 1978). On the cosmic context of the Trojan War, see B. Graziosi and J. Haubold: *Homer: The Resonance of Epic* (London: Duckworth, 2005), Chapter 2.

13. Hesiod, *Erga*, 650-7.

14. Sherratt: "The Trojan War", p. 7.

15. Hdt. 5.67.1.

16. *Iliad* 2.867-75; see Johannes Haubold: "Xerxes, Homer", in Emma Bridges, Edith Hall and P.J. Rhodes (eds): *Cultural Responses to the Persian Wars: Antiquity to the Third Millennium* (Oxford: Oxford University Press, 2007), p 59.

17. Hdt 7.43-52; for discussion see Haubold: "Xerxes' Homer", & Philippe Borgeaud: "Trojan Excursions: A recurrent ritual from Xerxes to Julian" *History of Religions* 49:4 (2010), pp.340-2, who offer very different interpretations of this episode.

18. See especially Hdt. 1.5.3, with its emphatic distinction between *oida* ('I know') and *legousi* ('they say'). On Thermopylae and Marathon, two of the key battles of the Persian Wars, see Aston and Leoussi in this volume.

19. Hdt 2.112-20; see too the sentiment he puts into the Persians' mouth at 1.4.2: 'we consider the abduction of women to be the mark of unjust men, zealousness in avenging them that of fools'. Stesichorus's 'palinode' to Helen is quoted by Socrates in Plato's *Phaedrus* (243a2-b7). It also supplies the dramatic pretext for Euripides' *Helen,* produced in 412 BCE.

20. Hdt 2.116.1.

21. Hdt 2.120.5.

22. Caroline Alexander: *The War that Killed Achilles: The True Story of the Iliad* (London: Faber and Faber., 2009) pp.20-21. For the Iliad in military circles see Shannon E. French: *The Code of the Warrior: Exploring Warrior Values Past and Present*, Foreword by Senator John McCain (Boulder, Co: Rowman and Littlefield, 2003) & Beatrice Heuser: "Der Krieger-Held in post-modernen Demokratien" in Eckhard Schinkel, Hannah Hettinger and Elham Moshefi (eds): *Die Helden-Maschine – Zur Aktualität und Tradition von Heldenbildern* (Essen: LWL-Industriemuseum., 2010).

23. Edward McCrorie (tr): *Homer: The Iliad* (Baltimore: John Hopkins University Press, 2012).

24. Borgeaud: "Trojan Excursions".

25. *De Bello Civili* 9.964-99.

26. Plut. *Alex.* 15.4-5, Arrian *Anabasis* 1.11.3-1.12.2; see Borgeaud: "Trojan Excursions", pp.342-3.

27. *De Bello Civili* 9.986-9.

28. Borgeaud: "Trojan Excursions", pp.344-6, see further Gergő Gellérfi: "Troy, Italy, and the Underworld (Lucan, 9, 964-99)" *Graeco-Latina Brunensia* 17:1 (2012).

29. Karen Ni-Mheallaigh: "Lost in translation: The Phoenician Journal of Dictys of Crete" in T. Whitmarsh and Stuart Thomson (eds): *The Romance Between Greece and the East* (Cambridge: Cambridge University Press, 2011).

30. R.E. Asher: *National Myths in Renaissance France: Francus, Samothes and the Druids* (Lanham, MD & London: Edinburgh University Press, 1993), pp. 9-43.

31. Ronsard, 1572 Preface to the *Franciade*, quoted from Marc Bizer: *Homer and the Politics of Authority in Renaissance France* (New York: Oxford University Press, 2011) p.84.

32. Bizer: *Homer and the Politics of Authority*. pp.17-58, 68-79.

33. Jonathan Shay: *Achilles in Vietnam: Combat Trauma and the Undoing of Character* (New York: Scribner., 1995) & Jonathan Shay: *Odysseus in America: Combat Trauma and the Trials of Homecoming* (New York: Scriber, 2002); see too Lawrence A. Tritle: *From Melos to My Lai: War and Survival* (London & New York: Routledge, 2000).

34. Peter Meineck: "'These are men whose minds the Dead have ravished': Theater of War/ Philoctetes Project", *Arion* 17:1 (2009) & Bryan Doerries: *The Theater of War: What Greek Tragedies can Teach us Today* (Melbourne & London: Scribe, 2015).

35. See for example Edith Hall, Fiona Macintosh and Amanda Wrigley (eds): *Dionysus since '69: Greek Tragedy at the Dawn of the Third Millennium* (Oxford: Oxford University Press, 2004) & Fiona Macintosh et al. (eds) *Agamemnon in Performance 458 BC to AD 2004* (Oxford: Oxford University Press, 2005).

36. Alexander: *The War that Killed Achilles* & Alice Oswald: *Memorial: An Excavation of the Iliad* (London: Faber and Faber, 2011).

37. Ibid., p.2.

38. On Longley see L.P. Hardwick: "Degrees of Intimacy: Michael Longley's poetic relationship with Homer", Poetry Database of the Project: *Classical Receptions in Drama and Poetry in English from c.1970 to the Present* (United Kingdom: Open University, 2007) http://www2.open.ac.uk/ClassicalStudies/

GreekPlays/PoetryDB/longley/poetrylongleyintro.htm [accessed 19 Aug. 2016]; on First World War poets and Trojan material, particularly evident among those who participated in the Gallipoli campaign, see Elizabeth Vandiver: *Stand in the Trench, Achilles: Classical Receptions in British Poetry of the Great War* (Oxford: Oxford University Press, 2013).

39. Lucy Pollard: *The Quest for Classical Greece. Early Modern Travel to the Greek World* (London: I.B. Tauris, 2015). Although now somewhat out of date (it predates Manfred Korfmann's important excavations in the 1990s), Michael Wood: *In Search of the Trojan War* (London: British Broadcasting Corporation, 1985) based on the BBC documentary of the same name, provides an engaging introduction to the historical and archaeological evidence for the real Troy.

40. Robert Wood: *Ruins of Palmyra, Otherwise Tedmor, in the Desart* (London:1753) & Robert Wood: *Ruins of Balbec, Otherwise Heliopolis, Coelosyria* (London:1757).

41. Robert Wood: *An Essay on the Original Genius of Homer* (London:1769) & Robert Wood: *An Essay on the Original genius and Writings of Homer, with a Comparative View of the Ancient and Present State of the Troad* (London: 1775); a good introduction to his travels and writings is David Constantine: *In the Footsteps of the Gods: Travellers to Greece and the Quest for the Hellenic Ideal* (London: I.B. Tauris, 2011), Chapter 3.

42. Wood: *An Essay on the Original Genius of Homer*. p.ii.

43. Heinrich Schliemann: *Ilios: The City and Country of the Trojans* (London: John Murray, 1880), p.3.

44. On Calvert see Susan Heuck Allen: "Finding the Walls of Troy: Frank Calvert, Excavator", *American Journal of Archaeology* 99:3 (1995); for a short introduction to Schliemann, see David Traill: "Heinrich Schliemann and Sophia Schliemann, 1822-90 and 1852-1932: Searching for Homer's World" in Brian Fagan (ed): *The Great Archaeologists* (London: I.B. Tauris, 2014).

45. On Dörpfeld, who excavated with Schliemann in the 1880s and continued in the 1890s, after the latter's death, see Ernst Pernicka and Diane Thumm: "Wilhelm Dörpfeld, 1852-1940: Scientific Excavation at Troy", in Brian Fagan (ed): *The Great Archaeologists* (London: I.B. Tauris, 2014).

46. The object (NM 624) is dogged by controversy, not least over whether or not it is the one Schliemann himself associated with Agamemnon. See Oliver Dickinson: "The 'Face of Agamemnon'" *Hesperia* 74:3 (2005).

47. The best summary of Korfmann's excavations and their importance remains that of Joachim Latacz: *Troy and Homer: Towards a Solution of an Old Mystery*, translated by Kevin Windle and Rosh Ireland (Oxford: Oxford University

Press, 2004). See too Trevor Bryce: *The Trojans and their Neighbours* (London & New York: Routledge, 2006).

48. See for example Eric Cline: "Introduction: The Ahhiyawa Problem" in G.M. Beckman, T. Bryce and E.H. Cline (eds): *The Ahhiyawa Texts* (Atlanta: Society for Biblical Literature, 2011), p.3: 'Ahhiyawa must, essentially by default, be a reference to the Mycenaeans' vs. Sherratt: "The Trojan War", p.11: 'there is nothing (apart from wishful thinking) to link the land of Ahhiyawa and its successive kings in the Hittite texts with anywhere on the Greek mainland let alone with any Mycenaean palace yet known to us.'

49. Beckman, Bryce and Cline: *The Ahhiyawa Texts,* pp.101-122. For brief discussion of the linguistic arguments identifying Ilion and the Achaeans with Wilusa and the Ahhiyawans, see Latacz: *Troy and Homer,* pp.73-100, 120-136.

50. UNESCO: "UNESCO World Heritage Committee Adds 30 Sites to World Heritage List" Press Release (2 Dec. 1998) http://whc.unesco.org/en/news/64 [accessed 23 June 2016]

51. Sherratt: "The Trojan War", pp.17-18.

Chapter 3. Marathon 490 BCE and European Identity

1. This essay is based on a public lecture that I delivered at the British Museum, in London, on 7 October 2016. I should like to dedicate it to my brother, Paul Leoussis, without whose amazing knowledge of universal history, the essay would have been all the poorer.

2. According to the Chinese archives, the conversation was with Henry Kissinger. See, Richard McGregor 'Zhou's cryptic caution, lost in translation', *Financial Times,* June 10, 2011, https://www.ft.com/content/74916db6-938d-11e0-922e-00144feab49a, Accessed 14 April 2017.

3. As noted by Christopher Carey and Michael Edwards, editors of *Marathon – 2,500 Years,* a book based on a colloquium held at the University of Peloponnese, Kalamata on 7-10 October 2010 (London: Institute of Classical Studies, 2013), p.1.

4. Carey and Edwards: *Marathon,* p.1.

5. Herodutus, *Histories,* Book 1, http://classics.mit.edu/Herodotus/history.1.i.html, Accessed 14 April 2017.

6. Herodotus, *Histories,* Book 1.

7. Herodotus, *Histories,* Book 1.

8. Richard A. Billows: *Marathon: How One Battle Changed Western Civilization* (New York:Overlook Press, 2010, Uncorrected Proofs edition) p.191. I am very grateful to Professor Andrew Lambert, who has also contributed the chapter on

the Armada to the second volume of our *Famous Battles,* for recommending to me Professor Richard Billows' book on Marathon.

9. J. A. S. Evans: 'Herodotus and the Battle of Marathon', *Historia: Zeitschrift für Alte Geschichte* Bd. 42, H. 3 (3rd Qtr., 1993), p. 282.

10. Paul Cartledge: *After Thermopylae: The Oath of Plataea and the End of the Graeco-Persian Wars* (Emblems of Antiquity Series. Oxford: Oxford University Press, 2013), p.87. See also Nikolaus Overtoom: Review of Cartledge, Paul, *After Thermopylae: The Oath of Plataea and the End of the Graeco-Persian Wars*. H-War, H-Net Reviews. February, 2014. URL: http://www.h-net.org/reviews/showrev.php?id=39780. Accessed 20 April 2017.

11. Herodotus, *Histories*, Book 6.

12. Herodotus, *Histories*, Book 6.

13. Peter Krentz: *The Battle of Marathon* (New Haven: Yale UP, 2010). See also, 'Marathon and the development of the exclusive hoplite phalanx', in Christopher Carey and Michael Edwards (eds.), *Marathon*, pp.35-45.

14. J. A. S. Evans: 'Herodotus and the Battle of Marathon', *Historia: Zeitschrift für Alte Geschichte.*
Bd. 42, H. 3 (3rd Qtr., 1993), p.285.

15. Billows, *Marathon*, p.214.

16. Herodotus, quoted in Krentz, 'Marathon and the development of the exclusive hoplite phalanx', p.42.

17. Herodotus, *Histories*, Book 6.

18. Herodotus, *Histories*, Book 6.

19. Herodotus, *Histories*, Book 6.

20. Michael Jung: 'Marathon and the construction of the Persian wars in Antiquity and modern times', in Carey and Edwards (eds.), *Marathon*, p.266.

21. Houchang Nahavandi and Yves Bomati: *Les Grandes Figures de l'Iran* (Paris, Perrin: 2015), p.79.

22. Nahavandi and Bomati: *Les Grandes Figures de l'Iran*, p.78.

23. Alistair G. G. Gibson: *Robert Graves and the Classical Tradition* (Oxford: Oxford University Press, 2015), p.244.

24. Cartledge: *After Thermopylae.*

25. Herodotus, *Histories*, Book 6; Eleni Volonaki: 'The Battle of Marathon in Funeral Speeches', in Carey and Edwards (eds.): *Marathon*, p.175.

26. Evans: 'Herodotus and the Battle of Marathon', p.307.

27. Carey and Edwards: 'Marathon – 2,500 Years: Introductory Note', in Carey and Edwards (eds.), *Marathon*, p.1.

28. See Evans for one of the many scholarly discussions about the actual numbers of forces involved, although there is general agreement that the Persian force was disproportionately bigger than the Greek, in Evans: 'Herodotus and the Battle of Marathon', p.287.
29. See, for example, Evans: 'Herodotus and the Battle of Marathon', p.284.
30. See, for example, Volonaki's analysis of Lysias' *epitaphios*, written in 395-87BCE, in Volonaki: 'The Battle of Marathon in Funeral Speeches', p.170.
31. Haskins, Ekaterina V. "Philosophy, Rhetoric, and Cultural Memory: Rereading Plato's 'Menexenus' and Isocrates' 'Panegyricus.'" *Rhetoric Society Quarterly*, vol. 35, no. 1, 2005, pp.25-45.
32. Volonaki: 'The Battle of Marathon in Funeral Speeches', p.173.
33. On Plato see also Volonaki: 'The Battle of Marathon in Funeral Speeches', pp.165-79.
34. Evans: 'Herodotus and the Battle of Marathon', p.287.
35. Eugene Vanderpool: 'A Monument to the Battle of Marathon', *Hesperia*, Vol. 35, No. 2 (Apr. - Jun., 1966), p.101.
36. Claire Cullen Davison: 'Pheidias: The Sculptures & Ancient Sources', *Bulletin of The Institute of Classical Studies*, Volume 56, Issue S105P1, May 2013, pp.303–318.
37. Davison: 'Pheidias', p.307.
38. Neer, Richard. 'The Athenian Treasury at Delphi and the Material of Politics.' *Classical Antiquity*, vol. 23, no. 1, 2004, p.83.
39. Neer: 'The Athenian Treasury', p.67.
40. Neer: 'The Athenian Treasury', p.83.
41. Neer: 'The Athenian Treasury', pp.63-93.
42. Ian Jenkins: *The Parthenon Frieze* (London: The British Museum Press, 2009 [1994]), p.14.
43. Jenkins, *Parthenon Frieze*, p.14.
44. Herodotus: *Histories*, Book 1.
45. Max Weber: 'Critical Studies in the Logic of the Cultural Sciences: A Critique of Eduard Meyer's Methodological Views', in *The Methodology of the Social Sciences*, (New York: The Free Press of Glencoe, 1949), p.172.
46. Weber: 'The Logic of the Cultural Sciences', p.162.
47. Weber: 'The Logic of the Cultural Sciences', p.163.
48. Weber: 'The Logic of the Cultural Sciences', p.171. Here, reference is most probably made to the charter of 444 BCE that was granted to the priest Ezra, who was intent on enforcing the regimen of the Torah, by the Persian king Artaxerxes I. It made the Torah the imperial law for the Jews.
49. Weber: 'The Logic of the Cultural Sciences', p.171.
50. Weber: 'The Logic of the Cultural Sciences', p.172.

51. William St Clair: *That Greece Might Still Be Free: The Philhellenes in the War of Independence* (Cambridge: OpenBook Publishers, 2008).

52. Harold Talbot Parker: *The Cult of Antiquity and the French Revolutionaries: A Study in the Development of the Revolutionary Spirit* (New York: Octagon Books, 1965), p.118.

53. Parker: *The Cult of Antiquity*, p.142.

54. Jane Ellen Harrison: *Introductory Studies in Greek Art* (Memphis: General Books, 2012 [1885]), p.47.

55. Glenn Richard Bugh: *The Horsemen of Athens* (Princeton University Press, 2014 [1988)], p.78.

56. Royal Mint: http://www.royalmint.com/discover/sovereigns/st-george-the-dragon-slayer. Accessed 21 April 2017.

57. Paul Cartledge: 'Democratic Politics Ancient and Modern: from Cleisthenes to Mary Robinson,' *Hermathena*, no. 166, 1999, p.6. See also, Paul Cartledge: *Democracy: A Life* (Oxford: Oxford University Press, 2016).

58. See on-line version of Thucydides' *The History of the Peloponnesian War*, 431 BCE, Book 2, Chapter VI: http://www.gutenberg.org/cache/epub/7142/pg7142.txt, Accessed 24 April 2017.

59. Sir Edward Shepherd Creasy: *The 15 Decisive Battles of the World from Marathon to Waterloo* (Mineola, NY: Dover Publications, 2008 [1851]), p.29.

60. Nike Monument: http://greece.greekreporter.com/2010/10/29/nike-monument-unveiled-at-new-acropolis-museum/#sthash.qU3dH5rc.dpuf, Accessed 24 April 2017.

61. G. Lowes Dickinson: *The Greek View of Life* (London: Methuen,1929 [1896]), p.55.

62. Harrison: *Studies in Greek Art*, p.47.

63. Christina Koulouri: *Sport et société bourgeoise. Les associations sportives en Grèce 1870-1922* (Paris: L'Harmattan, 2000). See also, 'Athleticism and Antiquity: Symbols and Revivals in nineteenth-century Greece', *The International Journal of the History of Sport* 15 / 3 (Dec. 1998), pp.142-149. On-line access: http://panteion.academia.edu/ChristinaKoulouri.

64. Billows: *Marathon*.

65. For example, in April 2017, there was a range of full and half wheelchair Marathons held in Seoul, South Korea: http://marathons.ahotu.com/calendar/korea. Accessed 24 April 2017, p.273.

66. J.S.Mill: 'A review of the first two volumes of Grote's History of Greece' *Edinburgh Review*, October 1846. http://oll.libertyfund.org/titles/mill-the-collected-works-of-john-stuart-mill-volume-xi-essays-on-philosophy-and-the-classics. Accessed 24 April 2017.

67. Carey and Edwards (eds.), *Marathon*, p.1.

Chapter 4. Thermopylai 480 BCE: Geography and Landscape

1. ὧν τὰς ἀρετὰς τίς οὐκ ἂν θαυμάσειεν; Diodoros 11.11.1: the opening words of the author's eulogy on Leonidas and his fellow-Spartans.
2. On the composition of the painting, see S.A. Nash: 'The Compositional Evolution of David's "Leonidas at Thermopylae"', *Metropolitan Museum Journal*, Vol. 13 (1978), pp.101-112. On the political backdrop to its creation, see N. Athanassoglou: 'Under the Sign of Leonidas: The Political and Ideological Fortune of David's *Leonidas at Thermopylae* under the Restoration', *The Art Bulletin*, Vol. 63 (1981), pp.633-649.
3. For a wide-ranging discussion of the battle and its legacy, see P. Cartledge: *Thermopylae: The Battle that Changed the World* (Woodstock: The Overlook Press, 2006).
4. A comprehensive treatment of the battle's significance in eighteenth- and nineteenth-century Hellenism is supplied by I. Macgregor Morris: "To Make a New Thermopylae': Hellenism, Greek Liberation, and the Battle of Thermopylae', *Greece & Rome*, Vol. 47, (2000), pp.211-230.
5. E.T. Cotham Jr.: *Sabine Pass: The Confederacy's Thermopylae* (Austin TX: University of Texas Press, 2004).
6. The use of Leonidas' famous words μολὼν λαβέ by people protesting their right to bear arms is especially visible in Internet discussion. See for example an article posted on *American News Media* ('Grassroots journalism. Grassroots America.') by Janell Maria Troutt on 2 April 2013: http://anmnews. com/%CE%BC%CE%BF%CE%BB%CF%89%CE%BD-%CE%B-B%CE%B1%CE%B2%CE%B5-why-i-want-my-gun-rights/ (site accessed 01.06.16 at 18:43 pm).
7. R.H. Watt: '"Wanderer, kommst du nach Sparta": History through Propaganda into Literary Commonplace', *The Modern Language Review*, Vol. 80 (1985), pp.871-883; H. Roche: '"Wanderer, kommst du nach Sparta oder nach Stalingrad?" Ancient ideals of self-sacrifice and German military propaganda', in N. Brooks and G. Thuswaldner (eds.), *Making Sacrifices – Opfer bringen: Visions of Sacrifice in European and American Cultures - Opfervorstellungen in europäischen und amerikanischen Kulturen* (Vienna: New Academic Press, 2016), pp.66-86. On the long-standing history of German intellectual and cultural engagement with ancient Sparta, see H. Roche: *Sparta's German Children: The ideal of ancient Sparta in the Royal Prussian Cadet-Corps, 1818-1920, and*

in National Socialist elite schools (the Napolas), 1933-1945 (Swansea: Classical Press of Wales, 2013).

8. As McMullin remarks (p.59), 'Simonides appears to have been *the* poet for the Greeks allied against Persia.' R.M. McMullin: 'Aspects of Medizing: Themistocles, Simonides, and Timocreon of Rhodes', *The Classical Journal*, Vol. 97 (2001), pp.55-67.

9. Simonides fr. 22 Page; my trans. On the setting up of this and other inscriptions at the site, see J.H. Molyneux: *Simonides: A Historical Study* (Wauconda IL: Bolchazy-Carducci, 1992), pp.175-187. For an account of the monuments which differs slightly from that of Herodotos, see Diod. 11.

10. For the Greek phrase, see e.g. Hom. *Il.* 9.413.

11. Molyneux, *Simonides*, pp.185-187.

12. Note that the Greek dead at Plataia may well have been the recipients of regular worship in the style of cult-heroes. Boedecker thinks they were; Bremmer argues against it. D. Boedecker: 'Simonides on Plataea: Narrative Elegy, Mythodic History', *Zeitschrift für Papyrologie und Epigraphik*, Bd. 107 (1995), pp.217-229; J.N. Bremmer: The Rise of the Hero Cult and the New Simonides', *Zeitschrift für Papyrologie und Epigraphik*, Bd. 158 (2007), pp. 15-26.

13. Hdt. 7.225.1; Hom. *Il.* 17.274-277.

14. Strabo 9.4.16; trans. Jones, adapted. Note that Strabo transmits a slightly different version of the verse: however, the essential translation is not affected.

15. J. Elsner: 'Structuring "Greece": Pausanias' *Periegesis* as a Literary Construct', in S.E. Alcock, J.F. Cherry and J. Elsner (eds.), *Pausanias: Travel and Memory in Roman Greece* (Oxford: Oxford University Press, 2001), pp.3-20; M. Pretzler: *Pausanias: Travel Writing in Ancient Greece* (London: Bristol Classical Press, 2007), esp. pp.55-90.

16. Paus. 10.21.6-7; trans. Jones, adapted.

17. The attribution is not certain, but it is extremely likely. For the text and its authorship, see G. Martin and J. Grusková: '„Dexippus Vindobonensis"(?): Ein neues Handschriftenfragment zum sog. Herulereinfall der Jahre 267/268', *Wiener Studien*, Bd. 127 (2014), pp.101-120. It is to their edition of the text that the following two footnotes refer.

18. Folio 192, lines 16-19.

19. Folio 193, lines 17-19: 'οὐδὲ γὰρ οἱ πρό-/γονοι υμῶν ἐν τῶδε μαχόμενοι ἔσφηλάν ποτε τῆς / ἐλευθερίας τὴν Ἑλλάδα...' ('Your ancestors, fighting on this very spot, never failed to uphold the liberty of Greece...' [my trans.].

20. For this comment and the surrounding events, see M. Hill: *Diggers and Greeks: The Australian Campaigns in Greece and Crete* (Sidney NSW: UNSW Press, 2010), p.113.

21. Hdt. 7.172-174.

22. Hdt. 7.6. On the medism of the Thessalians, see H.D. Westlake: 'The Medism of Thessaly', *The Journal of Hellenic Studies*, Vol. 56 (1936), pp.12-24; N. Robertson: 'The Thessalian Expedition of 480 B.C.', *The Journal of Hellenic Studies*, Vol. 96 (1976), pp.100-120.

23. Herakleides *FGrH* 369A F 3: 'τάχα δὲ φήσουσίν τινες ἡμᾶς ἀγνοεῖν τὴν Θετταλίαν τῆς Ἑλλάδος καταριθμοῦντας, ἄπειροι τῆς τῶν πραγμάτων ὄντες ἀληθείας.' ('Some may perhaps say that we are ignorant in counting Thessaly as part of Greece – they don't know the truth of the matter.') The earliest reference to Hellas as a site in Thessaly is in the Iliadic Catalogue of Ships, where it is designated part of the territory of Achilles: Hom. *Il.* 2.683.

24. E.M.M. Aston: 'Friends in High Places: The Stereotype of Dangerous Thessalian Hospitality in the Later Classical Period', *Phoenix* Vol. 66 (2012), pp.247-271.

25. Kritias DK 88 B31 = Ath. *Deipn.* 14.662f.

26. E. Hall: *Inventing the Barbarian: Greek Self-definition through Tragedy* (2nd ed., Oxford: Clarendon, 1991).

27. As the ancients themselves noted, 'Hellas' was originally the name of a region of southern Thessaly, and 'Hellenes' the inhabitants of that place, before the name spread out to encompass more and more of Greece. See e.g. Herakleides *FGrH* 369A F 3 (a continuation of his statement in n. XX above); for discussion of the historical processes behind this shift in the names' use, see J. Hall: *Hellenicity: Between Ethnicity and Culture* (Chicago: University of Chicago Press, 2002), pp.125-154.

28. See esp. frs. 5 and 9 MW.

29. It is worth noting that Makedon, the ancestor of the Macedonians, is given a completely separate genealogy in this poem: the Thessalians are part of the Greek world, and their northern neighbour is firmly pushed away (Hes. fr. 7 MW).

30. Hom. *Il.* 2.681-685.

31. This term, the conventional transcription of the Greek verb μηδίζειν used repeatedly by Herodotos and later authors, means to side or sympathise with the Persians. For the term and its origins, see D.F. Graf: 'Medism: The Origin and Significance of the Term', *Journal of Hellenic Studies* Vol. 104 (1984), pp. 15-30; for the medisers in the Persian Wars, see D. Gillis: *Collaboration with the Persians.* (Stuttgart: Franz Steiner, 1979).

32. Hdt. 7.132.1 (my trans.; please note that Herodotos' Ionian name-forms have been changed to their more usual spelling to avoid confusion).

33. See Thuc. 2.101.2, 4.78.6, 8.3.1. For discussion of the relationship between Thessaly and its immediate neighbours, see S. Sprawski: 'Thessalians and Their Neighbours in the Classical Period', in *First International Congress on the History and Culture of Thessaly* (Thessaloniki: Alexandros, 2006).

34. The first complete list of the Amphiktyons is provided by Aischines (4th c. BCE) in *On the Embassy* (2.116), where he enumerates them as follows: 'Thessalians, Boiotians (not only the Thebans), Dorians, Ionians, Perrhaibians, Magnetes, Dolopians, Lokrians, Oitaians, Phthiotians, Malians and Phokians.' For the composition and organisation of the Amphiktyony, see P. Sánchez: *L'Amphictionie des Pyles et de Delphes: Recherche sur son rôle historique des origines au 2e siècle de notre ère* (Stuttgart: Franz Steiner, 2001), pp.466-488.

35. It should be noted that medism did not imply hostility to the Greek side. For example, Herodotos tells us that the Amphiktyons were responsible for many of the formal burials and monuments on the site of the battle. (Hdt. 7,228.)

36. See e.g. Hdt. 7.140; however, when the Athenians protest at the bleak words of the Oracle they are given a second utterance (7.141) which holds out some hope in the form of the famous 'wooden wall' instruction which Themistokles interprets (correctly, as it turns out) that they should rely upon their fleet to defeat the invaders.

37. Hdt. 9.81.1.

38. *ML* 27; M. Scott: *Delphi and Olympia: The Spatial Politics of Panhellenism in the Archaic and Classical Periods* (Cambridge and New York: Cambridge University Press, 2010), p.173. The omission of Phokis from the list is interesting, in the light of Herodotos' cutting remarks, discussed below.

39. Scott, *Delphi and Olympia*, pp. 81-88; Hdt. 8.121.

40. The oath: Hdt. 7.132.2.

41. Hdt. 6.72: Leotychidas is caught red-handed actually sitting on his bribe which takes the curious form of a glove stuffed with silver, and is banished from Sparta.

42. Hdt. 8.30.

43. R. Osborne: *Greece in the Making* (2nd ed., London: Routledge, 2009), p.325.

44. The Persian Wars as inspiration and encouragement for the Ten Thousand under Xenophon: Xen. *Anab.* 3.2.11. Isokrates refers to the Persian Wars in his exhortation to Philip of Macedon to invade Asia: Isok. 5, esp. 147-147. For the shift between fifth and fourth century views of pan-Hellenism, with particular reference to Simonides and Isokrates, see M.A. Flower: 'From Simonides to Isocrates: The Fifth-Century Origins of Fourth-Century Panhellenism', *Classical Antiquity* Vol. 19 (2000), pp.65-101.

45. Athenian envy of Spartan simplicity and endurance: see e.g. Xenophon's *Constitution of the Spartans (passim)*.

46. The quotability of Spartan sayings was recognised in antiquity too: Plutarch wrote a whole work called *Sayings of the Spartans*, cataloguing pithy utterances. Leonidas gets a section, of course (51), in which the immortal μολὼν λαβέ is just one of fifteen apophthegms.

47. On the moral simplicity of Simonides' Persian War poetry, see McMullin, 'Aspects of Medizing', pp.59-60.

Chapter 5. The Wars of the Ancient Israelites and European Culture

1. *The Assyrian Dictionary of the Oriental Institute of The University of Chicago* (Chicago: Oriental Institute, 1956-2010); David C. Snell, *Flight and Freedom in the Ancient Near East* (Leiden: Brill, 2001).

2. See Jacob Talmon, *The Unique and the Universal* (New York: G. Braziller, 1966); Edward Shils, 'Primordial, Personal, Sacred and Civil Ties', in *Center and Periphery: Essays in Macrosociology* (Chicago: The University of Chicago Press, 1975), pp.111-126; Steven Grosby, 'Primordiality' in A. Leoussi, ed., *Encyclopaedia of Nationalism* (New Brunswick: Transaction Publishers, 2001), pp.252-255.

3. Anthony D. Smith, 'Nation and Covenant: The Contribution of Ancient Israel to Modern Nationalism', *Proceedings of the British Academy* 151 (2007): 213-255; 'Biblical beliefs in the shaping of modern nations', *Nations and Nationalism* 21/3 (2015): 403-422.

4. *Sifre: A Tannaitic Commentary on the Book of Deuteronomy* (New Haven: Yale University Press, 1986), pp.343, 352.

5. Nahum M. Sarna, 'Israel in Egypt: The Egyptian Sojourn and the Exodus', in Hershel Shanks, ed., *Ancient Israel: From Abraham to the Roman Destruction of the Temple* (Washington, DC: Biblical Archaeological Society, 1999), pp. 33-54.

6. Simon Schama, *The Embarrassment of Riches: An Interpretation of Dutch Culture in the Gold Age* (New York: Random House, 1997), pp.104-113.

7. For the development of the idea of 'ancient liberties', see, for England, J.G.A. Pocock, *The Ancient Constitution and Feudal Law: English Historical Thought in the Seventeenth Century* (New York: W.W. Norton, 1967); for the Dutch, Hugo Grotius, *De republica emendanda* (The Hague: van Gorcum, 1984) and *On the Antiquity of the Batavian Republic* (The Hague: van Gorcum, 2000);

for the French, François Hotman, *Francogallia* (Cambridge: Cambridge University Press, 1972).

8. Smith, 'Nation and Covenant'; see also Casper Hirschi, *The Origins of Nationalism* (Cambridge: Cambridge University Press, 2012), and, for America, Eran Shalev, *American Zion* (New Haven: Yale University Press, 2013).

9. See, for example, Diane Kelsey McColley, *Poetry and Music in Seventeenth Century England* (Cambridge: Cambridge University Press, 1997).

10. For an overview of this literature of the 'Hebrew Republic', see Frank E. Manuel, *The Broken Staff: Judaism Through Christian Eyes* (Cambridge: Harvard University Press, 1992), pp.115-127; Eric Nelson, *The Hebrew Republic: Jewish Sources and the Transformation of European Political Thought* (Cambridge: Harvard University Press, 2010).

11. For the boundaries of that land, see Numbers 34.

12. The historical reality behind the pollution of the temple is likely a reference to the policies of the Seleucid Antiochus IV, circa 165 BCE. See 1 Maccabees 1:46-47.

13. See, for example, Kevin R. Brine, Elena Ciletti and Henrike Lähnemann (eds.), *The Sword of Judith: Judith Studies Across the Disciplines* (Cambridge: Open Book Publishing, 2010).

14. Certainly all the more so if Piero d'Medici's now lost dedication for the sculpture read 'dedicated this statue of a woman both to liberty and fortitude, whereby the citizens with unvanquished and constant heart might return to the Republic'; see Loren Partridge, *Art of Renaissance Florence, 1400-1600* (Berkeley: University of California Press, 2009), p.89.

15. See, for example, Nicholas Morton, 'The defence of the Holy Land and the memory of the Maccabees', *Journal of Medieval History* 36 (2010): 275-93.

16. For an online source of Guibert of Nogent's account, http://sourcebooks.fordham.edu/source/urban2-5vers.html accessed on 14 IV 2017.

17. Morton, 'The defence of the Holy Land', p.283.

18. Morton, 'The defence of the Holy Land', p.287

19. For a brief overview of 'Christian Hebraism', see Steven Grosby, 'Hebraism: The Third Culture' in Jonathan A. Jacobs, ed., *Judaic Sources & Western Thought: Jerusalem's Enduring Presence* (Oxford: Oxford University Press, 2011), pp.73-96.

20. See Smith, 'Nation and Covenant'; Smith, 'Biblical beliefs in the shaping of modern nations'; Steven Grosby, *Biblical Ideas of Nationality: Ancient and Modern* (Winona Lake; Eisenbrauns, 2002).

Chapter 6. The Battle of the Teutoburg Forest Commemorated: from the Arch of Germanicus to the Arminius Monument

1. The principal references are in Strabo 7.1.4; Velleius Paterculus 2.117-20; Florus *Epitome* 2.30; Tacitus *Annals* 1.3, 1.10, 1.43, 1.55-71, 2.7, 2.9-10, 2.41, 2.45, 2.88; Suetonius *Augustus* 23, *Tiberius* 17-18; Dio 56.18-24.

2. Tacitus *Annals* 2.9-10.

3. See L. Powell, *Eager for Glory: The Untold Story of Drusus the Elder, Conqueror of Germania* (also from Pen & Sword Books, 2011).

4. Velleius Paterculus 2.106.

5. Virgil *Aeneid* 1.278-9: *His ego nec metas rerum nec tempora pono; imperium sine fine dedi.* 'On this people I impose boundaries in neither space nor time: I have granted them empire without limits'.

6. Tacitus *Annals* 2.46.

7. See n.1: Dio 56.18 says that Varus was exacting taxation as part of a move towards settling the Germans in towns, and both he and Florus say that Varus' arrogance as a giver of laws enraged the tribespeople. Compare the roughly contemporary provincial census in Judea, with its disruptive movement and assessment of people, that forms the backdrop of the story of the nativity.

8. R. Syme, 'Some Notes on the Legions under Augustus', *The Journal of Roman Studies,* Vol. 23 (1933), pp.14-33.

9. Suetonius *Augustus* 101; Tacitus *Annals* 1.11.

10. Edward Luttwak, *The Grand Strategy of the Roman Empire: From the First Century A.D. to the Third* (Baltimore and London: Johns Hopkins, 1976) remains a classic study, distinguishing three phases of Roman attitudes and policies towards the frontiers of the empire.

11. Tacitus *Annals* 2.5, 2.26, 2.73.

12. Tacitus *Agricola* 39.

13. Tacitus *Annals* 2.82.

14. Tacitus *Annals* 3.10 ff. and the epigraphic record of the verdict, the *Senatus Consultum de Cn. Pisone Patre*: for the latter see W. Eck, A. Caballos and F. Fernandez, *Das senatus consultum de Cn.Pisone patre, Vestigia* 48 (Muncih: Beck, 1996), S. 38-51; *American Journal of Philology* Vol. 120 No. 1 (Spring 1999) 'Special Issue: The "*Senatus Consultum de Cn. Pisone Patre*": Text, Translation, Discussion'.

15. Tacitus *Annals* 2.83.

16. For a recent survey, see M. Beard, *The Roman Triumph* (Harvard: Harvard University Press, 2009).

17. See n.13 above.

18. The *Tabula Siarensis* and another overlapping bronze document proposing further honours for Germanicus (the *Tabula Hebana*) are published in M. H. Crawford, ed., *Roman Statutes, BICS* Suppl. 64 (London: Institute of Classical Studies, 1996), nos. 37 and 38. For a related third document, the inscription of the senatorial decree on the outcome of Piso's trial, see n.12 above. See also G. Rowe, *Princes and Political Cultures: The New Tiberian Senatorial Decrees* (Ann Arbor: University of Michigan Press, 2002).

19. Forma Urbis fragment 31U.

20. Tacitus *Annals* 2.64.

21. Josephus, *Jewish War* 7.5.4.

22. Suetonius *Augustus* 29; Plutarch *Marcellus* 30.

23. Suetonius *Grammarians* 21; Plutarch *Marcellus* 30.

24. The author gratefully acknowledges the late Dr Georg Heuser's contributions to this section on the German Arminius/Hermann myth.

25. R.E. Walker, *Ulrich von Hutten's Arminius* (Bern: Peter Lang, 2008).

26. *Chronica durch M. Johan. Carion vleissig zusamen gezogen, meniglich nützlich zu lesen* (Wittemberg: Rhaw, 1533)

27. For Boudicca, see Tacitus *Annals* 14.29ff. Her speech – 'such was the firm resolve of a woman – let the men live in slavery if they wished!' – is at 14.35.

28. http://www.kalkriese-varusschlacht.de/ See also W. Doyé 'Arminius' in E. François & H. Schulze (eds), *Deutsche Erinnerungsorte* (Munich: Beck, 2001-2002), Vol. III, 587-602, and R. Wiegels and W. Woesler (eds) *Arminius and die Varusschlacht: Geschichte – Mythos – Literatur* (Paderborn, 1995) for fuller surveys of works of literature and art that have been dedicated to Arminius than we have the space to cover here.

Chapter 7. The Battle of Hastings: 1066: Military History, Myth and Memory

1. William of Jumiéges: *Gesta Normannorum Ducum*, ed.& trans. E.M.C. Van Houts (Oxford: Clarendon Press, 1995).

2. William of Poitiers: *Gesta Guillelmi*, ed. & trans. R.H.C. Daivs & M. Chibnall (Oxford: Clarendon Press, 1998).

3. Anon.: *Carmen de Hastingae Proelio,* ed. & trans. F. Barlow (Oxford: Clarendon Press, 1999).

4. There are many editions of the Bayeux Tapestry. See, for example, Lucien Musset: *The Bayeux Tapestry*, trans. R Rex (Woodbridge: Boydell, 2005). The same publisher has produced a digital edition which is excellent for teaching: M. K. Foys (Woodbridge: Boydell, 2003).

5. All have been published by Oxford Medieval Texts (an invaluable resource): Orderic Vitalis' *Historia Ecclesiatica* ed. trans. M.Chibnall in 6 vols. (Oxford: Clarendon Press, 1968-80); William of Malmesbury; *Gesta Regum Anglorum*, R.M. Thomson et.al. 2 vols. (Oxford: Clarendon Press, 1998-99); Henry of Huntingdon, *Historia Anglorum*, ed. trans. D.Greenaway (Oxford: Clarendon Press, 1996).

6. Wace: *The Roman de Rou*, trs. by Glyn S. Burgess, with the text of Anthony J. Holden and notes by Glyn S. Burgess and Elisabeth van Houts (St. Hélier : Societe Jersiaise, 2002).

7. *Vita Edwardi Regis,* ed. & trans. F. Barlow (Oxford Medieval Texts, T. Nelson & Sons, 1962), pp.52-3.

8. William of Jumièges mentions an attempt to restore Edward to the English throne, which may be attributed to 1032-33. *Gesta Normannorum Ducum,* vol. ii, pp.76-79.

9. A detailed study of the campaign (with maps) and the subsequent conquest may be found in N. Hooper and M. Bennett: *Cambridge Atlas of Warfare: the Middle Ages 768-1487* (Cambridge: Cambridge University Press, 1996), pp.42-9.

10. Jim Bradbury: *The Battle of Hastings* (Stroud: Sutton, 1998), pp. 168-78. John Grehan & Martin Mace: *The Battle of Hastings 1066 – the Uncomfortable Truth* (Barnsley: Pen & Sword, 2012); Nick Austin: *Secrets of the Norman Invasion* (Crowhurst: Ogmium, 2010).

11. R. Porter: 'On the very spot': In Defence of Battle, *English Heritage Review*, vol. 7 (2012), pp. 5-17.

12. C. Warren Hollister: *Anglo-Saxon Military Institutions on the eve of the Norman Conquest* (Oxford: Clarendon Press, 1962).

13. E. John: *Orbis Britanniae* (Leicester: Leicester University Press, 1996); *Reassessing Anglo-Saxon England* (Manchester: Manchester University Press, 1996).

14. Wace: *Rou*, p. 181; *Carmen de Hastingae Proelio*, p.25.

15. Poitiers: *Gesta Guillelmi*, p.131.

16. Poitiers: *Gesta Guillelmi*, p.133

17. *Carmen de Hastingae Proelio*, p.33.

18. Wace: *Rou*, p.191.

19. T.A.Dorey: 'William of Poitiers: "Gesta Guillelmi Ducis", in T.A. Dorey et al (eds): *Latin Biography* (London: Routledge & Kegan Paul, 1967), pp.139-56.

20. Orderic Vitalis' *Historia Ecclesiatica,* vol. 2, pp.230-36.

21. Edward Gibbon: *Miscellaneous works* ed. John Lord Sheffield, 2.vols (London: s.e., 1796), and the following newspaper materials became available to me via the Library of Winchester University electronic resources.

22. 13 October 1896, p.8.

23. 19 October 1895, p.3.

24. Under the heading of: 'The Songs of France'.

25. Issue 5, 1862, pagination uncertain.

26. Thursday 14 April 1831, pagination uncertain.

27. A brief but pungent review by Marc Morris in *History Today* (April, 2012, accessed online) is critical of the author's methodology e.g. using vox pop responses as comparable to near contemporary historical commentary and producing jejune conclusions; these are valid concerns with the work.

28. Ibid., p.92.

29. Ibid., p.96.

30. Ibid., pp.127-8.

31. Ibid., p.142.

32. See: Matthew Bennett: *Campaigns of the Norman Conquest* (Oxford: Osprey, 2001), which I wrote in a popular format in order to reach a wider audience, has been widely accepted as a school text book.

33. Peter Rex: *The English Resistance: the Underground War against the Normans* (Stroud: Amberley, 2014).

34. I am grateful to the editors for providing me with this interpretation.

Chapter 8. The Massacre of Béziers, 22 July 1209

1. 'Caedite eos. Novit enim Deus qui sunt eus', Caesarius of Heisterbach, *Dialogus Miraculorum*, ed. Joseph Strange (Cologne, Bonn, Brussels: Heberle, 1851), vol 1., p.302.

2. Jasper Heinzen, 'A negotiated truce: The Battle of Waterloo in European Memory since the Second World War', *History and Memory*, 26 (2014) 39-74, p.43. The key sources for this chapter are Andrew Roach, 'Occitania Past and Present: Southern Consciousness in Medieval and Modern French Politics', *History Workshop Journal* 43 (1997), 1-22.; Emily McCaffrey, 'Memory and Collective Identity in *Occitanie: The Cathars in History and Popular Culture'*, *History and Memory*, 13 (2001), 114-138; also by McCaffrey, 'Imagining the Cathars in late twentieth-century Languedoc', *Contemporary European History*, 11. 3 (2002) 409-27. Philippe Martel, 'L'encombrant massacre de Béziers vu par la postérité', in *En Languedoc au XIIIe siècle : Le Temps du sac de Béziers*, ed. Monique Bourin (Perpignan : Presses universitaires de Perpignan, 2010),

pp. 27-45; Lawrence Marvin, 'The Albigensian Crusade in Anglo-American Historiography, 1888–2013', *History Compass*, 11 (2013),1126–1138.

3. Selected texts are available in Catherine Léglu, Rebecca Rist and Claire Taylor, *The Cathars and the Albigensian Crusade: A Sourcebook* (London: Routledge, 2014). John H. Arnold and Peter Biller, *Heresy and Inquisition in France, 1200-1300* (Manchester: Manchester University Press, 2016). Among the many excellent studies of this war, the following are among the most relevant for this chapter: Michel Roquebert, *L'Epopée cathare*, 5 vols (Toulouse, Privat, 1970-1998); Lawrence Marvin, *The Occitan War: A Military and Political History of the Albigensian Crusade, 1209-1218* (Cambridge: Cambridge University Press, 2008).

4. *Journal officiel de la République française* (JORF), décret N° 2016-1264, 29 September 2016. www.legifrance.gouv.fr/eli/decret/2016/9/28/INTB1617888D/jo/texte. (consulted 16 January 2018). Formerly Languedoc-Roussillon and Midi-Pyrénées.

5. Géraldine Jammet, L'Eglise demande pardon pour le massacre des cathares', *La dépêche*, 23 September 2016. www.ladepeche.fr. (consulted 16 January 2018). Gauthier Vaillant, 'Les Cathares', *La Croix*, 8 October 2016. www.la-croix.com. (consulted 16 January 2018).

6. Jammet, 'L'Eglise demande pardon'.

7. See the stress on the techniques of warfare in Marvin, *The Occitan war*.

8. Jacques Berlioz, « *Tuez-les tous, Dieu reconnaîtra les siens* » : *La croisade contre les Albigeois vue par Césaire de Heisterbach* (Portet-sur-Garonne: Loubatières, 1994).

9. Laurence W. *Marvin*, 'The *Massacre at Béziers* July 22, 1209: a revisionist look,' in *Heresy and the Persecuting Society in the Middle Ages: Essays on the Work of R. I. Moore*, ed. Michael Frassetto (Leiden: Brill, 2006), pp.195-225.

10. Marie Dejoux, 'Après la conquête, les enquêtes ? L'exemple des *Querimoniae Biterrensium* de 1247-1248', in *En Languedoc au XIIIe siècle : Le Temps du sac de Béziers*, ed. Monique Bourin (Perpignan : Presses universitaires de Perpignan, 2010), pp.269-288, pp.273-74.

11. Marvin, 'The Albigensian Crusade', pp.130-31.

12. Beverly Mayne Kienzle, *Cistercians, Heresy, and Crusade in Occitania, 1145-1229: Preaching in the Lord's Vineyard* (York: York Medieval Press, 2001). Uwe Brunn, *Des contestataires aux "cathares": Discours de réforme et propagande antihérétique dans les pays du Rhin et de la Meuse avant l'Inquisition* (Paris: Institut d'Etudes Augustiniennes, 2006).

13. Malcolm Barber, *The Cathars: Dualist Heretics in Languedoc in the High Middle Ages*, 2ⁿᵈ edn (London: Routledge, 2014).

14. Monique Zerner, *L'Histoire du catharisme en discussion: Le « Concile » de Saint-Félix (1167)* (Nice: Centre d'Etudes Médiévales, 2001); Jean-Louis Biget, *Hérésie et inquisition dans le midi de la France* (Paris: Picard, 2007). Mark Gregory Pegg, *A Most Holy War: The Albigensian Crusade and the Battle for Christendom* (Oxford University Press, 2008). These issues are discussed in *Cathars in Question*, ed. Antonio Sennis (York: York Medieval Press, 2016).

15. Jean-Louis Biget, 'Béziers, citadelle de l'hérésie?', in *En Languedoc au XIIIe siècle : Le Temps du sac de Béziers*, ed. Monique Bourin (Perpignan: Presses universitaires de Perpignan, 2010), pp.49-62.

16. Malcolm Barber, 'The Albigensian crusades: Wars like any other?', in *Dei gesta per Francos: Etudes sur les croisades dediées à Jean Richard*, ed. Michel Balard, Benjamin Z. Kedar and Jonathan Riley-Smith (Aldershot: Ashgate, 2001), pp.45-55.

17. Martel, 'L'encombrant massacre'.

18. Peter of Les Vaux-de-Cernay, *The History of the Albigensian Crusade*, translated by W.A. Sibly and M.D. Sibly (Rochester: Boydell Press, 1998), pp.289-90.

19. Sibly and Sibly, pp.48-51.

20. Sibly and Sibly, p.51.

21. *La Chanson de la croisade albigeoise*, ed. Martin-Chabot, with an adaptation by Henri Gougaud (Paris : Le Livre de Poche, 1989), p.58.

22. *Chanson de la croisade*, p.58.

23. *Chanson de la croisade*, pp.60-64.

24. Berlioz, *Tuez-les tous!*, pp.93-98.

25. 2 Timothy 2: 19, and Numbers 16:5. Berlioz, *Tuez-les tous*, pp.76-83.

26. Anne-Marie Lamarrigue, 'La Croisade albigeoise vue par Bernard Gui,' *Journal des savants*, 2 (1993), 201-233.

27. See McCaffrey, 'Memory'.

28. Arnaud Sorbin, *Histoire des Albigeois et gestes de noble Simon de Montfort* (Paris: Guillaume Chaudière, 1569); Benoist Pierre, 'La Parole publique des prédicateurs royaux au temps des guerres de religion : l'exemple d'Arnaud Sorbin (1532-1606)', in *La Parole publique en ville: des Réformes à la Révolution*, ed. Stefano Simiz (Villeneuve-d'Ascq : Presses universitaires du Septentrion, 2012), pp.61-84.

29. *Allegresse de la France pour l'heureuse victoire obtenue entre Coignac et Chasteauneuf, le 13 de mars 1569, contre les rebelles Calvinistes* (Paris: chez Guillaume Chaudiere, 1569).

30. Sorbin, *Histoire des Albigeois,* pp.5v and 25v.

31. Pierre, 'La Parole', pp.71-72.

32. Jean Paul Perrin, *Histoire des Chrestiens albigeois: Contenant les longues guerres, persecutions qu'ils ont souffert à cause de la doctrine de l'Évangile* (Geneva : Matthieu Berjon, 1618). Yves Krumenacker, 'La généalogie imaginaire de la Réforme protestante,' *Revue Historique*, 308 (2006), 259-289.

33. Perrin, *Histoire*, p.20.

34. Perrin, *Histoire*, p.23.

35. Perrin, *Histoire*, pp.24-25.

36. Randall J. Pederson, *Unity in Diversity: English Puritans and the Puritan Reformation, 1603-1689* (Leiden: Brill, 2014), pp.3-4, 25-26.

37. McCaffrey, 'Memory', pp.117-18. David D. Bien, 'Religious Persecution in the French Enlightenment', *Church History*, 3 (1961) 325-333, p.326.

38. McCaffrey, 'Memory', pp.118-120, and Roach, 'Occitania'. Napoléon Peyrat, *Histoire des Albigeois*, 3 vols (Paris : Librairie Internationale, 1872).

39. Stephen O'Shea, *The Perfect Heresy: The Life and Death of the Cathars* (London : Profile Books, 2000), pp.247-64.

40. Henri Martin, *Histoire de France populaire depuis les temps les plus reculés jusqu'à nos jours* (Paris: Furne, Jouvet et Cie, 1867), I, pp.223-69. Michael Glencross, *Reconstructing Camelot: French Romantic Medievalism and the Arthurian Tradition* (Woodbridge: D.S. Brewer, 1995), pp.110-13.

41. Martin, *Histoire de France populaire*, I, pp.268-69.

42. Martin, *Histoire de France populaire*, I, p.248.

43. Henri de L'Epinois, *Critiques et réfutations: M. Henri Martin et son histoire de France*, (Paris: Librairie de la Société Bibliographique, 1872), pp. 38, 112-15.

44. L'Epinois, *Critiques*, p.166-69.

45. McCaffrey, 'Memory', pp.120-22.

46. L'Epinois, *Critiques*, pp.153-57.

47. Otto Rahn, *Kreuzzug gegen den Graal* (Urban Verlag, 1933). Pierre Belperron, *La Croisade contre les Albigeois* (Paris: Plon, 1942; reprint Perrin, 1967) p.20. Marvin, 'The Albigensian Crusade', pp.1130-31.

48. Laura Gilmour Bennett, *A Wheel of Stars* (London: Penguin, 1990); Kate Mosse, *Labyrinth* (London: Orion, 2005).

49. Dan Brown, *The Da Vinci Code* (London: Bantam, 2003). Quotation from Mark Lawson's review, 26 July 2003, *The Guardian*: < www.theguardian.com. > (consulted 16 January 2018).

50. Gilmour Bennett, *A Wheel of Stars*, p.42.

51. Arthur Guirdham, *The Cathars and Reincarnation* (Jersey - London: Neville Spearman, 1970), and also by Guirdham, *We Are one Another: a Record of Group Reincarnation* (Jersey - London: Neville Spearman, 1974).

ENDNOTES

52. Arthur Guirdham, trans. by Claudine Brelet, *Les Cathares et la réincarnation*, preface by Lawrence Durrell, postface by René Nelli (Paris: Payot, 1972).

53. René Nelli, *La Vie quotidienne des cathares du Languedoc au XIIIe siècle* (Paris : Hachette, 1969), and also by Nelli, *L'Erotique des troubadours* (Toulouse: Privat, 1963). McCaffrey, 'Memory', pp.121-22.

54. Zoé Oldenbourg, *16 mars 1244 – Le bûcher de Montségur*, series : Trente journées qui ont fait la France (Paris : Gallimard, 1959).

55. Etienne Delaruelle, *Revue d'histoire de l'Eglise de France*, 50 (1964) 154-58. On Delaruelle, see McCaffrey, 'Imagining the Cathars', p.414.

56. *La Caméra explore le temps*, episode 46, 'Le Drame cathare', episode 47:'Montségur (L'Inquisition)'.

57. https://mediasethistoire.wordpress.com/2012/06/09/alain-decaux-et-la-television-33/ (consulted 16 January 2018). McCaffrey, 'Imagining the Cathars', p.417.

58. Gérald Forton and Michel Roquebert, *Aymeric et les Cathares,* and *Aymeric à Montségur* (Toulouse : Loubatières, 1978, 1981). *L'Histoire de France en bandes dessinées*, 10 vols (Paris : Larousse, 1976-77).

59. Renée Aurembou, *Le Trésor de Montségur*, Paris: Editions G.P., Collection Spirale, 1976), p.172.

60. *Mémoire de Cendres,* by Philippe Jarbinet, 10 vols (Grenoble: Glénat, 1995-2007).

61. Arnaud Delalande and Eric Lambert, *Le Dernier cathare*, 4 vols, I: *Tuez-les tous!* (Paris : Les éditions 12 bis, 2010). Arnaud Delalande, *L'Eglise de Satan* (Paris: Le Livre de Poche, 2004).

62. http://www.locirdoc.fr/. (consulted 16 January 2018).

63. Linda M. Paterson, *The World of the Troubadours: Medieval Occitan Society, c.1100-c.1300* (CUP, 1995), pp.4-6.

64. Heinzen, 'A negotiated truce', p.46.

65. http//: www.tripadvisor.co.uk, review consulted 16 May 2016.

66. (translation mine), www.beziers-in-mediterranee.com (consulted 16 January 2018).

67. http://www.culture.gouv.fr/Wave/image/merimee/PROT/PA00103379_DOC.pdf (consulted 16 January 2018).

68. http://thepot.blog.lemonde.fr/2012/03/31/abdel-a-la-manif-des-occitanistes/ (consulted 16 January 2018).

69. O'Shea, *The Perfect Heresy*, p.249.

Chapter 9. Courtrai 1302, the Battle of the Golden Spurs

1. The author thanks Beatrice Heuser for the invitation to contribute to this project and for her comments on the final version of this chapter; Athena Leoussi for coordinating the proofs; Samuël Coghe for valuable suggestions on the first draft of the text. He is also grateful to the staff of the museum 'Kortrijk 1302', who provided precious exposition transcriptions. Last but not least the author thanks the museum's former curator Véronique Lambert, who provided exceptional support throughout the research and writing process, including precious time for a personal exchange in June 2016.
2. Michael Schudson: "The Present in the Past Versus the Past in the Present," *Communication* 11, no. 2 (1989).
3. Xavier Hélary : *Courtrai : 11 Juillet 1302* (Paris: Tallandier, 2012).
4. Ibid., pp.35-57.
5. Ibid., pp.65-66.
6. Ibid., pp.74-77.
7. Due to the lack of sources regarding the composition of the Flemish troops, the estimations by Hélary are based on the usual size of the individual militias. Older historiographic sources indicate drastically lower numbers, but this may be motivated by a desire to further emphasize the asymmetry between the two armies.
8. Hélary: *Courtrai*, pp.79-91.
9. Ibid., pp.134-46.
10. Veronique Lambert: "De Guldensporenslag van Fait-Divers tot Ankerpunt van de Vlaamse Identiteit (1302-1838): De Natievormende Functionaliteit van Historiografische Mythen," *Bijdragen en Mededelingen tot de Geschiedenis van de Nederlanden* No. 115 (2000), p. 389.
11. Hélary: *Courtrai*, pp.139-40.
12. Quoted in: ibid., p.140.
13. Ibid., pp.119-25.
14. J. F. Verbruggen: *The Battle of the Golden Spurs (Courtrai, 11 July 1302): A Contribution to the History of Flanders' War of Liberation, 1297-1305* (Woodbridge: Boydell Press, 2002), p.41.
15. Hélary: *Courtrai*, pp.147-48.
16. Gevert H. Nörtemann: *Im Spiegelkabinett der Historie: Der Mythos der Schlacht von Kortrijk und die Erfindung Flanderns im 19. Jahrhundert* (Berlin: Logos Verlag, 2002), 196-226.
17. Ibid., pp.213-26.
18. Ibid., pp.213-14.

ENDNOTES

19. Ibid., pp.227-34.
20. Jo Tollebeek: «Le Culte de la Bataille des Eperons d'Or de la fin du XVIIIᵉ Au XXᵉ Siècle,» in Raoul C. Van Caenegem (ed.) : *1302, Le Désastre De Courtrai : Mythe Et Réalité De La Bataille Des Eperons D'or*, (Anvers: Fonds Mercator, 2002), pp.202-03.
21. Jo Tollebeek: "An Era of Grandeur: The Middle Ages in Belgian National Historiography, 1830–1914," in *The Uses of the Middle Ages in Modern European States: History, Nationhood and the Search for Origins*, ed. R. J. W. Evans and Guy P. Marchal (London: Palgrave Macmillan, 2011), p.118.
22. Nörtemann: *Im Spiegelkabinett*, pp. 240-44.
23. Ibid., pp.245-47.
24. Gevert H. Nörtemann: „'Flamen, Feiert Die Schlacht Der Goldenen Sporen!': Die Schlacht Von Kortrijk Als Flämischer Gründungsmythos Im 19. Und 20. Jahrhundert," in ed. Nikolaus Buschmann and Dieter Langewiesche (eds.): *Der Krieg in Den Gründungsmythen Europäischer Nationen Und Der USA*, (Frankfurt am Main: Campus Verlag, 2003), p.243.
25. Tollebeek: "Le Culte", p.204. The fact that the Belgian Ministry of Home Affairs asked him to write an official history of Belgium in Flemish language, the *Geschiedenis van België*, may illustrate this observation.
26. Joep Leersen: "'Retro-Fitting the Past': Literary Historicism between the Golden Spurs and Waterloo," in Hugh Dunthorne and Michael J. Wintle (eds.): *The Historical Imagination in Nineteenth-Century Britain and the Low Countries*, (Leiden / Boston: Brill, 2013), p.122.
27. Tollebeek: „Le Culte", p.208.
28. Nörtemann: „'Flamen, Feiert'„, p.241f.
29. Hendrik Conscience: *The Lion of Flanders* (1838, repr. Baltimore: John Murphy, 1912), vol. III, ch. VI.
30. Quoted in: Nörtemann: „'Flamen, Feiert'„, p.244.
31. Tollebeek: „Le Culte", p.208f.
32. Nörtemann: *Im Spiegelkabinett*, p.191f.
33. Throughout the novel, including during the description of the *Bruges Matins*, the friend-foe identification happens for the reader and for the protagonists alike through the appraisal of a person's lack of 'native' Flemish skills or, respectively, a person's bad mastering of French, the language of the 'occupiers'.
34. Nörtemann: *Im Spiegelkabinett*, p.103f.
35. Jeroen Dewulf: "'O Liebes Land', 'O Belgiens Erde': The Development of the German-Speaking Community in Belgium Reflected in the Light of the Flemish Struggle for Autonomy," *German Studies Review* Vol. 32, No. 1 (2009), p.68.

36. Robert Mnookin and Alain Verbeke, "Persistent Nonviolent Conflict with No Reconciliation: The Flemish and Walloons in Belgium," *Law and Contemporary Problems* 72, no. 2 (2009), pp. 157-59.

37. Aristide R. Zolberg: "The Making of Flemings and Walloons: Belgium: 1830-1914," *The Journal of Interdisciplinary History* Vol. 5, No. 2 (1974), p. 194.

38. Nörtemann: *Im Spiegelkabinett*, pp.110-18.

39. Tollebeek: „Le Culte", p.209.

40. Leersen: 'Retro-Fitting the Past', p.123.

41. Tollebeek: „Le Culte", p.211.

42. Nörtemann: „'Flamen, Feiert'„, pp.246-55.

43. Tollebeek: „Le Culte", p. 223f.

44. Nörtemann: *Im Spiegelkabinett*, pp.407-46.

45. Mnookin and Verbeke: "Persistent Nonviolent Conflict," p.159f.

46. Nörtemann: *Im Spiegelkabinett*, p.266.

47. Tollebeek: „Le Culte", p.225.

48. Nadim Farhat, Valérie Rosoux, and Philippe Poirier, "The Causal Pattern of Collective Memory in a Community Conflict: "Constant Causes" in the Belgium Case," *Nationalism and Ethnic Politics* Vol. 20, No. 4 (2014), p.411.

49. Personal conversation with Véronique Lambert, the former curator of the museum Kortrijk 1302, on 13 June 2016.

50. Transcript of the film 'Traditio Universalis' (Museum 'Kortrijk 1302': Courtrai, 2006), p.8.

Chapter 10. Famous Battles: A Typology

1. George Schöpflin: 'The Functions of Myth and a Taxonomy of Myth' in Geoffrey Hosking & George Schöpflin (eds): *Myths and Nationhood* (London: Hurst, 1997), p.19.

2. Ernest Renan: *Qu'est-ce qu'une nation?* (Paris: Calman Levy, 1882), p.27.

3. Monika Flacke (ed.): *Mythen der Nationen: ein Europäisches Panorama* (Berlin: Deutsches Historisches Museum, 1998).

4. Schöpflin: 'The Functions of Myth', pp.28-35.

5. This usually contained, not a cross, but the Greek letters XP for ΧΡΙΣΤΟΣ, Christ.

6. H.V. Livermore: *A New History of Portugal* (Cambridge: Cambridge University Press, 1966), p.52.

7. Saul António Gomes: *A Batalha Real: 14 de Agosto de 1385* (Batalha: Fundação Aljubarrota, 2014).

8. Thucydides: *Peloponnesian War* II.43, here in the translation of Rex Warner (London: Penguin, 1954).

ENDNOTES

9. Maurice Halbwachs: *La Mémoire collective* (19XX) dt.: *Das Kollektive Gedächtnis* übers. von Holde Lhoest-Offermann (Frankfurt/Main: Fischer Taschenbuch Verlag, 1991), p.71

10. György Dalos: 'Ungarn: Mythen, Lehren, Lehrbücher', in Flacke (ed.): *Mythen der Nationen*, pp.544-548.

11. Vít Vlnas and Zdeněk Hojda: 'Tschechien: ‚Gönnt einem jeden die Wahrheit", in Flacke (ed.): *Mythen der Nationen*, pp.508-512.

12. Georg Kreis: 'Schweiz: Nationalpädagogik in Wort und Bild', in Flacke (ed.): *Mythen der Nationen*, pp.460-464.

13. Ingrid Bohn: 'Schweden: Zu Grösse und Freiheit geboren…', in Flacke (ed.): *Mythen der Nationen*, pp.437-444.

14. Henke Slechte: 'Durch eigene holländische Kunst angeregt, fühle ich, dass ich Holländer bin', in Flacke (ed.): *Mythen der Nationen*, pp.242-246.

15. See both versions and many copies of Benjamin West's *The Death of Lord Nelson* (Liverpool: Walker Art Gallery, 1806, and Greenwich: National Maritime Museum, 1808), and his earlier *Death of General Wolfe* (Ottawa: National Gallery of Canada, 1770). See also Arthur Devis' *The Death of Nelson* (Greenwich: National Maritime Museum, 1807).

16. Joseph von Führich, Lithography of 1820-1824, in Flacke (ed.): *Mythen der Nationen*, p.511.

17. Olaf Isaachsen's *The shrouding of the corpse of St Olaf* (Oslo: National Gallery, 1880).

18. Bertalan Széjely: *The discovery of the corpse of Lajos II* (Budapest: Hungarian National Gallery, 1859).

19. Inscription on the war memorial, Square Montholon, Paris, put up 1874.

20. Schöpflin: 'Functions of Myth', p.29.

21. Slechte: 'Durch eigene holländische Kunst', pp.228-231.

22. Inge Adriansen and Birgit Jenvold: 'Für Fahne, Sprache und Heimat', in Flacke (ed.): *Mythen der Nationen*, pp.95-100.

23. Vlnas and Hojda: 'Tschechien', pp.520-525.

24. Quoted in François-Xavier Nérard: 'Les cimetières mémoriaux de Leningrad : l'impossible deuil?', in David El Kenz and François-Xavier Nérard (eds.): *Commémorer les victimes en Europe (XVI-XXI siècles)* (Champ Vallon : Seyssel, 2011), pp. 197-214, here p.201f.

25. Loc. cit. [Nérard: 'Les cimetières mémoriaux', p.202].

26. John Hussey: *Waterloo: The Campaign of 1815* in two volumes (London: Greenhill Books, 2017).

27. Ciro Paoletti: 'The Battle of Culloden: A Pivotal Moment in World History', *Journal of Military History* Vol. 81 No. 1 (Jan. 2017), pp.187-203.

28. Murray Pittock: *Culloden* (Oxford: Oxford University Press, 2016), p.117f.
29. Widukind of Corvey: *Res gestae saxonicae sive annalium libri tres,* written in the 960s and 970s. Significantly, Ekkehart Rotter's translation (Stuttgart: Reclam, 1981) translates 'Saxon' into 'German' (*deutsch/Deutsche...*).
30. Ulrike Schmiegelt: 'Russland: Geschichte als Begründung der Autokratie', in Flacke (ed.): *Mythen der Nationen,* pp.407-9.
31. Ilaria Porciani: 'Fare gli italiani', in Flacke (ed.): *Mythen der Nationen,* pp.210-213.
32. Witold Molik: 'Noch ist Polen nicht verloren', in Flacke (ed.): *Mythen der Nationen,* pp.301-305.
33. Yves Lacoste: *Vive la Nation: Destin d'une idée géopolitique* (Paris: Fayard, 1997), pp.251-260.
34. For the best collection of World War I art, see the collections of the Imperial War Museum in London.
35. *Im Westen nichts Neues* (Berlin: Propyläen Verlag, 1929).
36. Schöpflin: 'The Functions of Myth', p.27.
37. Both excerpts from the *Leningradskaya Pravda* quoted in Nérard: 'Les cimetières mémoriaux', p.201f.
38. Ibid. [Nérard: 'Les cimetières mémoriaux',] p.202.
39. David R. Shearer: *Policing Stalin's socialism: repression and social order in the Soviet Union, 1924-1953* (New Haven: Yale University Press, 2009), pp.405-436.
40. Sarah Halifa-Legrand & Vincent Jauvert: 'Extrême Droite', *L'Obs,* No. 2731 (15 March 2017), p.54.

Index

INDEX

INDEX

INDEX

Wolfe, General James, 145
Wolf, Christa, 22, 26
Wood, Robert, 29f

Xerxes, 26f, 41, 46, 51-3, 55, 57, 59-61
Yeatman, R.J., 16

Yugoslav Wars, 9

Zeus, 25, 49, 60
Zhou Enlai, Chinese Prime Minister, 35
Zorndorf, Battle of (1758), 14